£2.99
/52

The Political Philosophy of New Labour

The Political Philosophy of New Labour

MATT BEECH

TAURIS ACADEMIC STUDIES
LONDON • NEW YORK

Published in 2006 by Tauris Academic Studies, an imprint of
I.B.Tauris & Co Ltd
6 Salem Road, London W2 4BU
175 Fifth Avenue, New York NY 10010
www.ibtauris.com

In the United States of America and Canada distributed by
Palgrave Macmillan a division of St. Martin's Press
175 Fifth Avenue, New York NY 10010

Copyright © 2006 Matt Beech

The right of Matt Beech to be identified as the author of this work has been asserted by the author in accordance with the Copyright, Designs and Patent Act 1988.

All rights reserved. Except for brief quotations in a review, this book, or any part thereof, may not be reproduced, stored in or introduced into a retrieval system, or transmitted, in any form or by any means, electronic, mechanical, photocopying, recording or otherwise, without the prior written permission of the publisher.

International Library of Political Studies 6

ISBN 1 84511 041 2

EAN 978 1 84511 041 3

A full CIP record for this book is available from the British Library
A full CIP record for this book is available from the Library of Congress

Library of Congress catalog card: available
Printed and bound in Great Britain by TJ International Ltd, Padstow, Cornwall

For my parents, Roger and Laraine Beech

John 3:16

Contents

Acknowledgements		ix
1.	Introduction	1
2.	An Intellectual History of the Labour Party: 1900-1949	9
3.	An Intellectual History of the Labour Party: 1949-1979	37
4.	An Intellectual History of the Labour Party: 1979-1994	58
5.	An Intellectual History of the Labour Party: 1994-2004	100
6.	New Labour and Liberty	133
7.	New Labour and Equality	154
8.	New Labour, Community and Democracy	177
9.	Conclusion	206
Notes		213
Bibliography		245
Index		259

ACKNOWLEDGEMENTS

This book originated from my doctoral thesis that I completed in the Division of Politics and International Relations at the University of Southampton in 2003. Whilst at Southampton I was fortunate enough to come under the tutelage of two superb political philosophers. I would like to express my gratitude to my supervisor Raymond Plant for being an excellent teacher and friend. I would like to thank my co-supervisor Andrew Mason for his encouragement and valuable comments on my work and my doctoral examiners Dilys Hill and David Marquand.

I would like to thank the Thorneycroft Memorial Fund who awarded me a vital scholarship in the final year of my studies. Particularly, my thanks go to Stanley Crooks. Also, I would like to thank all of the interviewees who gave so freely of their time and knowledge and to Kevin Hickson, Noel Thompson and Mark Wickham-Jones for their help and encouragement. Thanks go to Lester Crook, Kate Sherratt and Elizabeth Munns at I.B. Tauris for their assistance and efficiency in producing this book.

At this point certain people deserve a special mention. My parents Roger and Laraine Beech for their constant generosity and belief in me. My brothers and sisters at Highfield Church for their prayers and encouragement. Finally, I would like to thank my wife Claire for editing the manuscript, but more substantially for her love, understanding and forbearance.

1

INTRODUCTION

This book is a study of New Labour's political philosophy. It attempts to explain and locate New Labour's philosophical values. Specifically, the study attempts to situate New Labour in the *intellectual* history of the Labour Party and analyse the traditional social democratic values of liberty, equality and community in relation to the ideas and policies of New Labour. The first half of the book charts the *intellectual* history of the Labour Party from its nineteenth century origins in the Labour Movement, through the twentieth century, up until 2004. The second half of the book evaluates the political values of liberty, equality and community in response to the New Right's political thought, various traditional social democratic perspectives and New Labour's contemporary social democratic interpretation.

This book claims that New Labour is a revisionist social democratic government that believes in a positive as well as a negative conception of liberty, holds to non-strict prioritarian and generous sufficiency conceptions of equality, and advocates a belief in state-level, regional-level and local-level community in the form of a communitarian social philosophy.

In addition to this argument the book makes some other important contributions to knowledge. The material gathered includes primary sources such as interviews with former Labour politicians, advisers and academics. This information has provided new and apposite insights into the development of New Labour's political philosophy. This is one reason why New Labour warrants a detailed research investigation and three further reasons exist. Firstly, because it has been argued that New Labour has no clear philosophical commitments that can be described as social democratic[1] or that New Labour is an amalgam of conservative, liberal and social democratic influences[2]. Secondly, New Labour has attempted to enunciate its political motivation and philosophical influences in a number of ways that have been ambiguous and short-lived.[3] Thirdly, because New Labour's political philosophy is largely under-researched and the little research that has been conducted has been in the form of newspaper and journal articles and not in the form of a thorough historical and philosophical evaluation.[4] Therefore, this study is concerned with discovering New Labour's philosophical commitments to a set of social democratic values and by doing so it will suggest that New Labour should describe itself by these value commitments and politically in terms of being a revisionist social democratic project in the Labour Party.

However, by attempting to discover New Labour's political philosophy this presupposes that New Labour has a political philosophy. A more precise research aim is to assess New Labour's commitment to a set of widely accepted social democratic values. Chapters 5-7 attempt to reveal New Labour's interpretation of liberty, equality and community. Yet when embarking upon political philosophy and especially an investigation of ideas and values which are notoriously hard to define, and systematise in a coherent way, a robust understanding of the historical context of the subject (in this case the *intellectual* history of the Labour Party) is necessary.

By the term *intellectual* history I refer in the book to the historical development of social democratic ideas within the Labour Party and the wider Labour Movement that have shaped the character and the attitudes of New Labour. I understand that some fellow political theorists question the historical approach I adopt in evaluating New Labour. Some have suggested to me that an intellectual history adds little to an understanding of New Labour's political philosophy and particularly to what they think about certain political values. In one sense I see this point. However, in methodological terms I am from another school of thought. I think that political values are best understood when located in their historical context. By applying an historical context to a contemporary subject one gains a fuller perspective on the evolution of political ideas and values. To this end, chapters 2-5 chart the main features of the Labour Party's *intellectual* history from its nineteenth century origins until 2004.

Due to the paucity of studies on New Labour's ideas and values particularly during its second term, the book uses primary interview material as well as secondary sources to draw its conclusions. I want to suggest that although the interviews are inherently subjective and few in number, they give the book a closer seat of observation on the actual views and priorities of New Labour. This is because the interviewees consist of former Labour politicians, advisors and academics; who include a former Labour Leader, a former Deputy Leader, a former Education Spokesman, a former Labour backbencher and New Labour advisor prior to 1997, a prominent 'New Labour' academic, a former General Secretary of the Fabian Society and a former Director of the Institute for Public Policy Research. What is clear is that the interviewees are, or have been, significantly closer to the key figures in New Labour than I, or the majority of academics researching New Labour. This does not diminish the existing academic work on New Labour, but it adds a further dimension of qualitative data that can be interpreted and factored into the evaluations made in the course of this book. Three specific research questions are raised in chapter 4 and were posed to the interviewees concerning the development of what we understand to be 'New Labour':

1. How far is the contrast between 'Old Labour' and 'New Labour' a rhetorical one and how real is this distinction?

2. What is the influence of the New Democrats on New Labour?
3. Was the 2002 Budget and the Comprehensive Spending Review (on which the investment in the public services was contingent) a reversion to 'Old Labour' principles or not?

Many other questions could have been posed to the interviewees but the empirical aspect of the chapter is meant to complement not replace the textual analysis of what New Labour claim to be and what they claim to believe in. Therefore, I chose three specific questions. The first question 'How far is the contrast between 'Old Labour' and 'New Labour' a rhetorical one and how real is this distinction?' was asked to discover whether these key Labour figures accepted or rejected the constructs 'Old Labour' and 'New Labour' and to gauge what they thought of the implied difference between these alleged two schools of British social democracy. The second question 'What is the influence of the New Democrats on New Labour?' sought to garner attitudes about a much talked of process in the development of New Labour, namely that Blair, Brown and other modernisers embarked on a similar process of internal and external modernisation as the Clinton New Democrats. Therefore, did the success of the New Democrats significantly influence New Labour? The third question 'Was the 2002 Budget and the Comprehensive Spending Review (on which the investment in the public services was contingent) a reversion to 'Old Labour' principles or not?' was asked because it is argued that the 2002 Budget and the Comprehensive Spending Review marked a step change in New Labour's approach in government. From then on one could see parallels with previous Labour governments in terms of wanting high levels of public spending to improve public services - this was a departure from the approach of the early years in office. The question wanted to judge whether this was a reversion to traditional social democratic governance or something else altogether.

A further point is that because there has yet to be published any book length, detailed analysis of New Labour's political philosophy this book has few texts to utilise. An advantage of this is that the book will add to this gap in research on New Labour, but the obvious disadvantage is that one must use to a greater extent speeches, lectures and policy documents authored by New Labour politicians when examining their philosophical commitments. This would have been a key part of the analysis if a number of core political philosophy texts had existed, but in this situation it increases the reliance of the researcher on such materials and places greater responsibility on the researcher's analytical skills.

The book is divided into nine chapters including the introduction. Chapter 2 begins the task of charting the *intellectual* history of the Labour Party. It takes as its starting point the Labour Party's nineteenth century origins before the establishment of the Labour Representation Committee in 1900 and surveys important thinkers and ideas up until 1949. Chapter 3 continues the *intellectual* history of the Labour Party between 1949 and 1979 and comments on the salience of the 'Great Debate' between the Gaitskellites and the Bevanites; the emergence of the New Left and Thatcher's first electoral victory. Chapter 4 continues the *intellectual* history of the Labour Party between 1979 and 1994 highlighting the key influences including the rise of the Bennite New left; the departure of the 'Gang of Four' in 1981 and the formation of the SDP; the revitalisation of ideas on the social democratic right of the Labour Party after 1983; and a plethora of internal changes of policy and direction between 1987-1994. Chapter 5 is the final chapter on *intellectual* history and focuses on the period 1994-2004. This chapter charts the birth, development and electoral successes of New Labour. It also includes interview material from former Labour politicians, academics and advisors. Chapter 6 marks the second half of the book and begins the philosophical examination of New Labour's commitment to the social democratic value of liberty. Chapter 7 focuses on the value of equality and chapter 8 on community with a discussion of the role of democracy and decentralisation within the communitarian framework that New Labour advocates. Chapters 6-8 begin with a discussion of New Right ideas concerning each of the three social democratic interpretations of these values, an evaluation of various social democratic perspectives on these values is then outlined and finally an analysis of New Labour's specific commitment to these values is offered. Chapter 9 is the conclusion and provides a summary of the main findings.

Following Driver and Martell[5], the book argues that New Labour is a post-Thatcherite political project and had to develop partly in an intellectual environment dominated by New Right ideas and partly in a period of electoral dominance by the Conservative Party. The fusion of New Right ideas in the Conservative Party and the general lack of faith of the British electorate in the Labour Party are interconnected factors that have played a role in the political commitments of New Labour. This book is a study that situates New Labour in the *intellectual* history of the Labour Party and reveals their philosophical commitments to conceptions of liberty, equality and community. Demonstrating that New Labour is a revisionist social democratic government that legitimately sits in the broad church of British social democracy. As a final introductory comment I believe that an analysis of the political philosophy of any subject whether an individual, a group or a political party must succeed in fulfilling certain tasks. It must be firmly rooted in an *intellectual* history of the subject; survey all of the relevant source material; interpret statements of doctrine and practice; construct a coherent framework of the subject's value commitments; and, if possible, gain access to material outside of the usual research remit with the aim of contributing something new to the body of knowledge on the subject. The outcome of this book, I hope, fulfils these tasks. Any errors are of course my own.

2

AN INTELLECTUAL HISTORY OF THE LABOUR PARTY: 1900-1949

To understand the political philosophy of New Labour and the values of the Labour Party in general, it is important to grasp a history of its personalities, internal struggles, policy achievements and its perspectives on socialism, to name several possible areas of historical study. This chapter, although by no means comprehensive in its history, will firstly attempt to provide an *intellectual* history of the first forty-nine years of the Labour Party. It will begin by looking back to the roots of the Labour Movement in the nineteenth century, analysing the political climate of the day and more specifically, the role of the working class in the beginnings of an organised labour movement in Britain. Secondly, the chapter will attempt to uncover the underlying values embedded within Labour Party history. This chapter begins the exercise of explaining and understanding the political philosophy of New Labour and therefore it must identify the notable *intellectual* themes and issues relevant to the study of New Labour's political philosophy. The book will contend, as Alasdair MacIntyre does that actions as opposed to physical movements embody ideas and values which are essential to their identification.[1]

Nineteenth Century Origins of the Labour Party

The early nineteenth century saw the rise of the new industrial working class who campaigned for greater enfranchisement since only two percent of the United Kingdom's population had the vote. Due to mounting civil protests and partly as a reaction to the French Revolution, the Whigs introduced the 1832 Great Reform Act. This brought greater enfranchisement and prompted the emergence of the trade unions in the latter half of the nineteenth century. However, in some cases the franchise was reduced including the situation regarding 'free borough'.[2] In 1867, the second Great Reform Act brought the introduction of partial enfranchisement to ratepayers in towns and cities. As the nineteenth century progressed, the two original parties evolved into the Liberal and Conservative parties. The Liberal Party was more of a coalition between the Whigs, Non-conformists and the Radicals, than a coherent ideological party. At first glance the radical liberal wing of the Liberal Party could be understood as the group of politicians most likely to support causes connected to working class life but, the Liberal Party also consisted of classical liberals, associated with the Manchester School of laissez-faire economics, who held ideas that were not compatible with issues of social justice and social reformism for the working class. Furthermore, nineteenth century Conservatism included a strong sense of social paternalism. In fact, the Tory paternalists under Disraeli, who was arguably the father of Tory paternalism and one-nation Conservatism, passed the Artisans' Dwellings Act which according to Greenleaf was a notable piece of legislation which attempted to:

'...tackle the problem of urban working class housing as a whole and (for) the first time public authorities were given responsibility for remedying defects in privately owned dwellings by compulsory purchase if necessary.'[3]

Disraeli's Tory Government also passed the Factory Act and statutes that encouraged Friendly Societies, made labour contracts more equitable and removed trade union activity from the remit of the conspiracy law, to name but a few pieces of legislation that such Tory paternalists enacted.[4] The collectivist strand in Tory ideology supports the claim that branches of Conservatism are paternalistic and statist in their approach to governance. W.H. Greenleaf asserts that:

> '...so many unhistorically minded critics persist in seeing the Conservative record anachronistically in terms of some misleading legend based on ideological hostility or in the exclusive context perhaps of the other, very different and anti-statist, strand in Conservative tradition. Whether one approves of it or not, the Tory Party effort and effect in this collectivist regard has been very substantial indeed.'[5]

Therefore, it is not quite accurate to view the Liberal Party as the natural party with outright concern for the working class and, in addition, it is disingenuous to view the nineteenth century Conservatives as being wholly unsympathetic to the problems affecting working class life. What can be argued is that even in the years after the second Great Reform Act, working class people were impatient at the rate and limitations of both Liberal and Tory social reform.

Socialist societies, socialist leagues and federations were forming mainly in London, Birmingham and some northern industrial towns. For example, in 1869 the Labour Representation League was established with the aim of promoting the registration of the working class vote and enabling working class men to stand as Labour candidates.[6] However, the League gradually dwindled in support and failed to maintain itself financially. Henry Pelling views this failure as indicating:

> '...the unwillingness of the Whigs and middle-class Liberals to see working men elected as their representatives.'[7]

Before the advent of the Labour Party in British politics, it was the Liberal Party and, in particular, the radical wing of the Liberal Party that claimed to represent the industrial working class and the majority of the industrial working class were Liberal supporters. Politically, it appeared that the working class was content with the Liberal Party with Gladstone at the helm, as he had championed the issue of working class suffrage a decade before. Nevertheless, the Conservative Party has always gained the support of certain elements of the working class. The class system which until recently was clearly identifiable and clear cut in social customs and practices, reinforced people's social status and therefore prompted elements of the working classes to show an attitude of deference to the upper classes. This type of deference was specifically applied to the Tory Party who have historically represented tradition, the establishment and the monarchy to select just a few of its main concerns.[8] Deferential working class Tories felt that the upper classes were meant to govern and would be best at governing and, because they were Tories, they embodied the class system and therefore that is one reason why deferent working class voters supported the Conservative Party and not the Liberal Party.

The 1880s were a period of dramatic change for many in the Liberal Party. The rise of 'New Liberalism'[9] had its roots in the 1880s and had its legislative impact especially in the period 1906-1914. New Liberalism was a distinct political philosophy and one which at best could be described as contradictory to classical 'laissez-faire' liberalism. Andrew Vincent and Raymond Plant connect the emergence of New Liberalism as a political philosophy with the growth in influence of the British Idealist philosophers in the last three decades of the nineteenth century.[10] The most significant of all the idealist philosophers upon the philosophical establishment of New Liberalism was the Oxford philosopher T.H. Green.[11] The philosophical thrust of New Liberalism was different from classical liberalism in three main ways.

Firstly, New Liberalism believed in state intervention as a positive tool to secure greater social justice for the masses. This flew against the traditional laissez-faire approach to free market economics that Liberalism had advocated for the previous half a century. C.F.G. Masterman was one of the first New Liberals, who realised the benefits of the collectivist and statist approach for the Liberal Party. W.H. Greenleaf notes that:

> 'While always opposed to the "insect state" of Socialism Masterman was early prepared to accept and urge the reconstruction of society "on a collectivist basis".'[12]

Masterman proposed an array of state-led, social policies to ameliorate social and economic ills in Britain in his 1901 publication, *The Heart of the Empire*[13] and then later in his 1909 piece, *The Condition of England*.[14]

Secondly and connected to the first point about the use of the state as a positive tool to implement social justice is New Liberalism's philosophical conception of positive liberty. Classical liberalism argued for a negative conception of liberty, inasmuch as the individual needed to be set free from as many legal and civil constraints as possible and that a free market produced the best conditions for the creation of wealth. In contrast, the New Liberals argued that a positive conception of liberty empowered the individual and could be a positive force through the mechanisms of state intervention in the market to secure necessary material goods and services for not just the rich and the able. In particular, L.T. Hobhouse espoused this positive conception of liberty in his notable piece of 1911, entitled, *Liberalism*.[15] Greenleaf suggests that Hobhouse's understanding of liberty was:

> '...built on a "more concrete" and "positive" conception of freedom; and was encapsulated in the oft-quoted epigram: "liberty without equality is a name of noble sound and squalid result".'[16]

The third philosophical position advocated by the New Liberals was the issue of social morality. They believed that individuals had not only personal morality to uphold and responsibilities to fulfil but also a social morality to uphold and social responsibilities to fulfil. One New Liberal, J.A. Hobson, criticised laissez-faire capitalism as being antithetical to such a vision of a communitarian and collectivist version of liberalism.[17] Thus, in short, the value of community responsibility came to the forefront of New Liberal thought.[18] The New Liberals, taking much of their political philosophy from the likes of the British Idealist thinkers and notably T.H. Green, also adopted philosophical perspectives from philosophers who influenced the British Idealists' conception of responsibility, community and rights, such as Hegel. Classical Liberals in contrast followed the Lockean perspective[19] that held that morality was personal and that responsibilities were individual and *ergo*, each man was to consider himself and his family. In Classical Liberal philosophy, little is mentioned about the wider notions of social morality and social responsibility particularly regarding the vulnerable, the underprivileged and the destitute. For the New Liberals, the Hegelian perspective on community and responsibility took precedence over the writings of John Locke.

David Marquand argues that the New Liberals influenced the revisionist right of the Labour Party during the mid-twentieth century. According to Marquand, the underlying political values of New Liberals such as J.A Hobson, L.T Hobhouse, C.F.G Masterman and of course, T.H Green were akin to those values advocated by Hugh Gaitskell and Anthony Crosland during the 1950s and 1960s.[20] This point about an evolutionary British tradition of leftist political philosophy is noticeable in Marquand's following quotation, speaking initially about the New Liberals, he notes:

> 'They redefined the core liberal principles of liberty and personal fulfilment to justify an active state, capable of securing 'positive' freedom as well as 'negative'. In the language of a later period, political citizenship was to be supplemented by social citizenship: constitutional democracy by social democracy.'[21]

However, the broad working class acquiescence with the Liberal Party was not the whole story of working class politics in the late nineteenth century. The Trade Union Congress was formed in 1871, meeting annually; it was regarded as the central parliament of labour.[22] This involved elected union representatives attending annual conferences, discussing the improvements that their unions wanted for their workers and the parliamentary committee was recognised for lobbying the Government on behalf of the trade unions.[23]

A notable event occurred in Germany which in turn raised the profile of socialism in Britain. In the election of 1877, the German Social Democratic Party won thirteen seats in the Reichstag.[24] This success was largely due to a change in the ideological trajectory of the Party after the adoption of the Gotha Programme of 1875.[25] The German Social Democratic Party was formally known as the Socialist Workers' Party of Germany but prior to this it was two separate and rival socialist parties: the Social Democratic Workers' Party and the General Association of German Workers. The Social Democratic Workers' Party was founded at the Eisenach Congress of 1869 and its members were thus known as the 'Eisenachers'. They were Marxist socialists who followed the teaching and instructions of Marx and Engels, under the leadership of Liebknecht, Bebel and Bracke. The General Association of German Workers followed the ideas of Ferdinand Lasalle and were henceforth referred to as the 'Lasallians'. They rejected Marxist socialism and desired a peaceful and democratic transformation of German capitalist society into a society committed to ideas of social justice. Both parties merged at the Gotha Congress of 1875 after an intense political struggle, which saw the German government intervene and undertake reprisals. The Gotha Congress also witnessed the proposal and acceptance of a programme designed by the Lasallians which was to change the official direction of the German Social Democratic Party and in turn, allowed them to gain a wider voter base and poll nearly half a million votes in the 1877 elections. One of the main protagonists in the development of the German Social Democratic Party was the thinker Eduard Bernstein whose ethical, evolutionary socialism will be discussed later in the chapter. Bernstein lived in England for a period of time and was influenced by the gradual evolutionary socialism of the early Fabians. Sidney Hook recounts how Bernstein found himself living, working and moving in left-wing circles in England in 1888, as a political dissident banished initially from Germany by Bismarck's anti-socialist laws:

'In Switzerland, where Bernstein remained in consequence of Bismarck's anti-socialist laws, he edited the official Party newspaper. In 1888, under pressure from Bismarck, Bernstein and the newspaper he edited was banished by the Swiss government. He then moved to London where he worked closely with Friedrich Engels the collaborator of Marx.'[26]

The 1880s were something of a watershed in socialist activity in Britain. Although socialist organisations were heterogeneous in make up, their leaders began to take on a more pragmatic outlook in order to appeal to broader elements of the electorate as opposed to merely the urban working man.[27] The decade saw the publication of numerous pamphlets, articles in newspapers and letters on the worsening economic and social conditions of the urban working class and their apparent expression of political defiance through the ideology of socialism, if one can call nineteenth century socialism in Britain's industrial towns an ideology. The point being made is simply that during the 1880s, for the majority of people involved with socialist societies and the working class agitators and activists, socialism was not a coherent economic doctrine. Socialism in Britain was not organised in the form of any national party until the collaboration of groups leading to the establishment of the LRC in 1900. Socialism, save a few

Marxists, was an expression of working class defiance at the political establishment of the day and a moral reaction to the drudgery of urban working class life, rather than a generally accepted and understood political ideology.

At that time other organisations connected to the Labour Movement began to organise themselves such as the Marxist, Social Democratic Federation.[28] The Social Democratic Federation founded in 1881, was not a social democratic party, as we would understand one to be today, but a Marxist federation that believed in economic determinism and saw capitalist society as unjust, involving a class struggle between the proletariat and the bourgeoisie.[29] The SDF like the Labour Marxists of the 1920s and the 1930s were always small in number and on the very margins of the Movement and the Labour Party. Their political thought consisted of an orthodox Marxist position concerning the determining factor of the mode of production, the exploitative capitalist system of wage labour, and the necessity of a class struggle, and the idea that 'labourism' and later social democracy are a compromise which seek only to ameliorate and not revolutionise the capitalist system. However, Labour Marxists and apparently Engels and Marx, believed that Britain's situation was different to continental capitalist democracies and, therefore, they accepted that with a large enfranchised working class, Marxism through the Labour Party, could be brought about by the ballot box.[30] H.M. Hyndman, the dominant figure in the establishment and the early years of the SDF, is an important figure in Labour Party history. Hyndman is important not for the direct impact his thought had on the Labour Movement, but because his ideas influenced a generation of Marxists who abandoned the SDF in favour of making the Labour Party a Marxist, working class political organisation.[31] Foote notes that as the lead player of the SDF Hyndman's approach was autocratic and, crucially, he rejected the trade unions as a vehicle for working class agitation. This rejection of the trade unions ostracised Hyndman from the Labour Movement and left the SDF with little influence.[32]

Another organisation was the Fabian Society, which was established in 1883 and comprised middle class intellectuals who believed in the democratic and gradual evolution of an unjust capitalist society in to a socialist society, through the means of state intervention and nationalisation.[33] Leading figures included George Bernard Shaw and Sidney and Beatrice Webb. Sidney Webb himself famously defined the character of Fabian Socialism with the phrase, 'the inevitability of gradualism'.[34] Therefore, Fabian socialism believed that progress and societal improvement was inevitable and that reforms would be incremental; each one taking a great deal of time and that in itself was necessary because democracy demanded gradual not revolutionary change. A further point warrants a mention regarding the tactics of Fabians in their quest for a socialist society. Foote argues that as a political group the early Fabians were more eager to permeate the Liberal and Conservative parties and further their ideas from within the existing structures and traditions of the two great parties of state, rather than co-operating with a working class party whose attitude to intellectual concepts and theories was often hostile:

> 'The Fabian leaders were constantly exasperated by the narrow-minded prejudice of the class which suffered most from the existing system, and looked instead to enlightened members of the two main parties, rejecting the ideas of an independent workers' party. Some Fabians, such as Hubert Bland, were more sympathetic to a workers' party than others, but the general attitude of the Fabian leadership was to permeate the Liberal and Conservative parties, municipally and nationally.'[35]

Arguably, the most salient contribution made by the Fabian Society in this era was a series of lectures organised by the society entitled, *The Basis and Prospects of Socialism*.[36]

These lectures were later published in 1889, edited by George Bernard Shaw under the new title *Fabian Essays in Socialism*[37], and received wide acclaim.

The year 1884 witnessed the third Great Reform Act, which enabled agricultural labourers to vote. However, poor men in towns did not receive the right to vote until 1918. Thus, by 1884 significant changes had taken place to the political map of Britain, nevertheless, as well as the poor urban men, women still had no political representation or voting powers. A further organisation was founded in 1893; it was known as the Independent Labour Party and led by the Scottish miner Keir Hardie.[38] The ILP was a group of very independent minded people who campaigned for democratic socialism. The ILP had MPs in the House of Commons before the Labour Representation Committee but it was a small and localised organisation. In 1900 the Social Democratic Federation, the Fabian Society and the ILP met together and formed the Labour Representation Committee. The purpose of which was to form a single political organisation that funded and campaigned to get its MPs elected to parliament. In 1900, the Labour Representation Committee had only two MPs, Keir Hardie and Richard Bell, but realised that the TUC could provide the necessary financial support to construct a formidable political force, representing the working classes in Britain.

The Labour Representation Committee and later the Labour Party[39] was promised Liberal votes in vital contested seats and a level of representation in parliament far beyond what it could have previously hoped for if campaigning on its own. It is perhaps worth noting that the Liberal Party would probably not have agreed to such a convenient pact with the LRC if it had been a substantially socialist party. In addition, the membership during the opening years of LRC history was a combination of some socialists and many working class 'labourites' and trade unions members. The term 'labourites' is used to identify MPs and members of the Labour Party whose cause was to improve the lives of the working classes through practical means. For example, through ameliorative measures such as wage rises, increased benefits and union representation, as opposed to British socialist doctrine in the early part of the twentieth century specifically advocating the nationalisation of industry. Labourites were not socialists by this definition and largely speaking were ambivalent to ideology, holding to a pragmatic, non-doctrinaire political outlook. It was not until the 1918 constitution was affirmed that the majority of the Labour Party would commit themselves to a political, social and economic doctrine and to what we would understand to be a form of democratic socialism.

Constitution, Communism and Keynesianism: 1918-1949

The year 1918 witnessed the Labour Party establish a constitution in the form of a document known as the *Programme for the Future*.[40] Henry Drucker notes the political background to why the Labour Party finally articulated its political aims in 1918:

'It was only at the end of the war, in light of the collapse of Liberalism in Britain, the success of the Bolshevik project in Russia, the increasing militancy of the shop stewards movement, the emerging socialism of some of the key unions, and the fear that if Labour did not adopt a programme others would and the movement would pass the party by…'[41]

This document outlining for the first time the Labour Party's constitution, included measures to:

'…transform the party from a loose federation of affiliated organisations to a national party with individual members in local constituency parties subject to central discipline. The party conference is to comprise delegates from national affiliated organisations and delegates from constituency parties in proportion to their affiliated membership.'[42]

In addition, the year 1918 was also of significant importance because it saw the Labour Party try to express its philosophical motivations in a programme committing the Party to democratic socialism. The document was entitled, *Labour and the New Social Order*.[43] It included commitments to the common ownership of the commanding heights of the economy and the means of production, distribution and exchange (notably the infamous Clause IV), universal enforcement of the national minimum (the pre-cursor of welfare state entitlements), full employment, a minimum wage, minimum working conditions for a maximum forty-eight hour week, progressive taxation, a capital levy to pay off war debts and a surplus for the common good.[44] However, Stephen Haseler argues that Clause IV was not a fair interpretation of the British ethical socialism of the Labour Party. He interprets British socialism as ethical rather than scientific or economic determinist. Bernstein originally put this distinction forward in his seminal piece of revisionist socialist thought, *Evolutionary Socialism*.[45] Bernstein highlights three main strands of thought that makes Marxism scientific socialism.

Firstly Bernstein argues that Marxism advocates the historical materialist interpretation of history. This materialist view of history:

'...means to trace back all phenomena to the necessary movement of matter....the movement of matter which determines the form of ideas and the directions of the will...'[46]

Secondly, he states that the political economy of Marxist socialism is distinct from other socialisms because it attempts to connect the method of production of the material things of life with determining the social, political and spiritual processes of life.[47]

Thirdly and finally, Bernstein highlights the necessity of a class war to Marx's strand of socialism that is not present in democratic forms of socialism. For Bernstein, democratic socialism is ethical and value based rather than scientific, economically determined and an inevitable historical process. Socialism for Bernstein is about democracy, social justice and greater equality. Furthermore, socialism according to Bernstein is inseparable from democracy and thus, it becomes a political project:

'Universal franchise is, from two sides, the alternative to a violent revolution. But universal suffrage is only a part of democracy, although a part which in time must draw the other parts after it as the magnet attracts to itself the scattered portions of iron. It certainly proceeds more slowly than many would wish, but in spite of that it is at work. And social democracy cannot further this work better than by taking its stand unreservedly on the theory of democracy - on the ground of universal suffrage with all the consequences resulting therefrom to its tactics.'[48]

This is yet another difference between Bernstein's revisionist socialism which is parliamentary and reformist and Marx's belief in an inevitable physical revolution and the eventual dictatorship of the proletariat. Sidney Hook states that one of the reasons why *Evolutionary Socialism* was regarded as heretical within Marxism was that it advocated the view that socialism should break with all notions of Utopianism:

'It must stop conceiving of itself as fulfilling a final goal, and constantly realize itself in the myriad of daily tasks, small or large, which confront the movement towards greater democratization. Whatever the ends of socialism, the means to achieve them must be continuous with these ends.'[49]

According to Hook, Bernstein believed there to be no predetermined socialist goals apart from democracy and it is because of this belief that Bernstein immortalised the phrase:

'...the movement means everything for me and that what is usually called "the final aim of socialism" is nothing.'[50]

Therefore, Bernstein had no vision of what socialism ultimately was, if it was anything other than a movement or a process of making democratic capitalist society more just and equitable through the means of reformist social democracy.[51] As was stated above, Bernstein was influenced by the early Fabians whilst living in exile in London, but what was his influence on British socialism? The answer is that it is difficult to measure because although the Gaitskellites in the Labour Party adopted the name 'revisionists' and one can see an ideological influence from Bernstein in the way the Gaitskellite revisionists attempted to revise mid-twentieth century British socialism, any further direct influence is not immediately obvious. That said, Crosland said in a letter to Philip Williams that he wanted to be a second Bernstein. Therefore, perhaps Crosland himself, in terms of his argument about needing to equate socialism with political principles and not specific policies (*vis-a-vis* greater equality as opposed to nationalisation) proved to be the main subject of influence of Bernstein's political thought.

Another strand of thought at the time was syndicalism. The syndicalist assertion of worker's management of industry appealed to G.D.H. Cole who was Chichele Professor of Social and Political Theory at Oxford University in light of his belief in the oppression of the working class through the wage system.[52] Echoing Marx, not only did Cole cite wagery as a structural ill of the capitalist system he called, as the syndicalists did, for a class war. Militant class-conflict in the form of industrial action was necessary and inevitable for Cole as the capitalist and working classes were opposed to each other due to the means of production of capitalism, which requires one class to exploit the other for profit. Cole explains his political thought on such matters in his 1928 piece, *The World of Labour: A Discussion of the Present and Future of Trade Unionism*.[53] Cole's socialism was libertarian as opposed to being collectivist in method, which was the approach of Fabian socialism. Foote posits the view that Cole was deeply critical of the Fabian brand of socialism because according to Cole they:

'...carried the anti-capitalist arguments to their logical conclusions in their call for nationalisation, but in so doing had forgotten that socialism was a human proposition as well as a business one...They saw nationalisation as the panacea for the problems of anarchical competition, and had failed to notice that capitalism itself had eliminated competition by means of creating an even deadlier enemy in the monopoly.'[54]

Guild socialism rejected the proposal of state monopolies advocated by many British socialists, on the grounds that transferring capitalist power from private owners to the ownership of the state bureaucracy was one and the same evil for the two following reasons. Firstly, workers were still not present in managing, decision-making and occupying positions of power within their role as producers. Secondly, capitalist power was being equally entrenched by Fabian socialists and such like who were advocating state ownership and management of industry. For Guild socialists, the fundamental issue of workers' control was missed by socialist ownership of industry through the state because mainstream socialist thought of the day ignored the question of the role of producers, (namely the workers) and focused on the method of distribution of the goods produced and the nature of capitalism.

Foote states that syndicalism, and he includes Guild socialism within that ideational bracket:

'...raised once again the point of view of the producers, but in a very one-sided manner. Whereas, the collectivist totally disregarded the producer, the syndicalist totally disregarded everything but the producer.'[55]

There is an element of truth in the claim that collectivist socialism focussed less on the workers' position in its concepts of socialising capitalism through state management and ownership of industry. However, collectivist socialists such as the early Fabians would perhaps argue that nationalisation as a policy of a Labour Government would be democratic common ownership and therefore individuals such as workers had an interest in the state bureaucracy controlling industry and not a capitalist or a board of shareholders.

Haseler quotes G.D.H. Cole referring to the socialism of the Labour Party as a,

'...broad human movement on behalf of the bottom dog.'[56]

This comment by Cole is perhaps particularly pertinent in that such an erudite man chose to sum up the philosophical thrust of the Labour Party's form of socialism with a vague and somewhat intuitive feeling about a movement existing for the less well off in British society. On the surface Cole's comment about the nature of British socialism may seem to imply that as a political philosophy it lacks a grounded philosophical thrust, however, the work done by Cole especially his writings on Guild Socialism establishes him as a clear and cogent thinker regarding his particular design for British socialism and one who was a significant influence on Hugh Gaitskell. His comment quoted above reflects the character of the British socialist movement, which differs philosophically from wing to wing and from faction to faction. Taken in this light, one could argue that British socialism is united in the fact that it exists for the worst off or 'bottom dog' in British society whilst at the same time differs significantly on precise political approaches and definitions of socialism.

Haseler claims that Clause IV was grafted on to the Labour Party in 1918 and that the Party has been trying to define its key motivations ever since and has often obscured the historical mission of representing the less fortunate in British society. This issue of defining and redefining the philosophical values of the Labour Party and in particular the struggle between those politicians on the one hand, who (not dissimilarly to Marxist socialists) have a fixed vision of what socialism is and can express it through the passing of specific policies (such as nationalisation, workers' councils and a certain approach to foreign policy issues) and those politicians on the other hand who have less of a fixed vision of socialism based around policy prescriptions but hold to a set of underlying values (like a positive conception of liberty, greater equality and community responsibility) as the yardstick to measure whether one is implementing socialism or not; was to resurface in the 'Great Debate' of the 1950s and was a precursor of the present debate surrounding New Labour.

The years after the Great War provided the Labour Party with a considerably wider voter base due to the gradual extension to universal suffrage and in particular, the introduction of the Representation of the People Act, in 1928. The mid-1930s saw the newly elected party leader Clement Attlee attempt to restrict the membership to democrats only. This event can be interpreted as part of a gradual process of removing or pressurising the Marxist elements of the Labour Party to leave. For example, 1901 saw the disaffiliation of the Marxist, Social Democratic Federation one of the founding organisations of the Labour Party. At the 1924 Party conference the Party banned all communists from membership and from adoption as candidates. The 1925 Party conference reaffirmed the ban on communists as individual members and requested that the trade unions not allow communists to be delegates at local or national conferences. The 1928 Party conference banned Communist Party members from attending conference as trade union delegates. The interesting point to note here is that not only were communists expelled but also what came to be known as the sympathetic wing or 'fellow travellers' within the Party. This act of removing supporters, advocates or members of the Communist Party came about after mounting support for the USSR during the 1930s in British universities, trade unions and amongst other sections of society. This was largely due to the global recession of the late 1920s and early 1930s that caused significant elements of the working class and the university educated middle class to view Marxism and in particular, the idea of a planned economy, as a viable alternative to the economic inconsistencies and ills of capitalism. Richard Crossman points out that the 1930s were the high-water mark of Marxist theory and communist influence in the Labour Party. Crossman states that:

'It is no exaggeration to say that Tawney, Laski, Strachey and the Webbs dominated the thought of young socialists in the 1930s and deeply influenced many practical politicians in the Shadow Cabinet. The Left Book Club replaced the Fabian Society as the home of the intellectual avant-garde.'[57]

R.H. Tawney is widely regarded as one of the seminal thinkers in the emergence of 'British Socialism'. Matt Carter suggests that it was through Tawney's attendance of Balliol College, Oxford and in his friendships with Edward Caird, the Master of Balliol and Charles Gore, then Bishop of Oxford whilst he was studying at Balliol that informed his philosophical outlook in keeping with the British Idealist tradition of T.H Green.[58] Carter states that when Tawney attended Balliol College it was, even after Green's death, a place imbued with his ideas:

'At the time Green's ideas were dominant and it would have been impossible for a young, socially aware Balliol student such as Tawney not to be strongly influenced by Green's lingering spirit...'[59]

Carter's argument is that Tawney can be viewed in the same philosophical heritage as Green and disciples of his such as Henry Scott Holland and Charles Gore who were Christians.[60] This is an important connection because it unites Tawney - arguably the main social democratic thinker and moralist of the twentieth century - with the political tradition and ideas of nineteenth century New Liberalism. The connection is not seamless, but according to Carter, it is genuine and historically accurate:

'Tawney's work rests on the same ideas that underpinned the work of Gore and Holland, strengthening the notion that there was a strong ideological connection between them. The three ideas are: a spiritual approach to life; emphasis on the moral aspect of human personality; and an organic view of society united by a common good.'[61]

'While Green wanted a Constructive Liberalism to revive the Liberal Party, and Tawney built an ethical socialism to support the Labour Party, the two doctrines were in essence the same. Indeed, making an argument used by Ball and other idealists previously, Tawney claimed that there was a close connection between liberalism and his version of socialism as the natural successor to liberalism and he believed that socialists must retain concerns about freedom to be successful.'[62]

If whilst at Oxford Tawney's political thought was influenced by New Liberal ideas, his later political thought is difficult to pigeon-hole within the various strands of British socialism as it changed emphasis in different periods of his life. Foote wisely comments on the difficulty in classifying Tawney's political thought:

> 'The difficulty of categorising him politically was underlined by his own political shifts; from an endorsement of a radical Guild Socialism in 1921 through his authorship of the gradualist Labour and the Nation in 1928, his savage attacks on gradualism in the 1930s to his endorsement of revisionism in the 1950s.'[63]

In the context of this section of the chapter one can regard Tawney's writings of the 1920s and 1930s and especially his 1921 publication, *The Acquisitive Society*[64] as at least indicative of his Labour left sympathies and at most an endorsement of quasi-Labour Marxism. This is why Tawney can be discussed with other thinkers of the time such as Harold Laski and John Strachey. *The Acquisitive Society*, more than any other of Tawney's works, influenced the Labour left. Tawney was influenced by Guild Socialist ideas whilst writing the piece and this type of syndicalist socialism is a variant of Labour Marxism.[65] Nevertheless, Tawney's ideas in the 1921 book were distinct from orthodox Marxism because he did not believe that private property *per se* was inherently exploitative and part of the class superstructure which systematically alienated and used workers for private gain. Tawney was hostile to the character of private property as was present in western capitalist states during the first decades of the twentieth century. However, Tawney believed that when private property was used for the common good, for the benefit of the community as opposed to the private financial benefits of the classes of property-owners, then property could be morally righteous and just.[66]

If Tawney's notion of the character of property was different to Marxist assumptions about private property, but still akin to Labour Marxist suspicions of private property as part of the illness of capitalism, then his main intellectual thrust in *The Acquisitive Society* was certainly in the Labour

Marxist tradition. This main intellectual point was simply that western capitalist societies had become societies preoccupied with acquisitiveness and that from Tawney's normative perspective was morally wrong and corrupt. Tawney notes that:

> 'Such societies may be called Acquisitive Societies because their whole tendency and interest and preoccupation is to promote the acquisition of wealth.'[67]

Leading on from the issue of acquisitiveness, Tawney stated that he believed it to cause two further social and moral ills. Firstly, such materialism and greed in individuals made them less compassionate towards the needy and therefore, poverty flourished relatively unabated. Secondly, the moral complexion of such acquisitive societies had been significantly diminished and self-interest had become, to greater or lesser extent, the prevailing social philosophy. However, if Tawney as a thinker diagnosed the sickness of western capitalism as acquisitiveness and noted that such a condition caused great poverty and a hollow and selfish morality, then what did he determine to be the point of origin for such acquisitive societies? Foote suggests that Tawney blamed two overarching events, firstly:

> 'Tawney traced this disorder to the foundation of capitalism, when individual rights were abstracted from any reference to the function played in society by the individual.'[68]

Secondly, Tawney emphasised the rejection by many in western capitalist societies of the Christian faith and specifically the rise in the idolatry of wealth and possessions instead of the worship of the Creator God. Christian morality was dwindling and the social and national character of such societies was being greatly demeaned. As Tawney himself recorded in his diary:

'Moral conduct by itself is not enough. Unless a man believes in spiritual things - in God - altruism is absurd...'[69]

Another important Labour thinker is John Strachey. Strachey was a one-time Labour Marxist and during the 1930s his Marxism was expressed in three publications; the 1932 book, *The Coming Struggle for Power*,[70] *The Menace of Fascism*,[71] published in 1933 and the 1935 book, *The Nature of Capitalist Crisis*.[72] According to his biographer, Hugh Thomas *The Coming Struggle for Power* was a sophisticated interpretation of Marxism whereby Strachey posited the orthodox Marxist theory of history, but in the context of twentieth century events:

'Twentieth century conditions...had brought with them monopoly, nationalism and, after 1919, unstable money. None of these things was the cause of the capitalist crisis, whose real nature derived from the essential features of capitalism, of the fact, that is, that capitalist production was carried on without plan, that its only regulating mechanism was the mechanism of the market, and that the wealth of the community was concentrated in the small number of persons who owned the means of production.'[73]

Strachey argued that actual crises in capitalism were as Marx suggested, due to its mode of production; the anarchical market with all of its shortcomings.[74] Strachey also argued that the only option open to capitalism and capitalist states who were experiencing economic crises was to engage in:

'Direct, open terror against the workers, violent aggression against its rivals, can alone enable a modern empire to maintain itself. A name for such a policy has been found: it is fascism.'[75]

The final section of the book is an appeal for communism in Britain, and communism by its orthodox means advocated by Marx himself through a workers' revolution. Strachey's 1933 book *The Menace of Fascism* was a shocking and deliberately alarming political tract about what was going to occur now that Nazism had won power in Germany.[76] Written primarily as a warning of the rise of fascism in Germany, it was not intended as a work of political thought or explicitly to convey Marxist politics.

Strachey's third book of the decade, *The Nature of Capitalist Crisis*, was an overt attempt to advocate the communist case. In this piece, Strachey criticised the economists Keynes and Robbins for being preoccupied with monetary issues and for ignoring the salience of Marx's labour theory of value. As Thomas asserts, Strachey thought that:

'This rejection was the fatal turning-point. Marx had not made this mistake, and made the critical distinction between labour and labour power: an artisan or peasant sells his labour embodied in a community on the market; a worker sells his labour power to a capitalist employer who then sells this worker's labour.'[77]

Nevertheless, Strachey's Marxism although influential and sincere, was not to endure. If the 1920s and 1930s were the zenith of Strachey's Marxism then the war years and postwar years were its abandonment in favour of social democracy. As Foote observes:

'...his reading of Keynes modified his earlier views and he became increasingly convinced that State direction of the economy could overcome capitalist crisis. He then played a prominent part in the Labour Party, becoming Minister of Food in the 1945 Government...'[78]

Harold Laski was another of the prominent Marxists of the 1930s but in the 1920s, he was influenced by the pluralism of J.N. Figgis and adopted federalist ideas regarding society.⁷⁹ This can be clearly seen in his 1925 publication, *A Grammar of Politics*.⁸⁰ Unlike Marx and Lenin, Laski viewed the state in a normative light. He argued that the state was coercive but nevertheless it could serve the needs of its citizens. The state was run by the ruling classes and this was problematic for Laski, but it could be run justly under a socialist government. One could say that Laski desired to legitimise the state through socialism not Marxism. This was the main argument developed in his 1935 book, *The State in Theory and Practice*⁸¹ in which he cogently remarked that:

'...the first duty of political philosophy is to examine the character of the State in its actuality rather than its idea.'⁸²

Thus, it was evident that for Laski and his political philosophy of Marxism in the 1930s the nature and practical role of the state was crucial to the nature of politics that it engendered. Nevertheless, to note that Laski's attitude towards the state was not orthodox Marxism is accurate, but his agenda was a radical departure from mainstream Labour socialism. However, the influence of Marxist theory was only temporary and soon died out due to communist opposition to the Second World War, which in turn divided and eventually ended the sympathetic Left Book Club. Furthermore, the 1945 election victory of Attlee's Labour Party reigned in the return of the Fabian approach to British socialism.⁸³

At the time of the publication of John Maynard Keynes' 1936 book, *The General Theory of Employment, Interest and Money*⁸⁴, the Labour Party was undecided on the most appropriate form of political economy to use to implement its policy aims. Much of the Labour left was not only influenced by the Marxist ideas of workers' collective ownership but also by the underconsumptionist ideas of the economist J.A Hobson. The Labour right had shown their indecision in the realms of economic ideas during the 1929-

1931 Labour Government when Chancellor Philip Snowden succumbed to the free-market and the authority of City bankers to co-ordinate economic policy. In his biography of Keynes, Robert Skidelsky argues that even shortly after the publication of *The General Theory* in 1936, the Labour Party continued to prefer a form of socialism as its economic doctrine although parts of the Labour Party were beginning to see how capitalism could be managed and controlled to further socialist causes.[85] When Skidelsky asserts that the Labour Party still preferred 'socialism', he is referring to the notion of a largely planned economy with a diminished private sector. This concept was certainly dominant on the Labour left and continued to be so. Nevertheless, Keynes and his economic theory were gradually affecting socialist ideas surrounding economics, and Keynesianism was emerging in some parts of the Labour Party as a possible economic approach for British socialism. As Foote notes:

> 'Keynes was putting forward a formidable challenge to a Labour intelligentsia which abhorred the cut-throat competition of private enterprise while having no realistic solution to the problems of the trade cycle and general unemployment.'[86]

Keynesianism appealed to much of the Labour Party.[87] This was for three main reasons. Firstly, because it rejected the classical economics of the free-market and that was consistent with the Party's philosophical values. Secondly, one of the primary goals of Keynesianism was its belief in the viability of full employment, therefore again demonstrating its convenience for the Labour Party with its moral detestation for high unemployment. Third and finally, Keynesianism as an economic doctrine legitimised through practical argument, the use of state institutions as a tool to maintain economic stability. Thus, Keynesianism provided the Labour Party with an economic argument for state intervention, which would in turn enable it to pursue its philosophical aims, such as the redistribution of income and wealth. An extra point relevant to the Labour Party's adoption of Keynesianism, made by Elizabeth Durbin, is that as an economic theory Keynesianism began to win support from leading Labour economists. Notably Douglas Jay, Evan Durbin, Hugh Dalton and Hugh Gaitskell who were members of the Labour economics group, the XYZ Club, which met under the guidance and organisation of Nicholas Davenport and Vaughan Berry.[88] Their endorsement of the theory aided the wider acceptance of Keynesianism in the Labour Party. However, as Elizabeth Durbin notes, not all socialist economists accepted Keynesian theories until around 1944 with the *White Paper on Unemployment*[89] which accepted the basic analysis of Keynesian ideas. This was because some were suspicious of Keynes' Liberal association and of theories which attempted to make the capitalist system workable and to ameliorate the ills of capitalism.[90] David Marquand argues that the years 1947-1949 of the Attlee administration saw the gradual adoption of Keynesian demand management as the Labour Party's official economic doctrine.[91] Marquand notes that it was during this period that:

'...ministers slowly abandoned their original vision of a socially-controlled economy in which resources would be allocated by political decisions rather than market-place haggling in favour of a mixed economy centred upon Keynesian demand management.'[92]

It was the Attlee Governments of 1945-51, who were the first governments in Britain to operate Keynesian economics. Adam Przeworski suggests that Keynesianism provided left-wing political parties with the:

'...ideological and political foundations for the compromise of capitalist democracy. Keynesianism held out the prospect that the state could reconcile the private ownership of the means of production with democratic management of the economy...Democratic control over the level of unemployment and the distribution of income became the terms of the compromise that made democratic capitalism possible.'[93]

Przeworski argues that Keynesianism provided social democracy with a political economy that suggested that the cause of unemployment was lack of demand, therefore what was required was for the state to use expansionist spending policies to stimulate production and reduce unemployment.[94] In addition, Keynesian demand management used methods that were compatible with political aims of parties of the left such as redistribution, state regulation and fiscal flexibility to raise taxes to invest in welfare and public services. This period of 1945-1951 is often seen as the starting point of Keynesian dominance over the debate about economic doctrine and as an intellectual framework of ideas it was at its zenith between 1945-1970.[95] This chapter has attempted to provide an *intellectual* history of the Labour Party from its nineteenth century origins up until 1949. It has also sought to introduce certain themes and values which are helpful in understanding the trajectory of social democratic thought and thus set the scene for examining the political philosophy of New Labour.

3

AN INTELLECTUAL HISTORY OF THE LABOUR PARTY: 1949-1979

This chapter will attempt to provide an *intellectual* history of events and ideas in the Labour Party from 1949-1979. It is particularly relevant to the formation of the revisionist strand of political thought within the Labour Party in the post-war era. The Gaitskellites, it will be agued, were revisionists of British democratic socialism and therefore, one can see them as being forerunners to New Labour in terms of revising specific underlying political values and revising the means to achieve those values. Understanding the 'Great Debate' is important in understanding the emergence and prominence of New Labour. Firmly on the Labour right and politically revisionist in attitude, Blair's New Labour is in part, the culmination of hard fought internal battles with the Labour left from the early 1980s onwards, the Labour Party's response to four successive electoral defeats and an updated social democratic response to the transformation of global politics and economics of the 1980s and 1990s. Therefore, I will argue that New Labour is similar to the vision Hugh Gaitskell had for the Labour Party of the 1950s and 1960s but also, that New Labour is a response to the factors outlined below. These factors are not dissimilar in character to the ones that the revisionist right faced during the 1950s and 1960s, namely philosophical battles with the left, three successive electoral defeats and the need to find a response to the 'affluent society'.

The 'Great Debate'

Domestic success did not mean domestic harmony within the Parliamentary Labour Party. In 1949, a dispute occurred between Herbert Morrison and Aneurin Bevan at the Labour Party Conference. However, the dates of the splits in the Parliamentary Labour Party are difficult to gauge. Haseler argues that:

'As early as 1946 certain sections of the Party were already becoming disillusioned at the lack of traditional socialist content in policy and the battle-lines for the fifties began to form.'[1]

Morrison, in what became known as his 'consolidation speech', argued for a halt in nationalisation because he believed that it had served its purpose and that there should be an end to the extension of nationalisation to all private industries merely for the sake of them being publicly owned. In contrast, Bevan wanted full-scale nationalisation, as he believed that it was what a democratic socialist government should do. This was the beginning of a much deeper philosophical dispute within local constituency branches but mainly amongst those on the National Executive Committee and members of the Parliamentary Labour Party. Drucker's opinion on the internecine struggle is that the Labour Party never adequately answered the question of what, after the Attlee Government of 1945-51 the:

'...implementing of socialism would actually mean.'[2]

This notion of uncertainty and the apparent 'where do we go from here?' attitude recorded by Richard Crossman in his 1951 essay, *Towards A New Philosophy of Socialism*[3] is imperative to understanding the factional disputes over what came to be known as the 'Great Debate' or the 'means and ends debate' in the Labour Party during the 1950s. The year 1951 witnessed a split in the Parliamentary Labour Party of unprecedented proportions. The split often characterized as the disagreement by the Bevanite left with the Gaitskellite right over the issue of nationalisation and the extent to which a Labour Government should nationalise the industries remained a thorn in the side of party unity until 1995.[4] However, some would state that this characterisation is too narrow an interpretation of the philosophical problems facing large elements of the Labour Party. The importance of the leaders of each of these groups is significant: both men became fierce rivals for the leadership of the Labour Party after the 1951 election, as it was expected that an aging Clement Attlee would be standing down after the next parliament. Therefore, not only was there a personal rivalry between the two figureheads, but also there was an ideological contest within the Parliamentary Labour Party between the revisionists or modernisers following Gaitskell and the traditionalists supporting Bevan.[5]

This section will not attempt to dissect the philosophical leanings of all elements within the Labour Party;[6] nevertheless, one can identify competing philosophical standpoints based on anecdotal evidence. Such positions include the left-wing or (traditional socialists), the centre and the right-wing or (social democrats). The centre group could just as easily have been labelled as adherents to 'Labourism', but are better understood to represent a wider group of MPs in the Party during the 1950s and early 1960s. Traditionally, the centre of the Party is seen as advocates of 'Labourism', which can be viewed as striving for the greatest advancement of the working classes and has historically been occupied by much of the trade unions. During the Party's problems in the 1950s, the centre was often seen as the 'Keep Calm' group committed to stabilising party unity between the Gaitskellites and the Bevanites. This included such figures as John Strachey, Michael Stewart and George Strauss.[7] Haseler asserts that the centre did not really exist in the Labour Party in any real form until the mid-1950s with the arrival of the ideological split in the Party and those members of the centre group opted out of the ideological factionalism of the time and appealed for unity behind the leadership of Attlee.[8] A further tension in the debate between the groups was that each one had its own power base within the structure of the Labour Party. Brian Brivati reveals in his biography of Gaitskell that although the Gaitskellites could claim support from the Shadow Cabinet, the majority of the Parliamentary Labour Party and the Trade Unions, the Bevanites had the general support of constituency parties and dominated the policy-influencing National Executive Committee from 1952 onwards.[9]

The debate over means and ends raised the question, 'what are democratic socialist values?' It is acknowledged that interpretations of the Bevanite[10] and Gaitskellite[11] socialist values are contestable, however, it is helpful for the chapter to attempt to unpack these concepts and thus gain a fuller understanding of the different perspectives on socialism in the Labour Party.

Bevan emerged as the standard bearer of the Labour left in the late 1940s. This group of left-wing MPs that rallied behind Bevan became known as the 'Bevanites'. The main unifying factor for this group of left-wingers within the Labour Party was their opposition to the Attlee Government's foreign and defence policy. The Foreign Secretary, Ernest Bevin, believed that Britain must continue her special relationship fostered during the Second World War with the USA if she wanted to retain a role in the global politics of the post-war era. This approach was known as 'Atlanticism' and it culminated in Bevin signing Britain up to the North Atlantic Treaty Organisation otherwise known as NATO. This organisation was a defensive alliance of Western states particularly with regard to defending their interests against the USSR. For the Bevanites this policy of allying Britain to the USA and demonising the USSR was unacceptable. Part of the disagreement inside the Labour Party was that some left-wingers argued that the moderate left could talk to and interact with the communist left of Soviet Russia. However, Bevan himself desired an independent middle way between siding with the USA or the USSR. This policy became known as 'Neutralism'. The second strand of unity for the Bevanites was their enmity for nuclear weapons and the Labour Party's acceptance of them as a necessary weapon in Britain's post-war arsenal. Moreover, the Bevanites were a group of MPs who were not particularly well organised in Parliament as many of them were passionate and independent individuals. Nevertheless, their speeches and articles were published in the Labour Party's left-wing magazine Tribune and in national newspapers such as the Reynolds News, the Daily Mirror and the Sunday Pictorial. With regards to a Bevanite political philosophy, Bevan authored a 1952 publication entitled, *In Place of Fear*[12] which sort to establish a coherent set of socialist policies for those MPs arguing for traditional democratic socialism. Therefore, as Brivati notes:

'The Bevanite group was not a direct challenge to the leadership but an attack on the complacency of the Labour front bench in the period 1951-5, and a blueprint for left-wing activity in subsequent decades.'[13]

In addition to Bevan, the Bevanites also included Richard Crossman, an academic and political thinker in his own right. Crossman penned several notable essays, in particular his 1951 piece *Towards A New Philosophy of Socialism*,[14] which was an essay discussing the direction that the Labour Party's form of socialism should take in light of its policy achievements between 1945-1951. However, Crossman's essay also outlined several Bevanite measures that the Party should focus on by claiming that the welfare capitalism delivered by the Attlee Government was not sufficient for a socialist party:

'Can an unhealthy concentration of capital be prevented without much greater extension of public ownership or, alternatively, a capital levy? Can inflation be countered, under conditions of full employment, without a national profits and wages policy? If not, how can such a policy be put into execution without some amendment by the trade unions of their cherished freedom of collective bargaining? Both these issues were avoided during the six years of Labour Government. They can be avoided no longer if the Labour Party is to face the future once again with a programme as challenging as that of 1945.'[15]

Crossman's 1956 essay *Planning for Freedom*[16] advocated a typically Labour left belief in central planning but contrary to usual criticism, Crossman argued that it enhanced freedom as opposed to restricting freedom. His piece, *The Affluent Society*,[17] written shortly after the 1959 electoral defeat casts doubt on the revisionist analysis that the nature of capitalism has been significantly reformed and that socialists parties need to adapt their economic objectives. In brief, Crossman is attempting to argue for a Bevanite perspective on the myths surrounding the 'affluent society' and argues for the view that Crosland's revisionist analysis, which is to be discussed shortly, is fundamentally flawed.

Bevanite assertions were largely the traditional values of the Labour Party as derived from the 1918 constitution. For the Bevanites, democratic socialist values would probably include widespread redistribution, extensive nationalisation of industry, an extension of trade union authority within the Labour Party and emphasising the class based nature of socialism. The Bevanites represented the 'ends' side of the great debate. They argued that nationalisation enabled the state to control the means of production and thereby enabled the government to enact socialist policies on behalf of working people. For example, nationalisation affected the conditions of the workers because the state was committed to pay its employees fair wage levels, allow and promote union representation and offered them the liberty to work as people with a stake in the nationalised industry. Thus, the nature of the workers position, their conditions and their relation to the industry is completely different to that of a privately owned and privately managed company.

For the Bevanites, nationalisation was intended to replace industries being privately owned by one individual or by a board of shareholders whereby the fundamental drive in the industry would be profit maximisation for the shareholders. Therefore, the policy of nationalising industry was of focal importance to those on the 'ends' side of the great debate. To nationalise was to be socialist. Thus, nationalisation was socialism in action.

At the time of the initial philosophical disputes, Gaitskell was Chancellor and later Shadow Chancellor and the leader of a group of MPs who backed him for Party Leader. They were on the right-wing of the Parliamentary Labour Party, pragmatic in outlook and inclined towards revisionism of Party policy. Notable Gaitskellites of the time included Tony Crosland, Roy Jenkins, Woodrow Wyatt, Christopher Mayhew, Arthur Allen, Patrick Gordon-Walker and Alf Robens. The Gaitskellites advocated a revisionist approach to Labour Party policy by discerning the benefits of these policies from their own democratic socialist values.[18] As Tony Crosland stated in *Socialism Now and Other Essays*[19], for the revisionists:

'Socialism in our view, was basically about equality. By equality, we meant more than a meritocratic society of equal opportunities in which the greatest rewards would go to those with the most fortunate genetic endowment and family background; we adopted the 'strong' definition of equality – what Rawls has subsequently called the 'democratic' as opposed to the 'liberal' conception. We also meant more than a simple (not that it has proved simple in practice) redistribution of income. We wanted a wider social equality embracing also distribution of property, the educational system, social-class relationships, power and privilege in industry - indeed all that was enshrined in the age-old socialist dream of a more 'classless society'.[20]

Gaitskell outlined his underlying political values in an interview with the BBC during the 1959 General Election campaign:

> 'I see no reasons whatsoever why we should have any doubts about the basic principles in which we believe. After all, one isn't in politics just for fun…we still believe…in equality and freedom at the same time, in equal opportunity, in a fair deal… in behaving decently and honourably to other nations. And these things are not temporary, not ephemeral, they're eternal things…But how they should be attained, how they should be interpreted and expressed to fit with… a modern generation, that always needs reappraisal, I think.'[21]

With regard to the great debate over means and ends, Gaitskell, along with his loyal lieutenants, had emerged during the early 1950's as the leading band of protagonists in the debate arguing that nationalisation as a policy of a Labour Government, should be a means to an end and not an end in itself. Philip Williams records that in principle, throughout his life, Gaitskell considered public ownership to be a means to the true socialist objective of a just, egalitarian, classless society rather than as an end in itself.[22] The sentiments of the 'means group' on the issue of how to build a democratic socialist society with consideration for the right and proper role that nationalisation should play are amply summarised in the following quotation from Crosland:

> 'It was therefore possible to achieve the goal of greater equality and other desirable ends within the framework of a mixed economy, with public ownership taking its place as only one of a number of possible means for attaining the ends in view.'[23]

Nonetheless, the 'means group' accepted that the private sector must not be allowed to be completely deregulated and for the market to rule the people. Their call was not the call for Adam Smith's invisible hand or as it is more commonly known, the laissez-faire approach to neo-liberal economics. The 'means group' saw capitalism as greatly reformed and socialised by the post-war consensus and that is why they felt that the Labour Party needed in some quarters to realise that capitalism was not diametrically opposed to democratic socialism. Writing in 1956, during the era of rising personal affluence, a boom in consumer goods and economic growth, Tony Crosland suggested that:

> 'Capitalism had been undergoing a slow, though painfully slow, metamorphosis since the turn of the century. Largely this was involuntary, in the sense that it was enforced by rebellion of the non-capitalist classes against the unpleasant consequences of industrial laissez-faire, and by the growing power of the political and industrial Left.'[24]

Crosland noted that as well as the opposition by the anti-capitalist classes; the business classes began to desire reform of traditional capitalism due to the economic shocks and the events of the 1930s and in addition to other problems such as:

> '...the gradual evaporation within the bourgeoisie of the old unquestioning self-confidence, the simple conviction that unregulated capitalism must be the best of all possible systems: the steady growth of a genuine moral conscience about the miserable social and physical results of capitalism: the political penetration of the middle-classes in the 1930s, culminating in the astonishing phenomena of the Left Book Club and of course the psychological change... associated with the gradual supersession of capitalist by managerial personnel in industry.'[25]

The issue of a change in the character of capitalism from owners to managers sometimes known as 'the managerial revolution' basically argued that capitalist owners took their decisions based exclusively on the profit motive, whereas this new generation of managers were not solely motivated by the profit motive because they were salaried employees and did not own the businesses in question and did not make direct profit themselves, therefore other considerations became important to them. Factors such as their own social status and managerial reputation of how they treated their subordinates all emerged as factors in their decision-making process. This, in turn, changed the character of capitalism and made it less cut-throat and 'more' socially responsible with regard to workers, wages and corresponding issues.

However, Crosland thought that these factors only had a relatively small impact on changing the character of capitalism. He argued for the view developed in *The Future of Socialism* that it was the Second World War and then the need for economic and social reconstruction which reformed the nature of British capitalism further than any other specific factor. This in Crosland's opinion was because:

> 'A predominantly Conservative Government was compelled by military exigency to introduce many of the reforms for which the Labour Party had vainly pleaded during year after year of peace: government-planning, full employment, redistributive taxation, new social services. The moral, that these measures were perfectly practicable and not merely the Utopian dreams of Left-wing visionaries, was not lost upon the electorate, which in 1945 firmly ejected the Conservatives for having neglected to do so in peace what they so readily did in war.'[26]

Another factor of significant importance in contributing to the change in character of traditional capitalism, according to Crosland, was the domestic achievements of the Attlee Governments of 1945-1951:

'Nationalisation, for example, embraced civil aviation, steel, road transport, and Cable and Wireless in addition to the industries listed in the official programme. Social service policy extended to family allowances, a comprehensive National Health Service, and a complete new structure, instead of minor improvements, of National Insurance. And in the fields of redistributive taxation, the level of employment, the Distressed Areas problem, the working-class standard of living, and government control over the economy, much more was achieved than most pre-war writers ever anticipated.'[27]

In summary, the 'means group' position outlined by Tony Crosland, saw by the mid-1950s, a capitalism greatly reformed due to the rise in power of the industrial left, the anti-capitalist classes and the Labour Party but more importantly because of a technical change in the management of capitalism from owners to mangers who, along with swathes of the middle-classes, were repulsed by the degradation and squalor which large sections of the British working classes had to endure during the ills of laissez-faire capitalism in the early part of the century. The moral change amongst the electorate kept out the Conservatives and enabled a radical Labour administration to reconstruct a welfare capitalism with social provision and regulation the likes of which had never been seen before.

Crosland's second major work *The Conservative Enemy*[28] was a political programme for Labour in the 1960s, and an attack on the Conservative Party and what he believed were the conservative elements in the Labour Party's social democracy. As a book it offered no new ideas on political economy that *The Future of Socialism* had not already enunciated. In fact, Crosland defended his main arguments set out in *The Future of Socialism* and as Foote notes he echoed J. K. Galbraith in highlighting the gap between private affluence and public squalor and suggested a range of egalitarian measures to counter this situation.[29]

In the introduction to the second edition of *The Future of Socialism*[30] published in 1964, Crosland accepted that he had been over-optimistic in his predications about the level of growth that western economies, but especially the British economy was capable of producing. This in turn, affected the amount of revenue available to invest in public spending and on welfare measures. His 1974 book *Socialism Now and Other Essays* was a collection of essays on a range of issues that Crosland had ministerial experience of such as the environment, housing, and education. The opening essay *Socialism Now* was an evaluation of his revisionist thought and most importantly an argument suggesting that the revisionists need not revise their version of socialism.[31] Two notable admissions were made in the essay. Firstly, Crosland stated that the economic policy of the 1964-1970 Wilson Labour Government had been a failure as unemployment was higher, inflation more rapid and economic growth was slower than when the Conservatives left office in 1964.[32] Secondly, Crosland concedes that his earlier writings had been overly optimistic concerning the pace and ease by which socialist goals could be implemented:

> 'Looking back with hindsight, the early revisionist writings were too complacent in tone; they proposed the right reforms, but underrated the difficulty of achieving them in a British context.'[33]

Finally, *Socialism Now* contained a brief list of priority areas that a future Labour government ought to focus on and these priorities included the reduction of poverty; the further provision of decent housing; taking developmental land into public ownership; the redistribution of capital wealth; the elimination of selection and segregation in the education system and an extension of industrial democracy.[34]

An essential point to remember in understanding the philosophical debate over nationalisation was that this debate was also about Clause IV. The great debate over means and ends was in part a debate about the relevance of Clause IV and the role of nationalisation as Party policy. Clause IV, point four of the Party Constitution to be precise, was an explicit commitment to extend public ownership throughout the economy. It was, therefore, an anachronism from 1918 and for many Labour people it was neither a realistic nor a desirable policy objective. Nevertheless, Gaitskell and several leading revisionists, at least initially, believed that it would be appropriate to redraft Clause IV in line with the kind of society that the Labour Party wanted to create.[35] This ambition of Gaitskell's was fuelled by recent election defeats, as he believed that it enabled the Conservatives to misrepresent the intentions of the Party's economic outlook. Gaitskell redrafted Clause IV and it was approved by the N.E.C. in March 1960 but as Williams notes:

'...within four months, four of the six major unions had refused to amend the constitution and, facing certain defeat at Conference, Gaitskell had to downgrade the "New Testament"[36] to a mere "valuable expression of the aims of the Labour Party in the twentieth century", while leaving Clause IV intact.'[37]

The unions and the pressure of the wider Parliamentary Party were against Gaitskell's revision of the Constitution. The Labour left were buoyant albeit without their leader Bevan, who was by spring 1960 seriously ill. The confidence of the Labour left enabled them to move swiftly on to their next internal battle with the leadership, namely the Party's policy on nuclear weapons.[38]

The spring of 1960 gave rise to the issue of the Labour Party's position on the nuclear deterrent and defence, which became a sticking point for the Party as it had been in the past. Williams suggests that it became a conflict about the character of the Party, whether it wanted to be a protest movement or a prospective government.[39] After the crucial event of the Government cancelling the American 'Blue Streak' rocket they had to decide whether Britain needed an independent nuclear deterrent, collective conventional and nuclear security of NATO or whether Britain should be neutral and adopt and encourage a non-nuclear policy. This, in turn, meant that the Labour Party had to have a policy position on the subject. The Labour left was traditionally suspicious of arms build-ups and became increasingly vocal in its support of unilateralism. The unilateralist cause took shape in an organisation known as the CND or the Campaign for Nuclear Disarmament, which was formed in 1958 by a group of Bevanites, Christian pacifists and New Left intellectuals. Its purpose was to argue for Britain to set a moral lead by unilaterally condemning nuclear weapons. The influence of the unilateralist cause reached its zenith in 1960 when it temporarily succeeded in getting it adopted as Labour Party policy. The unilateralist cause was most strongly argued by Stuart Hall in his 1958 piece, *Breakthrough*[40]. Foote suggests that Hall's argument pointed to the loss of moral high ground against the USSR because it enabled the Soviets to interpret the Western nuclear deterrent as a realistic military threat. This in turn, reduced the chance of democracy evolving in the Soviet satellite states of Eastern Europe. Paraphrasing Hall's argument, Foote argues that Western rhetoric and defence policy was responsible for:

'...preventing democratisation in Eastern Europe, solidifying the hold on power of Stalinist bureaucracies who could always defuse any threat to their rule by pointing to the Western threat.'[41]

The right of the Labour Party believed that by not having an independent nuclear deterrent Britain would be dependent on the United States for security against a threat from the Soviet Union.[42] This debate in the Party became known as the 'unilateralist-multilateralist debate'. It deepened the philosophical divisions in the Party and was not fully resolved until the late 1980s when the clear majority of Labour MPs and Party members supported the multilateralist cause. To summarise this tumultuous period in Labour Party history, the Conservatives won the 1959 General Election with Harold Macmillan capturing 50% of the working class vote. The two main wings of the Party persistently clashed with each other and in 1963 Gaitskell suddenly died and Harold Wilson, a figure of the Labour left, beat off challenges from Jim Callaghan and George Brown both figures of the right, for the leadership of the Party. It appeared to some that under Wilson the Labour Party would perhaps change its direction.

The Crisis of Keynesianism: 1966-1979

The decline of Keynesianism as the economic doctrine of social democracy and of the Labour Party can be interpreted in two ways; internationally and domestically. Robert Skidelsky argues that Keynesianism as an economic theory began to break down for a number of domestic reasons. Firstly, Skidelsky argues that one of Keynes' shortcomings was that he omitted from his theory, many causes of unemployment.[43] For example, Keynes acknowledged that demand-deficiency resulted in unemployment but failed to note that supply-side problems like the immobility of labour and the slowness of adaptation to change also can cause unemployment.[44] These supply-side factors accumulated over time and their net effect eventually contributed to stagflation. The next reason for the decline of Keynesianism posited by Skidelsky is that in fact Keynesianism was not the exclusive reason for the 'golden age' of the late 1940s until the start of the 1970s when western economies were productive and unemployment was relatively low.[45] When Keynesian economies experienced rising prices and rising unemployment and low economic growth this alternative view suggests that this had only been delayed by the 'catch-up' effect whereby economies after the Second World War had recently benefited from technology and high consumer demand for goods coupled with industrial adaptability.[46] The argument follows according to Skidelsky that:

'The reconstruction of industries and industrial relations on the Continent of Europe were the products of defeat, not Keynesian policy. The victorious nations, Britain and the United States, which were also most influenced by Keynesian ideas, exhibited the weakest tendency to structural reform.'[47]

The third problem identified was that of demands for wage increases. This issue was as political as it was economic.[48] Keynesians in Britain implemented incomes policies in the hope that as the Government kept aggregate demand high, trades unions would accept controls on wages and would refrain from industrial action, which would lead to lower productivity.[49] In fact, trades unions were unsatisfied with the level of wages set by the incomes policies and this caused rising inflation.[50] Skidelsky notes a fourth and more significant factor in the decline of Keynesianism namely, fiscal mismanagement.[51] He suggests that Keynesian economists:

'...have always known that, beyond a certain point, taxes encounter tax resistance... What became clear in the 1960s was that tax resistance developed much sooner in the working classes than in the middle and upper classes, for whom it was mitigated by guilt and noblesse oblige.'[52]

The fifth factor not separate, but connected to fiscal mismanagement, was that the working classes in some trade unions demanded lower public spending so they could receive high wages. This can be seen as a 'compensating wage-push', but it was not the only result of fiscal policy. A knock-on effect was the development of budget deficits due to large amounts of money invested and the Exchequer, because of tax resistance, was not collecting enough revenue.[53]

With regard to international economic factors, there are several issues. Firstly, Andrew Gamble argues that the problems of the mid-1960s were exacerbated in the early 1970s through a greater appreciation of their scale.[54] The problems of the mid-1960s were the gradual increase in inflation and unemployment and a slow level of economic growth. In particular, this was caused by the collapse of the Bretton Woods system of fixed exchange rates in 1971/1972. This was followed by the quadrupling of the oil price in 1973 and the generalised world recession which then occurred. Secondly, the collapse of the Bretton Woods system, the oil price rise and the world recession caused inflation and unemployment to rise steeply. Therefore, soon, the economic problem of stagflation was occurring in economies and it became apparent that successful economic management was going to prove to be increasingly more difficult than it had been in the 1950s and 1960s. It was around this time in the early 1970s that Gamble notes that the economic priority had changed in some Keynesian economies. Controlling inflation assumed priority over maintaining full employment, public expenditure programmes suddenly appeared very expensive and were being reined back and tight controls were placed on wages. Thirdly, a further issue that Gamble alludes to is that the disappearance of economic growth in the early 1970s was interpreted as a temporary phenomena but it gradually became apparent that the economic problems of the early 1970s were not short-term and represented something more deep-rooted in the international economic system.[55] It was this perception of the increasing economic problems of the 1974-1979 Wilson and Callaghan Governments that presented the revisionist right as unable to manage an economy that could sustain growth and provide policies that could bring about greater social equality simultaneously. This thesis advocated the use of Keynesian demand management as the tool to secure greater economic and social equality and Crosland argued it with most force in the Labour Party. Fourthly, Gamble argues that it was around the early 1970s that the monetarist economic approach began to be discussed and taken seriously by some politicians and economic commentators, particularly by people such as Keith Joseph in the Conservative Party.[56] In short, monetarism appeared to have the answers to the economic problems of the 1970s.

The New Right Challenge: 1979 Onwards[57]

Margaret Thatcher's Conservative Party and their radical New Right political philosophy of neo-liberalism and social authoritarianism was the dominant political philosophy in Britain during the 1980s and 1990s. The Labour Party systematically failed to win general elections and convey to the British public their vision for British society. Furthermore, they failed to articulate what they stood for as competently as they articulated their repudiation of Thatcherism. Philosophically, neo-liberalism appeared to be hegemonic during the Conservative years and yet only two fifths of the electorate voted for it. New Labour is a post-Thacherite political project and must be analysed in light of what went before it and how neo-liberalism has affected the change in political thinking in the Labour Party that produced New Labour.

The 1979 general election saw the Conservative Party argue the case for their New Right philosophy.[58] Callaghan and the Labour Party campaigned on the fact that the new radicalism of Thatcher's Conservatives was untried and untested and that Labour was the 'safety' option for the electorate. Nevertheless, the Conservative Party won with a majority of forty-four seats, which involved a 5.1% swing away from Labour to the Conservatives. The adoption of the New Right philosophy by the Conservative Party in the mid to late 1970s was a radical step unusual for conservatives. The New Right as it is widely known is identified with several political assumptions. They include the opposition of state involvement in the economy, criticisms of high public expenditure on welfare, thus making the case for a rolled back welfare state with minimal social provisions.[59] However, to conceive the New Right as a unified philosophy is incorrect, as Kenneth Hoover and Raymond Plant argue in their book *Conservative Capitalism in Britain and the United States*.[60]

> 'Throughout their histories, the Conservative Party in Britain and he Republican Party in the United States have contained traditionalists and individualists, those who believe in using authoritative institutions to secure social and economic ends, and those who preferred to see the operation of the market wherever and whenever possible.'[61]

One could describe the conflicting tendencies in the New Right philosophy as the conservative New Right and the liberal New Right and they collide on issues such as political culture, national defence and civil society.[62] However, whilst accepting philosophical tensions in New Right politics and alluding to the fault line between a neo-liberal economic approach which emphasises negative freedom and a 'hands-off' approach to economics and the rather different social authoritarianism in the personal and social sphere of life, a student of Labour's political thought must respond to the cogent and well defined philosophy of neo-liberalism.

Philosophically, neo-liberalism is united in its common enemies. Politically, in Britain, it is obviously the Labour Party but philosophically, it is explicitly the workings and values of Keynesian social democracy. The neo-liberal responds to the moral and ethical values of social democracy in several ways and he or she counters the social democratic critique of their political thought with a number of defences. Firstly, regarding social justice, neo-liberals claim that as such, it does not exist and is therefore an illusion.[63] Exponents of neo-liberalism claim that social justice is a moral illusion because markets do not cause injustice, as an injustice arises from an intentional act and market outcomes are not intentionally trying to cause injustice. Unintended outcomes in the market system are misfortunes not injustices and therefore the state has no responsibility to mitigate these misfortunes.[64] Secondly, in their critique of social justice, neo-liberals like Hayek argue that social justice is a contested term with many versions attached to it and to its vehicle, namely distributive politics. Hayek states that because both social justice and distributive politics are subjective they cannot be upheld philosophically.[65] Thirdly, the assault on social democratic political thought from neo-liberals comes in the form of the rejection of a positive conception of liberty. Neo-liberals such as Keith Joseph suggest that advocates of a positive conception of liberty confuse freedom and ability.[66] According to neo-liberals, freedom is the absence of interference and ability is one's capacity to act and make certain choices. Thus, 'freedom to' in other words a positive conception of liberty is incorrect because it links the concept of freedom with the notion of ability. Freedom is not about being enabled or empowered or assisted in the pursuit of material possessions or life opportunities as it is about leading an unconstrained life, free from interference from the state and from others in the market place and in society.[67] Fourthly, neo-liberals reject the role of large scale public provision because they argue that it does not create a more equal society but in fact benefits the middle classes disproportionately.[68] Although they are not concerned about reducing inequalities and therefore the plight of the working classes, they use such an argument to disarm the social justice and egalitarian responses for a large welfare state against social democrats. Neo-liberals believe that the welfare state can be reduced to a minimal safety net for those who truly cannot provide for themselves. This in turn, reduces the tax burden on individuals and lessens the state's role in people's lives, thus freeing them from state interference. The reduction in the welfare state would also be a morally sound thing to aim for because neo-liberals allude to the fact that a culture of welfare dependency has developed which encourages individuals not to aspire to their full potential but instead to accept a 'free lunch' from the state.

This chapter has attempted to chart the *intellectual* history of the Labour Party from 1949 to 1979. In addition, the more pertinent factor is that by 1979 the Conservative Party came to office with a new radical political philosophy in the form of the New Right; economic neo-liberalism combined with a brand of social authoritarianism. The way in which the Labour Party would respond to the neo-liberal challenge and the effects that Thatcherism would have on the Labour Party would shape its history for a generation to come. The following chapter attempts to analyse the ensuing travails of a Labour Party responding to Thatcherism and the specific internal political and philosophical debates that gripped the Party from 1979 until the mid-1990s and contributed to the political philosophy of New Labour.

4

AN INTELLECTUAL HISTORY OF THE LABOUR PARTY: 1979-1994

This chapter will attempt to provide an *intellectual* history of events, ideas and the battle for power in the Labour Party in the 1979-1994 period. This chapter identifies four factors that helped to shape the history of the Labour Party and in turn, were factors in the evolution of what we understand to be the political project of the modernisers or in other words New Labour. These four events are the rise of the Bennite left; the departure of the Gang of Four; the revitalisation of social democratic ideas by the traditional right-wing of the Labour Party; and a succession of events after the 1987 election defeat up until the election of Tony Blair as Party Leader in 1994.

The Rise of the Bennite Left

The rise of the Bennite left in the Labour Party was not an immediate reaction to the 1979 general election defeat. The Bennite left was a movement in the Labour Party long before Tony Benn assumed the leadership of this new left-wing agenda. The terms 'Hard left', 'Far left' or 'New left' have all been employed when identifying the policy designs and main motivations of Tony Benn and his colleagues from 1979 onwards. However, this chapter will use the term 'New left' to identify the Bennites from 1979 onwards as it is understood that the Bennite left was the modern continuation of the extra-parliamentary and radical left-wing agenda from the 1960s, which was termed the New left.

The New left had its origins in the late 1950s and early 1960s in issues and campaigns wider than the Westminster political village. Notable academics leant support to causes of the New left such as opposition to NATO, the Campaign for Nuclear Disarmament, the idea of transferring economic power from capitalists to workers through workers' councils, opposition to the entry of the Common Market and working class cultural politics. Such thinkers and former members of the Communist Party included Stuart Hall and Raymond Williams.[1] These two academics sat on the editorial board of the *New Left Review* when it was established in 1960 but they owed an inheritance to E.P Thompson[2] and John Saville who instigated dissident communist thought[3] and discussion around the 1957 journal the *New Reasoner* which in turn merged with the *Universities and Left Review* in 1960, to become the *New Left Review*.[4] However, most importantly for the ideological framework of the New left was the work of Stuart Holland. Holland's book, *The Socialist Challenge*[5] provided the New left and as it was to be later known under the leadership of Tony Benn, the Bennite left, with a counter economic strategy to the Labour Party's Keynesian demand management approach. More notably however, was the Bennite left's desire to change the Labour Party Constitution to enable them to make the Party adopt and follow left-wing policies. As David and Maurice Kogan point out:

'Between 1973 and 1981 small groups of activists sought to change the Labour Party's constitution in order to secure their own policies.'[6]

These groups of activists used legitimate constitutional processes that in a relatively short space of time altered the internal structure of the Labour Party.[7] With regard to the Labour left, one can see similar policy trajectories between the traditional Old left or Bevanite left as it was sometimes known and with the New left. As previously stated, the Old left under the leadership of Aneurin Bevan were left-wing

MPs united around issues such as a neutral foreign policy between the USA and the USSR, greater nationalisation of industry, support for unilateral nuclear disarmament and scepticism towards the ameliorating ability of social democracy in humanising capitalism, to name but a few issues of contention. It was in these last two areas, the issue of unilatertalism and scepticism about reforming the unjust nature of capitalism (which the social democratic right of the Labour Party believed in), that the New left adopted from the Old left.

As we have noted, the New left was developed before it decided to gravitate around the leadership of Tony Benn within the Parliamentary Labour Party. Nevertheless, Benn outlined his brand of socialism in his 1979 book, *Arguments for Socialism*[8] but it is with his principle of radical democratisation that Benn and his New left supporters shaped the Labour Party. Benn's belief in greater democracy is most clearly argued in his 1981 publication, entitled, *Arguments for Democracy*[9]. Not only does Benn's book set out his reasons for a radical democratisation of the Labour Party but also it suggests that democratisation is needed in institutions ranging from the Civil Service to the Press and to the security services. However, for the purpose of this chapter the examination of Benn's principle of radical democratisation will be kept to the structures and practices of the Labour Party.

Benn's contribution to political ideas in the Labour Party is a controversial subject because he is not an original thinker nor should any credit be ascribed to him for the New left's political economy, which was the mainstay of their political philosophy. The credit for authorship of the philosophy of the New left in the Labour Party should be reserved for Holland and his acclaimed critique of welfare capitalism and Croslandite social democracy. As Foote says:

'It was Stuart Holland who proved to be one of the principal sources of theoretical inspiration behind the 1973 Programme. Holland had worked as an economic assistant to the Cabinet Office and then to the Prime Minister in 1966-8, and his studies of the Italian models of public enterprise fed his work on the various sub-committees set up by the Labour NEC to work on its radical programme. It was in defence of this programme that he wrote *The Socialist Challenge...*'[10]

Holland argued that the crises in western capitalism such as high inflation and simultaneously high unemployment were caused by changes in the structure of power within capitalism. As he says:

'Recent acceleration in the tend to monopoly and multinational capital has eroded Keynesian economic policies, and undermined the sovereignty of the capitalist nation state.'[11]

Therefore, Holland's thesis was that the nature of western capitalism had changed and given rise to a form of monopoly capitalism on a global scale. In essence, he was highlighting the point that western capitalism was entering a multinational, and to some extent, globalised era. Holland referred to this build up of corporate power as *meso*economic power:

'But the trend to monopoly and multinational capital has set a new mode of production *in between* the Keynesian macroeconomic and microeconomic categories. This is the new *meso*economic sector which controls the commanding heights of big business in the national and international economy (Greek: *mesos* = intermediate).'[12]

The point that followed this diagnosis of economic change was that Keynesian demand management was unable to manage the economy in the same way as before. Furthermore, that British socialism required a new economic doctrine to secure socialist goals in a *meso*economic system. In effect, Holland was implying that Keynesian social democracy and therefore Crosland's thesis was ill equipped to face the economic and social problems brought about by the rise in monopoly and multinational capitalism. Holland proposed a series of economic measures which had largely been outlined in the Labour Party's 1973 manifesto, such as a programme of extended public ownership, a state holding company, strategic planning agreements and workers' democracy.[13]

With this in mind, Benn's principle of radical democratisation may not be entirely new nor fully his own, but his espousal of it in a publication outlining certain ideas warrants examination. In the preface to *Arguments for Democracy*, Benn summarises his purpose for the book and his reasons behind the need for a radical extension of democracy:

'This book has been written for those of us who want to see the people of this country take control of our own destinies and use the power of democracy to resolve the many pressing problems we face in our daily lives, including unemployment, injustice and the threat of war... Popular demands for political, economic and social rights have been a constant theme throughout our history. Since these demands were for equality in the control of political power it follows that when that power is acquired the next demand will be to use it to achieve greater equality of treatment in every aspect of life. This is the bridge which links democracy with socialism and merges the arguments for one with the arguments for the other.'[14]

Benn in support of the aims of the New left, wants to see people empowered to a far greater extent so they may participate more fully and acquire greater material equality by the means of radically democratising national institutions and the economy.[15] In part, Benn's call for a radical democratisation of British civic life is a means to guarantee greater material and social equality for individuals in the tradition of British radicalism that first won the right to vote and then focused on economic and social entitlements through the vehicles of the Liberal and Labour parties. Understood in this way, Benn's radical democratisation highlights the fundamental relationship between socialism and democracy. Therefore, when Benn argues for a radical democratisation of institutions he is tapping in to a powerful strand of socialist aspiration that states that without democracy socialism can never exist and without socialism democracy is only partial. It is merely the empowerment of individuals up to a point of equal political rights. The reasoning behind this is simply that socialism defined in Benn's terms as democratisation of all spheres of life, requires his form of radical institutional democratisation for society to truly be 'socialist' as those institutions are currently not democratised. Furthermore, Benn's argument gains even more credence when viewed as a continuation of the campaign of guaranteeing rights and entitlements for all, be they religious, political, legal, social or economic in character.

However, if one does not believe that Benn's 'socialism' is most adequately examined through the terms of the history of securing democratic rights then another thesis regarding Benn's socialism needs to be constructed. Firstly, it must be decided whether the principle of greater and radical democratisation is a means to achieve a socialist society, whether it in itself is an end and socialist in character or whether it is both a means and an end. This is crucially important because it appears that Benn desires radical democratisation in certain spheres for other political purposes that his fellow Labour Party members and people on the left would prefer to resist. For example, he desires radical democratisation of the internal structures of the Labour Party because he has his own 'socialist' agenda that wants to reduce the influence of MPs and increase the authority of the trade unions (at a time when several large unions were led by sympathetic leaders to Benn's brand of socialism). Secondly, such a radical democratisation of the Labour Party, Benn hopes, would enable people to such an extent that they would insist on the withdrawal of Britain from the EEC regardless of its legitimate mandate with the national party. Thirdly, a general criticism is that Benn's proposed application of this principle in the format of his suggested reforms, in practice lack popular appeal within the national and Parliamentary Labour Party and in the electorate at large. If one was to condense the basic criticism of Benn's principle of radical democratisation into a sound bite or brief summary, one could argue that it is the democratisation of British institutions without a democratic mandate from the electorate. This in itself is not a sufficient reason for not advocating the principle of radical democratisation but it does balance the analysis of a polemical thesis in *Arguments for Democracy*.

By the mid-1970s, the New left was resigned to the fact that it must change the Constitution of the Labour Party if it was to succeed in getting left-wing policies adopted by the Parliamentary Labour Party. However, the realisation that left-wing policies would only be taken seriously if the Party Constitution was changed was older than the Bennite left of the late 1970s. The most important groups in campaigning for constitutional reform and as it would turn out, the most important group within the New left was the Campaign for Labour Party Democracy or the CLPD for short. The CLPD was established in 1973 and as Kogan and Kogan point out it evolved into the driving force behind the constitutional New left agenda.[16] The adoption of left-wing policies was crucial for the New left because since the early 1950s the Labour left had won a considerable number of seats on the National Executive Committee and could sometimes get polices adopted by the Party Conference, but less often did it convince the Parliamentary Labour Party to accept these policies.[17]

It is at this point that the Labour left splits into two factions. The Old left had a 'Whiggish' respect for Parliament and believed that debate and dissent were the best tools for advancing their cause. The New left took a different approach, which entailed a radical reformation of the Labour Party Constitution to shift the balance of power as they saw it away from the right-wing Party leadership, trade unions and majority of the Parliamentary Labour Party to the NEC, the constituency parties and small groups of radical activists.[18]

The New left's motivation in turning to constitutional reform of the Labour Party was a general feeling of disillusionment, widespread on the Labour left and amongst constituency parties, that the Wilson Government of 1964-1970 and the Wilson and Callaghan Governments of 1974-1979, had failed to live up to their radical potential.[19] They dismissed the Wilson-Callaghan years as a wasted opportunity to make a socialist impact on the inequalities of British society and argued for the redressing of power in the capitalist system in the form of greater industrial democracy and workers' councils. The New left under Benn took its economic influence from Holland's thesis and advocated alongside the workers' councils, planning agreements, a national enterprise board, radical redistribution of wealth and the withdrawal from the Common Market.[20] Furthermore, the New left grew more discontented by conflicts concerning two sitting MPs. The Lincoln constituency party over disagreements about Britain's membership of the EEC finally removed Dick Taverne, the EEC enthusiast. In a similar fashion, the Newham North-east constituency party eventually succeeded in removing Reg Prentice as their MP after a long and drawn out conflict. The reason for this conflict was that Prentice expressed right-wing views that the constituency party felt were completely opposed to its collective viewpoint. Moreover, as the New left gained influence at the national level through securing a majority of seats on the NEC, their activists at local level were inspired and embraced the New left's emphasis on local socialism and greater devolved power for constituency parties.[21] In short, once the NEC was once again dominated by the New left from the late 1970s onwards, its extra-parliamentary and radical ideological appeal widened to the local level, particularly in London boroughs and other inner-city areas. Therefore, by 1979 the New left was spearheaded by Tony Benn and offered the Labour Party an alternative economic strategy, radical left-wing policy proposals and a determination to reform the Party Constitution to secure the means by which to instigate 'socialism' in the Labour Party.

The Departure of the Gang of Four

To understand the calamitous departure of David Owen, Shirley Williams and Bill Rodgers from the Labour Party in 1981, accompanied by Roy Jenkins (who had recently been President of the European Commission and formerly a Labour Home Secretary and Chancellor) and many Labour MPs, one must interpret the political manoeuvrings of certain dominant groups within the Labour Party in the 1980-1981 period.[22] The right of the Labour Party by 1980 was in a state of turmoil. This was due to three main reasons. Firstly, because of the sudden death of Tony Crosland, the intellectual driving force behind revisionist social democracy in the Labour Party. Crosland died in January 1977 and his death could not have come at a more difficult time for those who believed in the validity of his revisionist thesis. Secondly, the revisionist thesis itself was being fiercely criticised by a resurgent left and by the neo-liberals in the Conservative Party.[23] Both the Labour left and the neo-liberals pointed to Crosland's over-optimism about the ability of economic growth to maintain full employment and deliver the conditions so that a more equal society could be constructed. Obviously, the Labour left and neo-liberal conclusions were contradictory but their observations were similar and equally damning. This forced the Labour right into a period of reflection whereby they questioned the appropriateness of Crosland's revisionist thesis to the economic and social problems facing Britain in the 1980s. Thirdly and most crucially, several notable Labour right-wingers and supporters of Crosland were becoming concerned with the direction that the Labour

Party was moving under the influence of the New left. Bernard Crick notes in his 1984 Fabian pamphlet, *Socialist Values and Time*[24] that some of the social democratic right-wing Labour MPs who joined the Social Democratic Party could have stayed in the Labour Party because theirs was not a difference in doctrine but as he notes:

' ...a political misjudgement and a failure of nerve at the crucial moment.'

This can explain the departure of some of the social democratic right-wing Labour MPs because more right-wing MPs stayed in the Labour Party than left and joined the SDP. Nevertheless, by 1980 Williams, Owen and Rodgers were considering leaving the Labour Party and setting up a new social democratic party as the Labour Party in their opinion had become extremely left-wing and no longer represented their views. As Kogan and Kogan assert:

'On 1 August 1980 David Owen, Shirley Williams and William Rodgers published a letter in the Guardian declaring their beliefs in policies almost wholly contradictory to the general trend of constituency opinion, though perhaps not the views of Labour voters at large.'[25]

At this juncture, it is worth discussing the political ideas of the Gang of Four. David Owen, perhaps more than Shirley Williams, Roy Jenkins and Bill Rodgers had a coherent political philosophy that was distinct from traditional Labour right thought and written down and published by 1981 in the form of a book, entitled *Face The Future*[26].

Owen's book attempts two main things. The first is to outline his brand of social democracy and one can assume the brand that the SDP would be arguing for. The second task that Owen undertakes is to provide historical evidence to support the values of his brand of social democracy. The main tenets within Owen's social democracy are decentralisation of power, fellowship/community, a degree of greater equality and a concept of freedom. Concerning the decentralisation of power, Owen suggests that social democracy requires less central government control and further localised decision making. His argument is that social democratic thinkers have been consistently centrist and collectivist. Owen highlights the socialism of William Morris as an example of the decentralist democracy he believes to be necessary. As he says:

'For Social Democrats intent on reviving the decentralist strand of thinking and in advocating specific policies for the 1980s it is worth first re-examining the historical debate. The socialist societies of the 1880s and 1890s, with their mixed membership of socialists and anarchists, focused most of their attention on the issue of decentralised worker-control versus nationalisation. William Morris, although not an anarchist, criticised both the Fabian definition of socialism and the means by which the Fabians expected socialism to be realised.'[27]

Owen, obviously influenced by the decentralisation of nineteenth century socialists such as Morris and the twentieth century Guild socialism of G.D.H Cole suggests that those principles of decentralisation and greater participatory democracy by workers and voters in various ways needs to be once again adopted by social democrats.[28] As a forgotten principle within the tradition of social democracy, Owen's advocacy of a decentralist brand of social democracy to devolve power and re-engage the public through greater participatory democracy was an interesting concept for social democrats of the time. However, as a 'liberal' principle it appealed not only to Liberals but to certain Conservatives as well. This does not reduce its legitimacy as a counter measure against an increasingly centralist state and against a significant build up of power in the Government, however, one can appreciate the ambivalence such a principle received in traditional quarters of the Labour Party. Moreover, the strongest counter argument to the principle of decentralisation of power is that greater devolution of power leads to different people enacting a plurality of measures in various regions of the country. Therefore, the goal of nation-wide equality in public services is immediately called in to question.

A second principle that Owen elaborated on was more widely appealing to the Labour Movement and social democrats in the SDP. The emphasis on fellowship/fraternity or taken synonymously, 'community' is one that that many social democrats today pay lip service to. What is interesting about Owen's contribution is that he not only advocated the value of community but he argued that for many decades it had been overlooked and to a large extent forgotten by social democrats. This was remarkably accurate:

'For more than a century political thought has been dominated by the interaction and balance between liberty and equality, but surprisingly little attention has been given to the other element of this historic triad, fraternity, representing the sense of fellowship, cooperation, neighbourliness, community and citizenship. This neglect of fraternity, particularly by socialist thinkers, has meant that the espousal of equality has lacked a unifying force to bridge the gaps and contradictions between equality and liberty.'[29]

Owen goes on to argue that the debate surrounding equality has subsumed any appreciation of how the principle of community needs to be applied.[30] Nevertheless, Owen deserves recognition for realising such a trend in the intellectual history of social democracy, but at the same time, reminded that within the last century certain socialist thinkers have valued community such as R.H. Tawney. Tawney's book *Equality*[31] which was not merely about the need for greater material equality but also the need to recognise that the motivation for battling for equality was a sense of fellowship and brotherhood that humans posses and must demonstrate in order to fulfil their humanity.

Tawney's motivational principle was community and this produced his practical desire for greater equality.[32] This point is directly related to the discussion about 'means and ends' or motivational principles and problem solving principles. This will be discussed at length later.

Owen did not discard the principle of greater equality but he, like other members of the Gang of Four and later members of the SDP did suggest that the best economic model was a mixed economy with a dynamic market sector. This in itself could produce higher rewards for some and at the same time produce income inequalities that some in the Labour Party would want to resist. This issue proved deeply damaging for Owen, as many believed he was accepting core principles of Thatcherism and a full-blooded free-market theory of economics. However, such portrayals of his views were exaggerated. Discussing his belief in equality, he suggests that:

'Equality is a noble idea. We know it will not be achieved, but that of itself does not invalidate an aspiration - any more than the fact that wages and salaries will reflect different responsibilities and opportunities means that it is wrong to strive for a system which endeavours to make financial rewards fairer.'[33]

An accusation that Owen like the other social democrats had jettisoned equality is simply incorrect. In many ways, Owen and the SDP were ahead of their time in accepting a greater role for the market in the economy as social democratic parties around the world were beginning to see the impact of globalisation. Social democracy began to accept that the market economy could generate significant goods and that they had to think afresh about how to mitigate the social evils that it also generated.

Owen's concept of freedom is less explicit in his book. Owen classified his brand of social democracy as the:

'...radical democratic libertarian tradition of decentralised socialism...'[34]

This definition sheds little light on his view of freedom except that his emphasis on decentralisation of power coupled with a desire for greater participatory democracy increases personal freedom in theory. The greater choice involved by voting more at local level for local issues and to be given a greater say in how public services are to be organised and provided, would have the net effect of widening choice and in a sense would affect individual's political freedom to a greater extent. Furthermore, political accountability is transferred from the central state to local government or regional assembly in theory and the argument implies that therefore individuals as consumers and the local electorate at large have an increased say in the governing of their locality. Therefore, services are more responsive to the culture of accountability and in the process individuals are empowered. Thus, freedom of sorts is increased. However, all of this is dependent on the accountability and responsiveness of devolved government to individual, the consumer and to the electoral demands at a regional level. In practice decentralisation of power from central government to local government does not preclude centralist and elitist tendencies. Local councils have long been accused of being too powerful and *etatiste*. The culture of organisations and bureaucracies that would be established at local level would provide the real test of accountability, responsiveness and empowerment for individuals. Furthermore, and on a slightly different note, one can only assume that Owen would support freedom defined in the positive as well as the negative conception of liberty which is typical for the social democratic tradition. This can be inferred from a section in his first chapter which asserts that:

'Liberty-Equality-Fraternity the old radical cry still emphasizes an eternal truth: that none of these three can properly be fulfilled without being combined in some measure with the other two.'35

Although, Owen does not adequately unpack his advocacy of freedom, one can argue for the view that he believes that greater freedom can only come about to a certain extent when greater equality and community are established.

Therefore, if the three aforementioned factors were central in the departure of the Gang of Four in 1981, what had occurred between 1979-1981 within the Party to warrant some Labour MPs to consider leaving the Labour Party? As we noted in the previous section above, the New left had grown in prominence and power particularly by 1979 on the National Executive Committee. Furthermore, it had become apparent to Benn and his supporters that if they were ever to see the Labour Party embrace their brand of socialism they would require internal constitutional change so their external policies could be accepted and thus, one day implemented. The New left became fundamentally occupied with reform of the internal constitution of the Labour Party, which was influenced by the CLPD from the mid-1970s onwards. The creation of the CLPD was like much left-wing dissent at the time, a reaction against Wilson's rejection of the Party's left-wing manifesto of 1973. As left-wing activists, the CLPD easily fitted in to the practices of the New left and on their creation they ushered in a new format of inner-group politics to the Labour Party. It is important to note that Tony Benn and his supporters realised the salience of the CLPD's approach and consciously decided to work with them. Kogan and Kogan seek to understand this relationship:

'Benn, however, has become the figurehead of the movement led by the CLPD and the umbrella organisation, the Rank and File Mobilising Committee[36], which members of CLPD formed and shaped.'[37]

The CLPD was the means by which the New left could implement its ends. By the late 1970s the CLPD and the New left were part of the same movement and had three main aims. The first aim was the mandatory reselection of MPs. In 1978, shortly before the Party Conference, the NEC established a working party to discuss the reselection of Labour MPs. The working party recommended that constituency parties should be encouraged to consider the suitability of their sitting MPs to remain as candidates for the next election. This decision on MPs suitability to remain as future constituency candidates was to be decided by their behaviour in Parliament during the previous term.[38] The recommendation of the mandatory reselection working party was taken to the 1979 Party Conference and when a vote was held the Party Conference endorsed the NEC's recommendation of mandatory reselection of Labour MPs by a majority of four votes to three. This, according to the New left, would give constituency parties greater control over their sitting MP. It would empower them to reselect or deselect their MP on grounds of his or her record in Parliament. The question of the correct criteria to measure the suitability of a candidate appears somewhat vague and casts doubt over the intention of the New left because each constituency party could decide on a whim if their MP had been left-wing enough or not and therefore reselect or deselect them as they saw fit.

The second aim concerned the right to give the NEC final decision-making power over the Party manifesto. Once again, the New left argument for such a reform was so greater democracy was ensured over the decision-making of the manifesto and that the Parliamentary Labour Party and the Cabinet in particular, could not dominate discussions regarding the contents of the document which Labour Party members throughout the country had an interest in. Conversely, one can argue that this constitutional change was increasing the democratic deficit by ensuring that the New left who dominated the NEC at that time, had the final veto over the manifesto. However, the rhetoric of the New left was one of greater democracy, accountability and transparency. Although one could argue that a constitutional change should reflect the interest of the majority of the Party, which during the high watermark of the New left, the manifesto clearly did not. This objective was also taken to the 1979 Party Conference and it was passed by a majority of four to three.

The third main aim that the New left embarked upon was the establishment of an electoral college to elect the Party Leader. In 1979, the NEC set up a Committee of Enquiry to recommend constitutional changes to the Party Conference in the following year.[39] The Committee was comprised of seven NEC members, all of whom were left-wingers, the trade unions chose five representatives from across the Party spectrum and the Parliamentary Labour Party chose two representatives for the Committee, namely, Michael Foot from the Old left and the Prime Minister, Jim Callaghan from the right of the party. The salient point to note regarding the Committee of Enquiry is that the NEC deliberately chose a left-wing delegation to represent them on the Committee. In short, the New left dominated the Committee of Enquiry and because it was the NEC which established the Committee to recommend constitutional changes to the Conference, it can be interpreted as a deliberate campaign by the New left to mobilise their political agenda using the power base of the NEC. The Committee of Enquiry's findings were to recommend an electoral college to choose the Party Leader. Fifty percent of the college votes would be cast by MPs, twenty-five percent by the trade unions, twenty percent by the constituency parties and five percent by other affiliated bodies of the Labour Party. It was agreed that a special conference would be held to decide how to implement the principle of an electoral college into the Party's Constitution. Interestingly, the Committee of Enquiry's recommendation was criticised by both the left and the right of the Party. The left thought the college would support the right of the Parliamentary Labour Party, as MPs had fifty percent of the vote in the college and most right-wing MPs thought that the principle of an electoral college would erode the independence of MPs and put them at the mercy of the block vote of a single trade union.[40]

The last stage in the history of the electoral college was the Wembley Conference in January 1981. This was the occasion not only when the Party would approve the system of the electoral college but also, when the 'Gang of Three' would be joined by Roy Jenkins, become the 'Gang of Four' and would announce their intention to leave the Labour Party and establish the Social Democratic Party. This announcement took place a day after the conference ended and was called the Limehouse Declaration. The official creation of the SDP was March 26th 1981 and thirteen Labour MPs left the Labour Party and joined the SDP and another thirteen Labour MPs joined in 1982.[41] No further analytical narrative of the SDP[42] needs to be mentioned for the benefit of the chapter save a telling quotation from Denis Healey's autobiography, when he remembers the fate of the Gang of Four's breakaway from the Labour Party:

'Like all rightwing breakaways from leftwing parties, the SDP achieved nothing significant on its own account, but did grievous damage to those who shared many of its views in the party it deserted. The departure of twenty-nine opponents of the extreme Left shifted the balance of power inside the Parliamentary Labour Party.'[43]

It perhaps should be mentioned that such a comment about the SDP is predictable from a social democrat like Healey who chose to remain in the Labour Party. However, the formation of the SDP and its revisionist approach to social democracy can be seen to a certain extent as a forerunner to the revisionist approach to social democratic politics undertaken by New Labour, and in this instance one can appreciate the relevance of such a revisionist approach. In addition, Callaghan still Party Leader, decided to resign before the introduction of the new rules of the electoral college came in to being. Callaghan's main motivation was to prevent the election of a candidate from the Labour left, particularly Benn. Callaghan had hoped that Healey would succeed him and in doing so would begin to turn the tide against the Labour left in the Labour Party. However, Benn was advised by his supporters not to stand under the old rules as it was not a legitimate election in the view of the New left and it would appear hypocritical. John Silkin from the Old left, and Peter Shore from the ambiguous centre-ground, along with Healey from the Labour right and a reluctant Michael Foot put himself forward as the favoured candidate from the Labour left. Most of the New left would support Foot in securing a left-wing leader. Healey won the first ballot followed by Foot therefore eliminating Silkin and Shore. The second ballot, however, held no good fortune for the Labour right; it saw Foot defeat Healey by ten votes, one hundred and thirty-nine to one hundred and twenty-nine. Foot, therefore, assumed the Party Leadership and immediately asked Healey to be Deputy Leader, which Healey dutifully accepted.[44] In 1981, Benn challenged Healey for Deputy Leadership of the Labour Party. Benn's motivation was three-fold. Firstly, he made no secret of desiring one day to lead the Labour Party and therefore the Deputy Leadership was a step towards that political ambition. Secondly, Benn saw the contest as a chance to defeat Healey, the standard bearer of the Labour right. Thirdly, Benn saw the possibility of a successful outcome as strengthening the position of the New left particularly in the trade unions, which were traditionally allies of the Labour right. In addition, John Lansman, a crucial member of the CLPD, thought that Benn's challenge of Healey gave the New left an opportunity to test the machinery of the electoral college. Lansman thought that by using the electoral college the Party would get used to the new constitutional arrangement and to a certain extent the electoral college would become domesticated.[45]

In addition to those three explicit aims was an action instigated by the New left at the 1979 Party Conference at

Brighton, which had a considerable impact on the internal politics of the Labour Party for the next six years. This notable event was the relaxation of the proscribed list of organisations, which could legitimately join the Labour Party.[46] Whether such a motion was as important to the New left as mandatory reselection, an electoral college or control of the manifesto by the NEC is unlikely, but as an act of reform by the New left through their majority on the NEC it strengthened their movement. By relaxing the proscribed list, the New left consciously added more foot soldiers to their ranks, foot soldiers who were zealous and uncompromising. This in effect allowed fringe Marxist socialist and Trotskyite groups and individuals to infiltrate the Labour Party on the pretence that they were democratic and committed to parliamentary reform. Such groups included the infamous Militant Tendency (who dominated the Labour Party Young Socialists in this period),[47] the Socialist Workers Party, International Marxist Group, and The Workers Revolutionary Party, to mention the main organisations although several other small groups were prevalent during this time.[48]

The Revitalisation of Ideas on the Social Democratic Right in the Post-1983 Era

This section of the chapter attempts to highlight and examine the political ideas of thinkers on the Labour right or what will be termed the social democratic right of the Labour Party. Several thinkers and politicians during this period aided the revitalisation of social democratic ideas and values[49], however, this section seeks to analyse the work of five of these figures.[50] The five thinkers are the economist Alec Nove, the political philosophers Raymond Plant and Bernard Crick, the Deputy Leader of the Labour Party from 1983-1992 Roy Hattersley and the one time Shadow Trade and Industry Spokesman Bryan Gould. This era was crucial for the social democratic right of the Labour Party and some would say for the survival of the Labour Party itself, particularly because the political backdrop was one of such dominance by the New left from 1979-1983. In the words of Foote:

'...the period since the 1983 election has witnessed an evolution, rather than an end, to Labour's political thought, and it is an evolution which bears a strong mark of continuity with the British radical tradition.'[51]

The process of revitalisation of the ideas on the social democratic right of the Labour Party was two-fold. Firstly, it was about reconnecting the British electorate with what the Labour Party believed in, in terms of underlying values. Secondly, it was an exercise in strengthening the position of the social democratic right within the Labour Party. However, before the social democratic thinkers could allude to their favoured policy prescriptions that they believed the Labour Party should take to regain electoral popularity, a more fundamental lesson needed to be learnt by the Labour Party and crucially by the British electorate. That lesson and, therefore, the initial task of the thinkers on the social democratic right was to recover the place of social democratic values and to communicate to the electorate what the Labour Party believed in. This was an important process because the electorate had lost its understanding of what the Labour Party stood for. This is understandable when during the high watermark of the New left between 1979-1983, the Labour Party was described in terms of specific policy positions such as against the nuclear deterrent and for Britain's withdrawal from the European Community and not in terms of philosophical and ethical values, such as greater equality. For example, if one takes a cursory glance at the works of Nove, Plant, Crick, Hattersley and Gould in the post-1983 era, one notes that their works emphasised certain social democratic values. This was also an exercise in revitalising the ideas and values of the Labour right because historically the social democratic right from Hugh Gaitskell to Tony Crosland had described their democratic socialism or social democracy in terms of ends, underlying values. Conversely, the Labour left had described their political ends in terms of policy prescriptions but gave some role to political values. However, it was less clear what the Labour left in general and what the Old left and then the New left in particular, held to be their underlying values. This played to the strength of the social democratic right because the electorate were tired of the specific policy approach used to characterise what the Labour Party stood for. This approach was especially problematic for the Labour Party because the Conservative Party under Thatcher had a reasonably coherent political philosophy in the form of neo-liberalism and then attached certain policies to the values and subsequently sold those values to the electorate. In comparison, the Labour Party was incoherent and appeared like radical, single-issue campaigners devoid of understanding the needs of ordinary people.

In his study of the Labour Party's political thought, Foote notes that the economist Alec Nove in his 1983 piece, *The Economics of Feasible Socialism*[52] proved notably influential in the Labour Party in the post-1983 era.[53] In short, Nove argued that Soviet style socialism with its non-democratic, authoritarian philosophy led to an inefficient and stagnant economy. Nove went on to argue that without the market system of supply and demand, the Soviet Union was left with a hugely bureaucratic and incompetent economic system that made economic decisions on behalf of millions of people through fixing prices from above. Nove concluded that socialism required a market mechanism with a mixed economy and an element of state planning.[54] This critique of Soviet Communism is essential in understanding the change of attitude towards the centrally planned economies and anti-market rhetoric within elements of the Labour Party. Nove's work, therefore, was indicative of the reaction that many social democrats within the Labour Party were feeling towards the traditional mixed economy and the process of warming towards the benefits of the market to provide goods and services. Two points of clarification need to be made at this juncture. Firstly, many on the social democratic right accepted wholeheartedly the mixed economy, with therefore, an active role for the private sector and thus the market. However, the economic problems from the mid-1960s onwards and the popularity amongst the electorate of the ideas which underpinned the free-market such as competition, dynamism and choice became more acceptable to the social democratic right especially once it became so obvious that the Soviet planned economies were deeply flawed. Secondly, the debate about economic doctrine had not by 1983 really come of age. The social democratic right were still advocates of Keynesian demand management and many within the Labour Party saw this commitment to Keynesianism as a philosophical difference between Thatcher's neo-liberals and their commitment to monetarism. Thus, the abandonment of Keynesianism as Party economic policy had not quite begun and neo-liberalism was still viewed by the majority of the Party as being synonymous with monetarism.

Raymond Plant's initial contribution to the revitalisation of social democratic ideas came in the form of his 1984 Fabian Pamphlet, *Equality, Markets and the State*[55] that proposed several philosophical issues apposite for the strengthening of British social democracy. Firstly, Plant rebuffs the main claims, both moral and intellectual, of neo-liberalism.[56] Secondly, he constructs a defence of positive liberty and asserts that liberty and equality are intertwined and not mutually exclusive, as neo-liberals would argue.[57] Thirdly, Plant posits the view that although markets have their place in society there are moral limits to how far society should become market orientated:

'I do not want to deny that markets are important and should be kept within a socialist society; rather the arguments I am seeking to deploy are aimed to weaken the idea that markets should be the dominant mode of allocation and that therefore egalitarian socialism is a threat to the values which markets represent.'[58]

Fourthly, Plant criticises the notion that the pursuit of equality and, *ergo*, egalitarian politics, necessarily equate to an over-powerful bureaucratic state, which in turn causes a diminution of personal freedom. He notes that libertarians on both the right and the left concern themselves with the size and the tasks of the state and understands that although they reach different conclusions about equality neither presents a persuasive case for abandoning a central economic governmental approach to providing a high quality and equal standard of welfare and public services.[59]

The fifth and final task that Plant undertakes in his pamphlet is to endorse the kind of vision of equality that the American political philosopher John Rawls termed 'democratic equality'. Plant dismisses the neo-liberal equality of opportunity and the Marxist equality of outcome and settles for a measure of greater equality allowing only legitimate and justifiable inequalities in society.[60]

Plant's other significant contribution was his 1988 Fabian Pamphlet, *Citizenship, Rights and Socialism*.[61] In this piece, Plant had one main aim which was to establish the notion of 'democratic citizenship', borrowed in part from the New Liberals of the nineteenth century, to act as the framework within which social democratic values could be expressed and then put in to policy.[62] Plant's citizenship is basically, an expression of the aims of social democracy in terms of a communitarian conception of the citizen and society.[63] It is part of the British radical tradition and contrary to the traditional Labour left and Marxist framework which is elaborated in class-based language and understood through the ideas of economic alienation, capitalist exploitation and class confrontation.[64] Plant realised the conflict that the citizenship approach to social democracy stimulates when proposed against the class based approach and he believed that the values of citizenship could be the foundation of political agency to secure entitlements for individuals. The term 'democratic citizenship' has limitations and is better understood using the term 'communitarian citizenship'.

Democratic is true enough but it states the obvious that citizenship reflects democratic rights. In essence, Plant is using the term much more widely to embrace economic and social entitlements as well as political entitlements. Lastly, communitarian socialism or social democracy has a different emphasis to libertarian socialism and different thinkers are aware of their differences. One could also remark that the term 'democratic' received widespread abuse in the Labour Party particularly by the Bennite New left in the early 1980s and is best avoided as it leads to confusion.

Plant addressed his idea of citizenship as primarily an intellectual and moral means or vehicle for the Labour Party to espouse their underlying values such as greater equality, community and a positive conception of liberty. Nevertheless, it also acted as a defence against the rugged individualism of neo-liberalism which wants to emphasize the rights of the individual consumer whilst simultaneously negating the role of the individual in society, in communities and with responsibilities as well as rights. Although like most social democrats of the time, Plant accepted a greater role for market forces and appreciated the benefits that markets can supply, he considered and rejected the view that the market is the best mechanism for providing 'needs' when 'needs' are objectively and consensually understood as basic human requirements.[65] In addition, Plant highlighted the flawed nature of neo-liberal negative rights that portray positive rights, that is entitlements to goods as:

'...resources which are in themselves scarce and cannot therefore be considered to be objects of rights.'[66]

Simply put, Plant's argument is that there is no conceptual or categorical distinction between negative rights - the right to be free from interference and coercion and positive rights - rights to resources. Plant then states that the communitarian approach is consistent with previous trends in British socialist thought and that the market is compatible with a socialist society conceived in a communitarian citizenship framework, acknowledging at the same time the market's limitations and the injustice that it throws up. Plant asserts that:

'...markets have a central role to play within a socialist society. But they must operate within a set of community values where outcomes will not be regarded as impersonal visitations but adjusted within a framework of social justice.'[67]

Bernard Crick introduces his Fabian pamphlet, *Socialist Values and Time* with the precise intention that was noted above, namely opening the discussion of social democratic values to a wider audience and emphasising values ahead of policies:

'And it must argue not over the *minutiae* of party programmes, but over the broad direction of the economy and the whole quality and equity of our national life.'[68]

Crick argued that out of the triumvirate of values associated with social democracy through its history; equality, liberty and fraternity, only equality is explicitly social democratic.[69] Moreover, Crick suggested that when social democrats link all three of these values together, then both liberty and fraternity take on a distinctly social democratic form.[70] From this initial comment on the traditional social democratic values and their interconnected nature, Crick posits the view that equality is the normative value but the goal or the exact desired end is an egalitarian society. Crick clarifies this point in two ways. Firstly, he argues that a belief in equality and thus a desire for an egalitarian society does not mean that social democrats are advocating a literal equality of outcome that is suggested by some Marxists.[71] Secondly, that by giving up on equality as a value and in turn its goal of an egalitarian society, social democracy is left with:

'...a directionless pragmatism and the paternalism of benevolent hierarchies.'[72]

Crick expects neo-liberals and Marxists to misunderstand the merits of an egalitarian society and therefore, the merits of the value of equality. Nevertheless, his criticism is particularly harsh on what he sees as social democrats that have abandoned the cause. Crick is directly referring to the breakaway social democratic MPs who joined the SDP. As has been noted above, Crick believed that when liberty and fraternity are linked to the value of equality they too take on a social democratic form. With reference to this Crick argues that liberty takes on a positive character that can:

'...open doors, to create an open society; but then we do not just sit admiring so many choices of ways forward or to exist, we need to choose, by free and open debate, the best doors to go through...'[73]

Therefore, a positive conception of liberty is the outcome of connecting liberty to equality. Regarding fraternity, Crick realises that it is clearly the most intellectually underdeveloped of the social democratic values and he fails to analyse fraternity in sufficient detail. However, Crick does on the other hand, attempt to connect fraternity and liberty to demonstrate social democracy's end goal, namely a free and communal society:

'Fraternity without liberty is a nightmare, liberty without fraternity is competitive cruelty but fraternity with liberty is humanity's greatest dream.'[74]

In summary, Crick argues persuasively for the elevation of values instead of policy prescriptions, highlights equality, liberty and fraternity and criticises the neo-liberals for refuting, the Marxists for misinterpreting and the pragmatic Social Democrats for giving up on equality and an egalitarian society.

In Roy Hattersley's 1987 book, *Choose Freedom*[75] his first task was to argue for the importance of a clear Labour Party conception of social democracy and an explicit espousal of its core political values:

'If the Labour Party is to attract the support that will ensure a working majority, we cannot allow the voters to have any doubt about the ethical principles on which democratic socialism is based. Paradoxically, unless we strike out our ideological boundaries and defend them against external assault and internal subversion, we will not attract to our cause the millions of unideological supporters who are necessary for our victory.'[76]

Secondly, Hattersley sets out a positive argument for greater equality and not merely a version of equality of opportunity. He dismisses the two main counter-arguments against greater equality namely its negative effect on liberty and its necessity for economic success of society posited by the neo-liberals.[77] In renouncing these views, he rejects the purely negative conception of liberty that neo-liberals in the Conservative Party commit themselves to. Hattersley identifies four structural and political changes that took place during the post-war era which in turn, have led people away from the Labour Party and its traditional approach to its principles. The first was the fact that the political and social map of Britain had changed due to the movement between classes, the reduction in traditional manufacturing and increased affluence.[78] This meant that the Labour Party suffered because there was less class identification in politics and its natural strongholds in Scotland, Wales and the industrial north had diminished as many people fled to the affluent south-east of England. Secondly, economics had become increasingly unpredictable and the Keynesian approach had lost significant intellectual appeal.[79] The market was something that social democrats had to accept and this in turn meant there was a lesser degree of control that social democratic government's could exert. Thirdly,

Labour Party supporters had become increasingly middle-class.[80] Fourthly, ideological politics had re-emerged since the 1970s and thus, the Labour Party had to set out its ideology in terms of underlying values and not through specific policies. Hattersley concluded his first chapter by stating what he believed social democracy stood for:

> '...what we stand for is freedom. That is the ultimate objective of socialism.'[81]

The first part of the book was an attempt to justify social democratic values under the banner of greater equality which will lead to greater freedom through a positive conception of liberty. The second part of the book concerned itself with setting out the conditions and methods that social democrats could use to secure greater economic and social equality. Hattersley systematically analyses the benefits and drawbacks of varying social democratic methods including the market. He suggests that, on occasions, the market will be suitable for the purposes of social democracy and at other times, it will not be suitable.[82] Hattersley discusses nationalisation and concludes that state monopolies are not ideologically social democratic in themselves but accepts that they could be used in certain circumstances as a means to an end.[83] Hattersley mentions the issue of state planning and argues that stark lines of economic demarcation in the areas of public and private should not divide a mixed economy. A mixed economy should have companies with a variety of owners.[84] Hattersley concludes his examination with the method of redistribution. In each case, Hattersley revises some of the myths and shibboleths surrounding such practices and consistently emphasizes that greater equality within society will lead to greater individual liberty which should be the purpose of social democracy. Hattersley concludes that Crosland summed up the relationship between a positive conception of liberty and greater equality in a succinct phrase:

'Socialism, he said, is about the pursuit of equality and the protection of freedom - in the knowledge that until we are truly equal we will not be truly free.'[85]

Foote contends that the one time Labour Shadow Trade and Industry Spokesman Bryan Gould borrowed Plant's ideas concerning the relationship between equality and liberty and the task of reconnecting the electorate to an overall vision of the society that the Labour Party wanted to create through the implementation of its underlying values.[86] Gould published a noteworthy book in 1985 that contributed to the debate of social democratic values entitled, *Socialism and Freedom*.[87] This presented a detailed analysis of liberty from both the negative and positive schools of thought and he advocated the notion that freedom must be conceived in a positive framework:

'The absence or denial of a 'condition of freedom' if it prevents the exercise of that freedom and is socially ordained, must surely be a constraint upon freedom. This is because freedom is not, at bottom, an abstract but rather a practical thing. A freedom without the practical possibility of it being exercised is no freedom at all and has no meaning. It would be as paradoxical as a sight that could not be seen.'[88]

Gould then moves on to discuss different models of socialism such as the Soviet Communist model as well as democratic socialism. In particular, Gould believes that one of the main tasks of socialism is to resist large concentrations of power as he asserts that such occurrences will eventually impinge on individual liberty:

'The socialist on the other hand…operates to prevent and counteract the concentration of power which poses such a huge threat to individual liberty.'[89]

Finally, Gould's decentralist argument, which asserts that individual freedom will be protected as power and money are devolved to regional bodies fails to consider two issues. Firstly, as egalitarians, the decentralisation of state power would possibly cause different standards of services and benefits from one region to another due to different group abilities in providing those services and different ways of regional bodies spending money. Secondly, the state has traditionally occupied a key role in enacting socialist measures for socialist governments. Would a devolved and less centralised structure be as effective at implementing these policies? Perhaps they would but Gould does not consider the gap that decentralisation would leave in the political economy of the Labour Party.

The second important contribution made by Gould in this period is his 1989 publication, *A Future For Socialism*[90] in which he considers several large areas of political interest to social democrats ranging from the change in traditional political economy, to the rise in support for New Right ideas, to the case for decentralising state power. It is in this last area that Gould like Crick, parts company with Plant as Plant is suspicious of the inequalities in distribution that decentralisation may throw up. Plant is cautious about this issue because he thinks that at least with a central bureaucracy resources are intentionally equally distributed to the nation in the form of public services and welfare benefits.

The 1987-1994 Era

The Labour Party lost the 1987 general election and whilst it was a modest improvement on the 1983-election result because the Labour Party polled just over ten million votes, won 229 seats and gained 30.8% of the votes cast, whereas in 1983 the Party polled less than eight and a half million votes, secured only 209 seats and gained 27.6% of the vote;[91] the electorate still refused to give the Labour Party the responsibility of forming the Government. One can interpret the 1987 general election defeat as a catalyst for undertaking the Policy Review. When viewed historically, 1987 was the Labour Party's third consecutive election defeat and the cumulative effect on the morale, psyche and confidence of the Party at large and the leadership in particular was the motivating factor for such a review of aims, values, policies and prospects. The Party conference in October 1987 passed a motion commissioning a full Policy Review at the request of the Kinnock leadership.

The initial act was the *Labour Listens* campaign whereby senior Shadow Cabinet ministers toured the country listening to people's opinions on Labour's policies and attitudes on an array of subjects. Largely speaking, this was not successful and yet at least it showed that Labour was serious about enacting a policy rethink. The first decisive action of the Policy Review was the establishment of seven review groups according to certain themes as opposed to departmental issues. They were: *People at Work*; *A Productive and Competitive Economy*; *Consumers and the Community*; *Democracy and the Individual*; *Physical and Social Environment*; *Economic Equality*; and *Britain in the World*. As well as the seven thematic review groups the Party leadership wanted to revise the Party's statement of political values. Butler and Kavanagh suggest that this desire had been in place since 1985 and was based on three reasons. Firstly, it would enable the Party to re-evaluate its values in line with British societal changes of the 1980s. Secondly, it would counter the political misrepresentation made by the Conservative Party, as the original statement emphasizes class in a way that many groups in society no longer found appropriate and infers full scale nationalisation of industry, which in fact was never Labour Party policy. Third and finally, the redrafting of the Party's statement of values would enable the leadership to give some ideational coherence to the Policy Review and it would restate the Party's democratic principles and in doing so, would openly exclude undemocratic entryist groups such as Militant.[92] During 1987, Kinnock and Hattersley formulated the document entitled *Democratic Socialist Aims and Values*[93]. One can argue that the document initially appeared to act as a type of reformed constitution to rival the traditional Clause IV but as time passed and no motion to redraft Clause IV was offered by the leadership, *Aims and Values* appeared to be a test-balloon to measure the Party's willingness to reform in line with the changes of the Policy Review. Colin Hughes and Patrick Wintour note that when *Aims and Values* was published the Bennite left interpreted it as an assault on Clause IV.[94] However, they also note that the centre of debate in the Labour Party and inside the Shadow Cabinet was over the role of the market and the emphasis on individual freedom and, that these issues were largely raised by supporters of the Kinnock leadership.[95] Hughes and Wintour argue that *Aims and Values* was in essence, a half-hearted attempt by Kinnock to rebrand the Labour Party:

'Aims and Values was finally, for Kinnock, a staging post on the way to delivering the policy review. If Kinnock had genuinely wanted to write a new party creed, he could have slugged it out over the ensuing months...The main aim of the review was to persuade the world outside that Labour was changing; Aims and Values was the slipway.'[96]

Therefore, it is apparent that some members of the Labour Party took *Aims and Values* more seriously than the leadership. As is noted above, the Bennites saw it as an attempt to redefine the Labour Party's Constitution by supplanting Clause IV; others such as David Blunkett and Bernard Crick simply disagreed with its direction. The Labour leadership saw it as a marketing exercise and one that gave some ideational coherence to the Policy Review, rather than representing the Labour Party's own Bad Godesburg. Blunkett and Crick's document entitled, *The Labour Party's Aims and Values: An Unofficial Statement*[97] mainly argued that democracy is centrally about civic participation and this was the type of socialism that the

Labour Party should advocate. As Hughes and Wintour assert:

'Blunkett's personal preference was that Labour should rally around the notion of a participatory democracy – the approach which he himself adopted with considerable reward as leader of Sheffield city council. That meant, simply put, that socialism sought to involve every individual in those decisions which affect his or her life.'[98]

As we can see, *Aims and Values* was held with varying degrees of respect. Firstly, as a serious ideological statement of the Labour Party's social democracy and secondly, as a document that Labour members could support.

The next phase of the Policy Review was the submission of the review groups' preliminary reports to the Party Conference in 1988. All the groups filed reports apart from the defence group and industrial relations group which took longer due to the sensitive nature of their topics and their contingent policies. The following phase, approved at the 1989 Party Conference was the document, *Meet the Challenge, Make the Change* which was in essence the review groups' suggestions on the Party's values and principles. Then, in early 1990 the defence group concluded its discussions and made its recommendations. The final phase of the Policy Review was the launch in May 1990 of the programme, *Looking to the Future*. This document was an updated version of the *Meet the Challenge* paper. Butler and Kavanagh concluded their discussion of the Labour Party's journey for electability by asserting that the Policy Review remodelled not only policies but also the political approach of the Labour Party:

'Labour was now perhaps divided less on traditional left-right lines than between old Labour and new Labour. Old Labour was identified with the values and interests of the past, with high taxes, public ownership, trade unions, council housing, heavy industry and the north. New Labour sought to identify the party with skills training, new ways of working, improved public services, greater rights for women and families, and protection of the environment.'[99]

Stephen Driver and Luke Martell summarise the policy revisions that the Policy Review delivered:

'On the economy, the party became increasingly pro-market, limiting the role of government to the enforcement of competition and to market failures such as training, research and development and regional development. Labour's commitment to the renationalization of the privatised utilities-or, for that matter, public ownership at all, slowly disappeared...The Policy Review also saw the disappearance of Keynesian demand management and the withdrawal from the European Community. In their place the Labour leadership, in particular the shadow chancellor John Smith, advocated stable macro-economic management, including a commitment to low inflation, and membership of the European Community's Exchange Rate Mechanism. Increased spending on welfare was to be financed from economic growth except pensions and child benefits, where top tax rates would be increased. Trade union legislation would remain largely in place. And what was perceived as the party's albatross during the 1987 election, unilateral disarmament was buried.'[100]

In 1988, during the Policy Review, David Marquand published a book that significantly contributed to the debate about the future of social democratic politics, entitled *The Unprincipled Society*.[101] The book set out the political and economic reasons for Britain's relative decline and gave a thorough evaluation of the governing 'Keynesian social democratic consensus' and the factors which underpinned its successes and ultimately, its failure. In the first part of the book Marquand also commented upon two prominent doctrines seeking to assume the role left behind by Keynesian social democracy, namely neo-liberalism and neo-socialism.[102] These terms were used by the author to characterise the ideas and beliefs of the Thatcherite conservatives and the Bennite socialists and their accounts of the failings of Keynesian social democracy. The second part of the book focused on what Marquand termed 'realities' referring to the economic realities that a new philosophy would have to focus on and confront. This section also studied the nature of the state and the free market; an account of the relationship between public power and private freedom; and an examination of the institutions and conventions of the British state.

However, the salience of this book in relation to the changes in social democratic politics in Britain in the late 1980s is revealed in the third and final part of the book, which is a single chapter, entitled *The Public Realm*. It is here that Marquand suggests the basis for a new governing philosophy to rival both neo-liberalism and neo-socialism and to address the problems that Keynesian social democracy failed to remedy. Marquand states that:

'My central thesis is that the roots of Britain's adjustment problems are to be found in a coherent, though often unconscious, set of attitudes to politics and political man – to the relationship between man and society, between individual purposes and social purposes, and to the political dimension of these relationships – and in the reductionist model of human nature which lies behind them.'[103]

What Marquand finally implies is that Britain requires a form of communitarianism as its governing philosophy, with emphasis on local communities, decentralisation of power and decision-making, an attitude of politics as mutual education which is connected to a clear notion of British citizenship and an understanding of the 'common good'.[104] Marquand cites the lack of such a philosophy and the dominance of the market liberal philosophy as part of the cause of Britain's relative economic, social and political decline:

'All this puts the British crisis of maladaptation into a broader, but at the same time bleaker, perspective. As we have seen, the failures of adaptation of which it is the culmination all reflect the stubborn survival, both on the 'micro' level of the individual entrepreneur or producer group and on the 'macro' level of the whole society of the doctrines and – much more importantly – the ethos of market liberalism. These doctrines are, of course founded on the reductionist model of man which we have just been discussing. Though they are not solely British in origin, they have been propagated more insistently and for longer in Britain than anywhere else in Europe. And they, the ethos associated with them and – most of all – the conception of men which underlies them have nibbled at any notion of community or common purpose like pollution nibbling at an ancient building.'[105]

Marquand's contribution to the debates about the future of British social democracy in this period is less a prescription of policy solutions to difficult political problems and, more of a recommendation of a communitarian governing philosophy. Therefore, Marquand's book was a timely critical evaluation of Keynesian social democracy and one that suggested to social democrats that an emphasis on community, greater public participation in politics, decentralisation of power and a common notion of citizenship in the form of a communitarian philosophy was a worthy creed to challenge market liberalism.

Nevertheless, for all of its reformation and internal modernisation the Policy Review did not change enough of the British electorate's perception of the Labour Party. Issues such as economic competence and high taxation were still millstones around the Party's neck for much of the electorate and in turn were regarded as 'Old Labour'. The net result was the fourth consecutive election defeat for the Labour Party at the hands of John Major's Conservative

Party in 1992. Furthermore, not only was this election defeat a rebuff for Labour by the electorate it also continued the dominance of New Right ideas and principles in preference of modernised social democratic ideas proposed by Kinnock's Labour Party. The Conservative Party gained 41.9% of the vote compared to 34.4% by Labour, they won 336 seats as opposed to 271 Labour seats and polled just over fourteen million votes to Labour's eleven and a half million votes.[106] Nevertheless, the 1992 election created a close electoral result. The Conservative Party had only sixty-seven more seats than Labour and an overall majority of twenty-one seats. Butler and Kavanagh suggest that a one percent swing against the Conservatives would have resulted in a hung parliament and politically speaking things could have been completely different from 1992 onwards.[107]

In the immediate aftermath of the April 1992 General Election defeat, Kinnock and Hattersley resigned as Party Leader and Deputy Leader of the Labour Party. Three months later saw the leadership election with John Smith running against Bryan Gould. Smith polled 91% of the vote, assumed the Party Leadership and Margaret Becket comfortably won the Deputy Leadership contest securing 57% compared to John Prescott's 28% and Bryan Gould's 14.5 % (Gould's double ticket campaign did not win him either position of influence). The period from July 1992 until Smith's death in May 1994 was a crucial period in the manoeuvrings of the modernisers in the Labour Party who believed more policy reform and internal political reforms were required, against the leadership of Smith who, although a reformer, was more content with where the Party had arrived by the 1992 General Election. In this period three significant events occurred which furthered the ambitions of the modernisers.

The first event was Smith's incremental reduction in the trade unions' share of the vote at Party Conference. On winning the Party Leadership Smith had pledged to reform the Party's relationship with the unions and in September 1992 at the Party Conference, a motion was passed reducing the union share of the conference vote from 87% to 70%. Following on from this reform, Smith proposed to reduce the unions' share of the vote in leadership elections and constituency candidate selections in February 1993. The second significant event was the establishment of the Commission on Social Justice by Smith in December 1992. The Commission on Social Justice was an independent body organised under the auspices of the Institute for Public Policy Research and chaired by Gordon Borrie who was the former Director-General of Fair Trading. As the Executive Summary of the Commission's report states:

'The Commission's job was to carry out an independent inquiry into social and economic reform in the UK.'[108]

One can speculate that the impact of the Commission's findings would have largely shaped the economic and social policies of a Labour Opposition and Labour Government headed by Smith. What is certain is that the Commission's report has influenced New Labour. For example, David Miliband the then Director of the IPPR who organised the Commission, went on to become the Head of Blair's Policy Unit in Opposition and in Government and is currently Minister for Communities and Local Government. The contributions of academics, politicians and area experts provided a modern social democratic critique of, and suggested responses to, the ills of neo-liberal policies. Although, the 1987-1989 Policy Review designed policies on a range of social and economic issues and modified some of the social outlooks and economic commitments of the Labour Party at that time and proved to be an influential process in modernising party attitudes, the Commission on Social Justice was a more policy specific study and was a thorough academic examination in to the needs of British society in terms of the principle of social justice. The Commission's report defined its commitment to social justice as:

'...the equal worth of all citizens, their equal right to be able to meet their basic needs, the need to spread opportunities and life chances as widely as possible, and finally the requirement that we reduce and where possible eliminate unjustified inequalities. Social justice stands against fanatics of the free market economy; but it also demands and promotes economic success. The two go together.'[109]

In some of the concluding paragraphs of the Commission's report an appropriate summary of its main objectives are given:

'In our proposals for lifelong learning, for full employment in a modern economy and a new balance between paid and unpaid arrangements, for the development of health and community care, and the revival of distressed communities, we have set out the principle objectives that should guide government over the long term, as well as the steps towards these objectives that can be taken in the short and medium term...The longer the neglect of economic opportunity, social security, and civic health, the longer it will take to turn things round. The more marginalised the poorest, the more we will pay for their inclusion; the more insecure the labour market, the longer it will take for people to embrace change; the more centralised our political structures, the more difficult it will be to bring hope of renewal.'[110]

Some of these themes are now inherently thought of as New Labour themes, such as lifelong learning[111], revival of distressed communities[112], economic opportunity[113], secure and flexible labour markets[114] and decentralised political structures[115]. Therefore, the Commission on Social Justice proved to be an important process for generating modern social democratic policy proposals for the modernisers.

The third event of significance in the modernisers' project for the Labour Party was put forward at the Party

Conference of 1993. The Party Conference agreed on the introduction of One-Member One-Vote which meant that for Leadership and Deputy Leadership elections trade unions must ballot their members individually. This regulation also applied to constituency party sections of the electoral college. Furthermore, as part of the One-Member One-Vote proposal, the composition of the electoral college was also amended, reducing the trade unions' proportion of the votes from 40% to 33.3%. This specific reform meant that the electoral college became equally divided between the Parliamentary Labour Party, the trade unions and the constituency parties all of which have 1/3 of the vote.

Therefore, on reflection John Smith led further internal party reforms which evenly balanced the three main sections of the Party in terms of the electoral college. This can be interpreted as being another step towards a modern citizenship approach to Labour Party politics as opposed to the traditional class-based, union-preference approach that the Labour Party historically fulfilled. On a symbolic level, it let the public know that the Labour Party was more than a union supported political party, that it was committed to internal democratic processes which had become discredited due to 'democratic claims' by the New left between 1979-1983 which divided the Party and lost the respect of many sympathetic Labour voters.

Smith died suddenly in May 1994 and the Deputy Leader, Margaret Beckett became acting-Party Leader until a Leadership election was held. The following weeks between Smith's funeral and the result of the Leadership election has already gone down in British political folklore and the substance of whether Blair deliberately out manoeuvred Brown by announcing his candidacy for the Leadership or whether supporters of Blair, such as Peter Mandelson, orchestrated a Machiavellian plot to isolate Gordon Brown and his supporters, is fascinating in one respect but not necessary at this juncture in understanding the gradual evolution of New Labour under Blair.[116] In July 1994, the Leadership election was held with Blair, Becket and Prescott all standing. Blair gained 57% of the vote, under the new One-Member One-Vote regulations and Prescott defeated Beckett for the Deputy Leadership gaining 56.5% of the vote.

5

AN INTELLECTUAL HISTORY OF THE LABOUR PARTY: 1994-2004

In the previous three chapters, an *intellectual* history has been presented from the nineteenth century origins to the late twentieth century history of the Labour Party. This chapter will attempt in much the same way as the previous three chapters have, to provide an *intellectual* history of events and ideas in the Labour Party during the 1994-2004 period. This chapter identifies several factors that have significantly contributed and in turn, have shaped the Labour Party and assisted in creating what we understand to be 'New Labour'. These factors include the re-branding of the Labour Party by the 'modernisers' into New Labour; the distinction between 'Old Labour' and New Labour; the role played by the New Democrats in New Labour; the redrafting of Clause IV; the globalisation thesis; the specific policies of the 1997 election manifesto; Third Way ideas; and second term ideas 2001-2004.

Re-branding the Labour Party

I understand New Labour to be the modernised social democracy instituted within the Labour Party under the leadership of Tony Blair from 1994 to the present day. It is necessary to assert that although New Labour is now widely accepted as being the politics of Blair's Governments from 1997 and his Shadow Cabinets from 1994, it began as a process of changing the Labour Party's electoral appeal and policies. Steve Ludlam states that:

'The New Labour project that is popularly dated from Blair's succession to the Labour leadership in 1994 thus followed a long period of modernisation of the party's ideology, organization and policy.'[1]

When Blair was elected leader of the Labour Party in 1994 'New Labour' did not officially exist. The term 'New Labour' was applied publicly for the first time at the Party conference of 1994 in the phrase on the conference platform; 'New Labour: New Britain'.[2] However, it was Philip Gould who thought that the word could be used in conjunction with the Labour Party modernising in 1989. Gould states that it was a forgotten idea until it was brought back to the fore after Clinton's New Democrats successfully used the phrase to show a contrast between themselves and the 'old' Democrats.[3] Alistair Campbell suggested the phrase 'New Labour: New Britain' for the 1994 conference and it was from then onwards that Blair felt the notion of 'New' to be an appropriate next step for the Labour Party to take.[4] The importance of this is threefold. Firstly, one must note that the name 'New Labour' describes the politics and the political project of a powerful group of party modernisers rather than a nation-wide agenda of the Labour Party. The likes of Blair, Brown, Mandelson, Campbell, Philip Gould, political advisers and fellow kindred spirits who have largely comprised the Blair Cabinets since 1997 can be seen as representative of 'New Labour'.[5] Secondly, as a political project, it is a reaction to the past electoral failures of the Labour Party, the social and economic changes in Britain since the 1970s and a political response to the claimed intellectual hegemony of New Right ideas embodied in Thatcherism. As Mandelson and Liddle clearly state:

'The harder task of getting to grips with New Labour depends on understanding that, in giving renewed expression to the party's founding beliefs, it is a deliberate move forward from both the post-war Labour Party of

Wilson and Callaghan and the Conservative Party of Thatcher and Major – a political project requiring much greater radicalism and originality than simply 'moving right'.[6]

Therefore, New Labour is not a set of independent ideas that exist in the abstract but a response to the problems and requirements of British society. Its heritage is embedded in the recent history of the Labour Party as opposed to existing separately as a philosophy within the textbooks of social democracy. Third and finally, New Labour as I understand it, represents a genuinely new and distinct ideological position on the spectrum of Labour politics.[7] As we will see in the second half of the book, it will be claimed that New Labour has its own philosophical standpoints and is a different form of social democracy than has existed previously in the Labour Party. Therefore, New Labour was initially a political project and a political faction representing a distinct ideological position. That is not to say that New Labour has a single, new, cogent political philosophy, as it will be argued later in the book that it does not. What New Labour does appear to have is an interpretation of specific political values such as liberty, equality and community.[8]

The 'Old Labour'/New Labour Distinction

Martin Smith argues that for New Labour as the modernised social democrats in the Labour Party, the main political opponents are now those who can roughly be termed adherents to 'Old Labour':

'If there is an enemy left, and one that is strongly identified by certain elements in Blair's leadership, it is 'Old Labour'. The reality of Old Labour is that it is a combination of the right of the party, the left of the party and dissidents but its rhetorical importance is that it is a way of distancing New Labour from its past and indicating to the electorate that the Party has fundamentally changed.'[9]

At this point in the chapter it is beneficial to turn to first-hand interview material concerning the alleged distinction between 'Old Labour' and New Labour. The interviewees are former Labour politicians, advisors from the Blair era and academics. The question I asked was 'How far is the contrast between 'Old Labour' and New Labour a rhetorical one and how real is that distinction?'

In an interview with Matthew Taylor, the then Director of the Institute for Public Policy Research, he argued that the Old Labour/New Labour distinction is inaccurate and he points to three dominant strands of thought in the Labour Party which in his opinion is more reflective of the ideological divides that exist. Firstly, there is the 'hard left' or Trotskyite left who have a class-based analysis of society, are state-centrists and who entered the Labour Party in the late 1970s and early 1980s under the cover of democracy. Secondly, there is the 'soft left' which can be viewed as being the combination of two traditions; namely, the radical liberal and social democratic traditions. Individuals who occupy the 'soft left' are interested in themes such as equality, feminism, democratisation and quality of life. The third and final group are the *workerist* (labourist) right who have a bias towards the working class, are state-centrists concerned with winning power and who are interested in high public spending and universal provision in the welfare state.[10]

In contrast to Taylor and more in line with New Labour's ideological positions, the then Director of the London School of Economics, Professor Anthony Giddens believes that one does not have to use the terms 'Old Labour' and New Labour. Giddens acknowledges that there are divisions on the left, but distinguishes between the traditional and modernising left. According to Giddens, the traditional left advocates Keynesian economics, state-centrism and a collectivist approach to governance. The modernising left advocates a market economy and believes in decentralisation of power. In Giddens's view New Labour are attempting to sustain social democratic values in the modern world. Giddens regards the modernising left and therefore New Labour, as having a determination to maintain electability and to hold the centre ground of politics together. This is because Giddens believes that globalisation is reshaping the ideological map of politics across the world and that both the anti-globalisation left and the far right are competing political pressures on the centre ground of politics.[11]

Michael Jacobs, the then General Secretary of the Fabian Society asserts that 'Old Labour' is as much of a construct as New Labour. Jacobs suggests that Mandleson and Gould invented the terms simultaneously, as marketing devices in which one rebrands the Labour Party and contrasts it with the thing it used to be. Jacobs points out that the concept of Old Labour is inaccurate because the idea that Roy Hattersley and Tony Benn believed in the same type of socialism is absurd. Jacobs's main point is the need to separate rhetoric from reality. He believes New Labour's rhetoric has lost the traditional transformative language of socialism but the reality is more favourable with New Labour achieving more for social democracy than previous Labour Governments. Jacobs goes on to note that New Labour is different from various strands in the Labour Party, particularly regarding their favourable attitude towards private business. He thinks that New Labour believe that business operates largely in the public interest because they equate it with consumer interest. Furthermore, according to Jacobs, the socialism of Roy Hattersley would never have made such a claim. Finally, Jacobs states that New Labour does not privilege the public sector but Old Labour in all its forms did.[12]

David Marquand believes that it is politically expedient to distinguish New Labour from traditional Labour Party policies so to win the support of large numbers of the electorate who were deeply hostile to the Labour Party. Marquand suggests that New Labour had to do this if they were to build a social coalition that could match the achievements of the Thatcher years. Marquand also notes that New Labour's historiography is somewhat inaccurate. He says this because it was as if John Smith had never been Labour Leader.[13]

The then Vice-President of the European Commission, Neil Kinnock, argues that the only reason why the term Old Labour exists is because the term New Labour exists. Kinnock states the term is partly rhetorical and presentational and in those terms it is justifiable. Although he asserts that some individuals in New Labour want the 'New' to remain as the prefix to 'Labour' forever, therefore not merely being a new version of the Labour Party contrasted with previous versions but desiring the Labour Party to be something that it is not. Kinnock goes on to say that such people within New Labour want a complete change of values and a different analysis of how the world works.[14]

Giles Radice claims that the 'Old Labour-New Labour' distinction is largely a rhetorical contrast devised as a way of making the Labour Party electable by showing that it had changed. Radice comments that it is a very important political task of every generation to adopt a revisionist approach to party politics. Radice cites the redrafting of Clause IV as being the main revision of the New Labour modernisers.[15]

Roy Hattersley argues that ideologically there is a very real distinction between certain groups in New Labour and with certain elements of Old Labour. He gives as an example the ideas of Blair and states that there is a very real distinction between his ideas and those of egalitarian social democrats like Anthony Crosland. Hattersley would cite 'Old Labour' as a nametag for different types of Labour Party social democracy that are not New Labour.[16]

The opinions of the respondents can be categorised as follows: those who believe that the Old Labour/New Labour distinction is broadly accurate; those who think that the distinction is generally inaccurate; those who think that the distinction is to some extent accurate regarding political tactics, rhetoric and electioneering; and those who think that the distinction is to some extent accurate regarding ideas and policies.

I generally take the view posited by Taylor, Jacobs and Kinnock that as a method of distinguishing different ideological groups in the Labour Party the Old Labour/New Labour distinction is an inaccurate formula. Although I disagree with Taylor's analysis that the Labour Party can be broken down in to three ideological groups, namely: the Trotskyite left, the *workerist* (labourist) trade union right and the radical liberal/social democratic 'soft left'[17], I do accept that that there are historic distinctions which are largely due to different accounts of political economy and different interpretations of social democratic values.[18] Therefore, I do not accept the view that the Old Labour/New Labour distinction is broadly accurate. However, regarding the two other statements above namely: the 'Old Labour/New Labour distinction is accurate in terms of ideas and policy' and the 'Old Labour/New Labour distinction is accurate in terms of tactics and rhetoric' I again follow the views of Taylor, Jacobs and Kinnock because I do not think 'Old Labour' is, or ever has been a single, coherent ideological grouping in the Labour Party and thus, the distinction is not accurate in terms of differentiating ideas and policy. With regards to the Old Labour/New Labour distinction being about rhetoric and political tactics to win the electorate's trust, I would agree. The term 'New Labour' was used to demonstrate to a sceptical electorate that Labour policies would not be like the policies of the Wilson-Callaghan Governments in terms of the level of direct taxation and in terms of the tripartite approach to industrial relations. Furthermore, it was used to demonstrate that New Labour was a moderate social democratic party not an exceptionally left-wing party like the Labour Party was under the leadership of Michael Foot between 1980-1983 when the Bennite 'New left' dominated. What New Labour was attempting and succeeded in achieving was to demonstrate that they were not the 'Old right' or the 'Old left' or the 'New left' of the Labour Party but an ideologically moderate and significantly reformed social democratic party. In essence, the new right-wing of the Labour Party.

The Influence of the New Democrats on New Labour

Stephen Driver and Luke Martell suggest somewhat controversially that the New Democrats have been the most significant influence on the ideas and policies of the New Labour modernisers:

'Perhaps the most important influence on Labour modernizers has come from the USA. Bill Clinton's victory in the presidential elections in 1992 - the year of Labour's demoralising defeat by John Major - demonstrated that a party of the left could win power after a long period of conservative hegemony - but only if it moved onto the political centre ground.'[19]

Once again it is beneficial to turn to first-hand interview material concerning the alleged influence of the New Democrats on New Labour. The question that I asked in the series of interviews was, 'What is your view of the influence of the New Democrats on New Labour?'

Regarding the influence of the New Democrats on New Labour, Taylor argues that a student of Labour politics must separate out policy, tactics and presentation. Taylor believes the New Democrats were influential on New Labour's rhetoric and presentational approach. However, he notes that they were not overly influential on policy issues up to the point where there has been a systematic overemphasis of learning from the USA in comparison from learning from the European Union. Taylor asserts that because national policy decisions in the UK occur at the state level in the USA, the New Democrats at federal level have very little to teach the British Labour Government about education, health and pension reform. Furthermore, the welfare to work initiatives were borrowed as much from the

Scandinavians who have been operating them for the last thirty-five years as from the USA.[20]

Giddens suggests that the influence of the New Democrats on New Labour was mutual because Labour Party officials such as Peter Mandelson and Philip Gould worked with the New Democrats from the late 1980s. However, Giddens states that the New Democrats do have a theory of society and social change that New Labour has to some extent adopted. According to Giddens, the New Democrats argue that the industrial age has been supplanted by the information age and in the information age you need decentralisation of power, there is a shifting alignment in the politics of the electorate and new policies need to be formulated to respond to the social change.[21]

Jacobs believes that the influence of the New Democrats on New Labour is overstated. Regarding political strategy Jacobs believes the New Democrats taught New Labour how to use the media and play a continuous game of media manipulation, defence and attack. In particular, Jacobs noted that New Labour was influenced by the 'triangulation' approach, which enables a political party to triangulate between different sections of public opinion so they appear to be on the left and right simultaneously and therefore, become able to construct a consensus. Jacobs appears to be accurate in suggesting that 'triangulation' as a political technique was utilised by New Labour and enhanced its moderate appeal, because Philip Gould states that Blair was keen to transcend the traditional left-right barriers.[22] Gould connects Blair's desire to redefine the political dividing lines with the idea of Third Way politics.[23] In terms of policy, Jacobs like Taylor, argues that much of the welfare reforms about active labour markets are as Scandinavian and Dutch in origin as they are American. Therefore, Jacobs concludes that it is a bit of a myth to infer that New Labour borrowed its welfare state reforms and large-scale policy prescriptions from the New Democrats.[24]

Marquand is unsure of the extent to which the New Democrats influenced New Labour but his impression is that they have been quite a considerable political influence. Marquand cites the fact that in the 1990s when New Labour appeared on the British political scene, the New Democrats were the only comparable Western party who were winning elections. Marquand believes that New Labour viewed Bill Clinton as having achieved what they wanted to achieve, namely to win support from sections of the electorate who traditionally had been voters of the right. Marquand also suggests that Blair and Brown view the policies of the American New Democrats as a better guide in terms of what will 'play well' in Britain as preferable than the policies of the European social democrats.[25]

Kinnock argues that the influence of the New Democrats on New Labour is misleading. Kinnock notes that within both organisations there are some sharable values but the New Democrats work in a very different political environment from social democrats in Europe therefore, the actual political influence cannot be as substantial as some commentators believe. In addition, Kinnock notes that some Labour Party officials such as Philip Gould helped work on the 1992 Presidential election for the New Democrats and actually exported British electioneering techniques to America such as the rapid media rebuttal system.[26]

Radice believes similarly to Kinnock that the influence of the New Democrats on New Labour has been some what exaggerated. The only real area that Radice thought that New Labour might have been influenced was with regard to political techniques on how best to get elected and even so the influence appeared to be mutual.[27]

Hattersley is unsure of the influence of the New Democrats on New Labour but he feels that certain policies like the American 'Workfare' is similar to the Government's welfare to work schemes. In addition, he argues that Hilary Clinton originally discussed the Third Way ideas in public and he thinks that they have influenced elements of New Labour especially Blair. In campaigning and electioneering Hattersley accepts that people such as Mandelson and

Gould were probably influenced by tactics such as 'triangulation' and Dick Morris's 'rule of 50%' whereby a leader would never make a policy that more than 50% of the electorate would disagree with.[28]

The opinions of the respondents can be categorised as follows: those who believe that the New Democrats have in some way influenced New Labour; those who think that the New Democrats have influenced New Labour in terms of political tactics, presentation and rhetoric; those who think that the New Democrats have influenced New Labour in terms of ideas and policies; those who believe that the New Democrat influence is misleading; and those who think that New Labour have influenced the New Democrats in some way.

Regarding the question 'To what extent have the New Democrats influenced New Labour?' I take the view that the New Democrats have in some way influenced New Labour and therefore, I am in agreement with all of the respondents bar Kinnock who suggested that any idea of influence is misleading. It should be noted that this response from Kinnock is to be expected, as any response in the affirmative would imply that under his leadership the changes in the Labour Party were at least in part subject to some American Democrat influence and this is obviously a view he wishes to reject because he states that when he was Party Leader members of the Labour Party helped in Clinton's Presidential election campaign. Again, I agree with the arguments outlined by all of the respondents bar Kinnock that to some extent the New Democrats have influenced New Labour in terms of political tactics, presentation and rhetoric. In particular, I am convinced by the arguments of Jacobs that the New Democrats taught New Labour how to use the media to get its message out and by introducing it to electioneering techniques such as 'triangulation', which enabled them to appear to be moderately left as well as right on issues at the same time. However, like Taylor, Jacobs, Kinnock and Radice I believe that the New Democrats influence on New Labour ideas and policy is at best negligible and at worst completely absent. I follow the views put by Kinnock and Taylor; namely, that the New Democrats work in a different political environment and have quite different interest groups whom they claim to represent than social democratic parties in Europe and to claim that the New Democrats influenced significant amounts of New Labour ideas and policy prescriptions is untenable. This point is supported by the issue that Taylor raised which is because national policy decisions occur at state level and not federal level in the United States, the New Democrats at federal level have little to teach or offer New Labour on issues such as public services, pension reform and similar domestic issues. Finally, I am unsure of the extent if any, to which New Labour has influenced the New Democrats.

Redrafting Clause IV

The redrafting of Clause IV is perhaps the single most, far-reaching reform that has affected the character of the Labour Party and it is certainly the most symbolic act of reform by the New Labour modernisers. Philip Gould asserts that the redrafting of Clause IV was one of Blair's principle objectives. In a conversation with Blair, Gould recounts his intentions concerning that part of the Labour Party constitution:

'Past leaders lost because they compromised. I will never compromise. I would rather be beaten and leave politics than bend to the party. I am going to take the party on.' [29]

Furthermore, the decision to raise the issue of redrafting Clause IV at the 1994 party conference required the support of John Prescott. Gould quotes Alistair Campbell:

'There was no way we could have done it without John Prescott - not just John reluctantly agreeing, but John actually agreeing, giving his blessing to it... In the end it was

John who said if you are going to do this you have got to say it, you can't bugger about. That was when we wrote it in right at the last moment to review our constitution for a new age. That actually came from John - we were going to skirt around it.'[30]

Donald MacIntyre points out that the move to redraft Clause IV was the ultimate expression of Labour Party modernisation.[31] MacIntyre recounts that Blair was very keen on the idea because:

'...it would be a correspondingly symbolic break with Labour's socialist past.'[32]

However, he asserts that Mandelson was cautious about the redrafting of the constitution as he remembered the problems Gaitskell had after the 1959 election when he tried to redraft Clause IV, which ultimately led to failure and internal strife. Nevertheless, Blair's enthusiasm to redraft Clause IV was as much a demonstration of New Labour's break with 'Old Labour' as it was to remove a political albatross from around the Labour Party's neck, which the Conservatives occasionally made successful political capital out of.[33] MacIntyre views the redrafting of Clause IV as an early success by the New Labour modernisers:

'The replacement of Clause Four was an unalloyed triumph - not least because Blair's campaigning zeal up and down the country persuaded the party not only to change it, but, in the end, to want to change it.'[34]

However, as Mandelson and Liddle note, parts of the national Labour Party were hostile to any change to the constitution. These included some of the unions like the Transport and General Workers' Union and Unison who voted to keep the traditional Clause IV and the obvious and expected opposition from the Labour left, especially the MPs who gravitate around the publication, *Tribune*.[35] In addition, Philip Gould argues that the penultimate draft was inadequate and he persuaded Blair to write it himself. The redrafted Clause IV finally stated that:

'The Labour Party is a democratic socialist party. It believes that by the strength of our common endeavour we achieve more than we achieve alone, so to create for each of us a community in which power, wealth and opportunity are in the hands of the many not the few, where the rights we enjoy reflect the duties we owe, and where we live together, freely, in a spirit of solidarity, tolerance and respect.'[36]

Therefore, on 29th April 1995, the new Clause IV was adopted by a special conference of the Labour Party at Westminster Hall. The total vote endorsing the redrafted version was 65%, with 90% of the constituency parties supporting it and 55% of the Labour Party's affiliated organisations supporting it. The reduced support in the affiliated organisation category was due to the antipathy towards a modernised statement of Labour values by parts of the trade union movement. Martin Smith notes that once Clause IV was reformed the modernisers built upon their influence:

'Once Clause IV was reformed Blair quickly consolidated the reforms to the party machinery that Kinnock had begun. Blair strengthened one member one vote and through the development of the policy forum he effectively undermined the role of conference in policymaking. Likewise, the NEC, which at times had been a troublesome critic of the leadership, became increasingly Blairite whilst its policy role was significantly reduced.'[37]

The Globalisation Thesis

When New Labour came to power in 1997, eighteen years after last holding office, they entered a world significantly altered by economic, technological and geo-political change.

New Labour holds to a specific economic and sociological thesis of globalisation, which informs their aspirations and policy objectives. In the western world, mainstream politicians of all persuasions generally accept this thesis, although it is strongly criticised by some notable academics.[38] To refer to it as the 'globalisation thesis' is partly problematic as the term is contested and has become deeply politicised. However, for the sake of this chapter it will suffice. The globalisation thesis argues that the economic, technological and geo-political changes are all part of an observable phenomenon that has evolved in the last quarter of the twentieth century.

With regard to economics, the decline in operation of the doctrine of Keynesianism in the western world and the dominance of market forces has opened national economies to large flows of tradable goods and services. In short, many more countries are active in trading partnerships and are economically dependent on each other. Another change in economics is the expansion of world financial markets. These markets trade in actual time due to sophisticated telecommunications systems that allow huge flows of capital to be traded by vast numbers of traders in markets throughout the world.[39] In each day of trading on the world financial markets over one trillion dollars is 'turned-over' in transactions of currency.[40] Likewise, companies choose to invest in states whose workforces are well trained and highly skilled. Therefore, investor confidence in a national economy is central to companies staying in that state and central to the availability of jobs in the private sector. The flexible nature of capital means that multi-national companies can easily shut down factories and plants making job instability a significant aspect of the globalised economy. The positive side of such a situation is that firms wanting to harness favourable economic conditions in specific countries can create jobs rapidly. In the chapter entitled, *The Global Economy* in his book, *New Britain: My Vision of a Young Country*[41], Blair affirms this belief in the globalisation thesis:

'The driving force of economic change today is globalisation. Technology and capital are mobile. Industry is becoming fiercely competitive across national boundaries. Consumers are exercising ever-greater power to hasten the pace of this revolution. Travel, communications and culture are becoming more international, shrinking the world and expanding taste, choice and knowledge. The key issue facing all governments is how to respond.'[42]

Another aspect of the globalisation thesis that has contributed to the economic interdependence of nations in the global market is the communications revolution. By the term 'communications revolution' one is referring to the growth in information technology ranging from the widespread use of personal computers and email to website and satellite technologies.[43] All of these types of technology create a world of immediate communication and immediate flows of information.[44] For example, the twenty-four hour money markets depend on satellite and computer technology, television is now a global medium which provides information, entertainment and interactive communication due to digital technologies.[45] Therefore, globalisation is not only transforming the business sector of nations but also the entertainment, leisure sector and the nature of public institutions such as the NHS which runs a twenty-four hour, nurse-led, internet and phone based helpline known as NHS Direct which answers people's concerns about illness and health issues.

Geo-political change is a further aspect that has occurred due to globalisation. Economic blocs such as the European Union, NAFTA, OPEC and the Asian Tiger economies exert significant power over national economic policies. For Britain, in particular the decision to either join or withhold from the Euro is another crucial globalised decision to face. Military defence, global crime prevention and political convergence are all issues that the world faces through the lens of co-operation and partnership rather than as solitary island nation-states. Global fragmentation has occurred partly as a reaction to the collapse of the traditional political boundaries of the Cold War and the ensuing democratisation and economic liberalisation in regions such as eastern and south-eastern Europe, and partly as a reaction to the political instability that a globalised world brings. Globalisation has shrunk the world in terms of finance, time and space. This gives rise to opportunities for wealth creation inside and outside the Western world; it reduces the detachment the West used to have from global social problems; it means that different races, religions and cultures mix together in a smaller and more diverse world and it means that national and international co-operation becomes a necessity not an optional extra. However, globalisation also raises the spectre of cultural and religious clashes and international terrorism, and it highlights the ever-widening wealth gap between the North and the South. Political and economic instabilities have been exacerbated because of the world's interconnected and interdependent character. It is within this globalised world that New Labour has constructed its revised form of social democracy.

The 1997 Labour Party Election Manifesto

The 1997 Labour Party election manifesto is an important document to consider when charting New Labour's *intellectual* history. The manifesto makes clear that by 1997, New Labour had defined itself as a modern and internally reformed Labour Party, with altered outlooks and policy prescriptions:

'In each area of policy a new and distinctive approach has been mapped out, one that differs from the old left and the Conservative right. This is why new Labour is new.'[46]

In addition, the manifesto outlines two interesting points that are salient in a discussion of New Labour's evolution.

The first point of interest is that as a political party, New Labour claims to be a party of:

'...ideas and ideals but not of outdated ideology. What counts is what works. The objectives are radical. The means will be modern.'[47]

This statement is pertinent for a number of reasons. The commitment to ideas and ideals sits comfortably with the Labour Party's tradition yet the statement makes a blatant distinction between New Labour's ideas and ideals and what it views as the previous generation of Labour ideals which it terms 'outdated ideology'. It is one thing to claim that certain ideas are outdated and are thus, no longer appropriate but it is a different issue to label them as 'outdated ideology'. Ideology is a word that conjures imagery of the grand-narratives that claim to hold the answers for every conceivable human problem. It also makes one think of political extremism particularly of marxism, fascism, communism and religious fundamentalism. Therefore, New Labour's implication that traditional Labour ideas and ideals are 'outdated ideology' is as hostile as it is pejorative. The subtext to such a statement is possibly that New Labour only accepts 'new' and 'current' ideas and that to be 'modern' is what ultimately counts in social democracy. The second point of interest in the statement arises from the possible philosophical quandary that the second part of the statement conjures; namely, that New Labour's objectives or ends are radical and therefore, conventionally leftwing or social democratic but the solutions or means for achieving the objectives are 'modern'. On a political level, this suggests in New Labour parlance and in no uncertain terms, that issues of economy and society must be treated in modern not traditional terms. Thus, regarding the economy, New Labour implies that a market economy as opposed to a Keynesian demand management economy will be pursued. Regarding society, a communitarian, not a liberal world view will inform their social policies. Philosophically, the problem that arises here is that if one attempts to change the means of implementing an end or objective, it is possible that one could change the objective in the process. This is an issue that certain thinkers raise.[48]

The 1997 Labour Party election manifesto also states that New Labour are only willing to pledge:

'...a limited set of important promises and achieving them.'[49]

This can be seen as the cautious and conservative character of New Labour. A character forged in the recent electoral history of British politics, where grand promises scared an inherently conservative electorate into not risking Labour in government. The tone of the manifesto and the above quotation imply to some extent that New Labour's first term would be pragmatic and largely unambitious in legislative terms but that it would seek to secure a second term through its steady and competent handling of the economy during its first term. Related to this character of caution and the absence of a truly transformative ambition for British society, Blair accepts that New Labour will not unpick the legislation that he believes the Conservative Governments were right to implement:

'Some things the Conservatives got right. We will not change them.'[50]

Although, Blair does not directly state what areas of legislation New Labour believes the Conservatives were right to implement it is probable that he was referring to the majority of industrial relations legislation from the Thatcher era, the acceptance of the market as the primary economic mechanism for providing goods and services and implicit in that assumption is a pledge not to return to Keynesian demand management with price controls, tripartite negotiations and incomes policy.[51] A further indication of the policy areas that New Labour believe the Conservatives were right to implement and would not be repealed by a New Labour Government is given by Mandelson and Liddle; they include the removal of penal rates of income tax, and the emphasis on increased productivity in industry through privatisation.[52]

Third Way Ideas

In the post-1997 period, Blair attempted to define what New Labour stood for in philosophical terms. The sociologist and Third Way thinker, Anthony Giddens summarises the notion of the 'Third Way' in Britain:

'In Britain 'third way' has come to be associated with the politics of Tony Blair and New Labour. Tony Blair's political beliefs have frequently been compared to those of the New Democrats in the US, and indeed there have been close and direct contacts between New Labour and the New Democrats.'[53]

In 1998, Tony Blair published a Fabian Pamphlet entitled, *The Third Way: New Politics for the New Century*. In the introduction to that pamphlet, Blair stated that:

'The Third Way stands for a modernised social democracy, passionate in its commitment to social justice and the goals of the centre-left, but flexible, innovative and forward-looking in the means to achieve them. It is founded on the values which have guided progressive politics for more than a century - democracy, liberty, justice, mutual obligation and internationalism. But it is a third way because it moves decisively beyond an Old Left preoccupied by state control, high taxation and producer interests; and a New Right treating public investment, and often the very notions of 'society' and collective endeavour, as evils to be undone.'[54]

It can be argued that in a limited way Blair's introduction to his Fabian pamphlet is perhaps one of the clearest indications of New Labour's understanding of Third Way ideas and politics. Much time and scholarship has been spent debating the Third Way and a standard conclusion is the ambiguity of the position as a political theory.[55] This point is not disputed. However, it can be argued that the 'Third Way' is most appropriately interpreted as Blair's political philosophy rather than as New Labour's political philosophy. For example, Brown has yet to mention the phrase in any of his speeches or statements since New Labour has come to office. In addition, although between 1998-1999 Blair made speeches with Bill Clinton, Wim Kok, Gerhard Schroder and Massimo D'Alema on Third Way ideas, little is heard of it today as shorthand for New Labour's political philosophy.[56]

What is clear about Blair's enunciation of Third Way ideas is that he was attempting to place the politics of New Labour and himself in an historical context. Blair tried to suggest that New Labour was not a Labour Party version of Thatcherite neo-liberalism on the one hand or a reworked, media friendly form of 'Old Labour' on the other hand. Although perhaps more notably, that New Labour was not a half-way house or the centre of gravity between traditional Labour Party social democracy and neo-liberalism because that itself would require the abandonment of some traditional social democratic values that he and New Labour were not willing to sacrifice. Blair asserts that:

'The Third Way is not an attempt to split the difference between Right and Left. It is about traditional values in a changed world. [57]

A further point of importance that Blair raises in regard to the type of politics that he wants New Labour to represent occurs when he cites New Labour as an attempt to reconnect liberalism and democratic socialism. He says that New Labour:

'...draws vitally from uniting the two great streams of left-of centre thought - democratic socialism and liberalism - whose divorce this century did so much to weaken progressive politics across the West. Liberals asserted the primacy of individual liberty in the market economy; social democrats promoted social justice with the state as its main agent. There is no necessary conflict between the two, accepting as we now do that state power is one means to achieve our goals, but not the only one and empathically not an end it itself.'[58]

Specifically speaking one could assert that he means to reunite social liberalism with democratic socialism because liberalism can and has taken a number of philosophical positions from the right as much as the left. However, the problem with this (as is mentioned above) is that social democracy when it is viewed as not synonymous with democratic socialism but as a traditional Labour right political philosophy is the child of social liberalism and democratic socialism. Individuals like Giles Radice would consider themselves revisionist social democrats because they are different from liberals and, to Labour leftwingers who would usually describe themselves as democratic socialists and not social democrats due to their penchant for public ownership, a state centric approach to governance and an antipathy towards markets.

Finally, it appears that Blair has ceased to describe New Labour's politics in terms of Third Way rhetoric but perhaps he feels he has succeeded in defining what New Labour is and is not about in contemporary British politics. Arguably, the majority of his Cabinets and Labour MPs who would describe themselves as modern social democrats are reassured that the Third Way rhetoric has ceased as so few notable politicians and British academics bar Giddens truly gave intellectual credence to it as an accurate and rigorous political philosophy of modern social democracy.[59]

Second Term Ideas: 2001-2004

The 2001 Labour Party election manifesto is an important document when charting the recent *intellectual* history of New Labour because it contains one markedly different economic factor which was absent in the 1997 manifesto; namely, the continued commitment of high levels of investment in Britain's public services. One can argue that this single re-emphasis by New Labour has altered its political trajectory towards what can be understood as traditional social democratic means for changing society in line with its stated principles. In his introduction to the 2001 manifesto Blair states that:

'This general election is in many ways even more important than the last. Since May 1997 we have laid the foundations of a Britain whose economy is stronger, where investment is now pouring into public services...'[60]

This change in attitude came half way through the first term when Brown announced in his 1999 Pre-budget report that the Government was going to significantly increase public spending on education and the health service. This was a matter of sizeable debate for commentators of New Labour. After two full years of keeping to the previous Conservative Government's spending plans (arguably to prove to the electorate that a Labour Government could competently manage the economy) the Government finally began to invest in public services.[61] With this economic policy step change came the main difference in the 1997 and 2001 manifesto commitments. In Blair's own words:

'Now is the chance to build the future properly, to make the second term the basis for a radical programme of British renewal: to keep a firm grip on inflation, with low interest rates and the public finances sound, and then build the dynamic and productive economy of the future; to keep investment coming into public services and then making the reforms so we use the money well...'⁶²

Due to the announcements in the 1999 Pre-budget report, the 2001 manifesto clearly set out that there would be a commitment to further funding to improve public services. To ascertain whether New Labour had changed its political approach between the lead up to its first term and the end of the first term and whether such a change of approach had meant a change in its underlying values, I asked the interviewees the following question: 'Was the 2002 Budget and the Comprehensive Spending Review (on which the investment in the public services was contingent) a reversion to 'Old Labour' principles or not?'

Taylor argued that the 2002 Budget and Comprehensive Spending Review can be seen in a different light depending on whom one talks to. Taylor notes that people around Blair are more likely to say that the 2002 Budget and Comprehensive Spending Review are a response to the realisation that they could not improve public services without investing more money although when they first arrived in government that was their belief. Therefore, according to Taylor, the so-called 'Blairites' initially thought that creating high quality public services was not contingent on high investment. Taylor suggests that the 'Brownites' would argue that the 2002 Budget and Comprehensive Spending Review were things that they had always planned to do but that they had to appear to do it through pragmatism, to improve the public services that the electorate demanded, as opposed to do it because the Labour Party is a tax and spend party.⁶³

Giddens believes that because the Government built up a surplus of funds they were able to invest it in public institutions and the issue of raising taxation to fund further investment is, according to Giddens a difference from the first phase of New Labour governance. However, he does not view the 2002 Budget and the Comprehensive Spending Review as a reversion to 'Old Labour' if that means irresponsible taxation. Giddens suggests that 'Old Labour' tax and spend meant tax and overspend and that it incurred large debts and borrowings, which is not the New Labour approach. Finally, Giddens stated that he thought the first term prepared the way for the second term and that a key part of the New Labour philosophy is that you have to show that you (the Government) are delivering effective goods when using taxpayers money and spending it on part of the state.[64]

Jacobs stated that when answering questions concerning the policy and value distinction between 'Old Labour' and New Labour (especially in the second term of New Labour) it is not a simple choice between 'Old Labour' principles versus New Labour principles, because it is not always so clear where they start and finish. What Jacobs argued was that the emphasis on high level public investment is a definite shift in the way New Labour governs compared with the majority of the first term. New Labour Mark-I stated that they could reform and improve public services without significant amounts of investment, but this ceased to be the outlook during the first term and because of the new approach of raising taxes to fund high levels of investment, it suggests a major change in policy prescriptions and philosophy. Finally, Jacobs stated that because the 2002 Budget and the Comprehensive Spending Review is the centrepiece of New Labour's second term one has to say that it is inherently New Labour although accepting that New Labour Mark II is different to New Labour Mark I. At the same time noting that the continued emphasis on reform of the public services is distinctly New Labour and that 'Old Labour' would have been perhaps less concerned and more complacent about public service delivery due to the great faith it placed in all aspects of the public services.[65]

Marquand suggested that New Labour and Blair and Brown particularly, bought into the worst aspect of Thatcherism namely a deep distrust of public sector professionals; that they are in some sense monopoly seeking cartels who are protecting their own privileges and incomes from market forces. In addition, Marquand asserted that there was little patience with the delivery improvements in the public services by New Labour, although he conceded that 'Old Labour' perhaps was too enthralled with public service interest groups.[66]

Kinnock argued that the 2002 Budget and the Comprehensive Spending Review was not a reversion to 'Old Labour' principles but that it was just Labour. He noted that any Labour Party supporter and even floating voters realise that one needs to invest in the fundamentally important services like health and education because they determine a condition of life and affect real freedom. However, Kinnock speculated that the large-scale public investment should have perhaps come earlier in the Labour Government's tenure in office.[67]

Radice argued that the 2002 Budget and the Comprehensive Spending Review was not particularly 'Old Labour' or New Labour just what the Labour Party does, namely providing good quality public education and free health care. However, he praised New Labour's commitment to making sure the public gets value for money from the extra taxation they have to surrender in order to get better public services. Radice stated that the emphasis on value for money and auditing the performance of public services that get extra money is something that social democrats did not really comment on in the 1950s, 1960s and certainly not in the 1970s.[68]

Hattersley, when asked whether the 2002 Budget and the Comprehensive Spending Review was a reversion to 'Old Labour' principles suggested that it was clearly a step back towards what he considers to be traditional social democracy. He stated furthermore, that the 2002 Budget was a sign of great hope that New Labour would be willing to commit to better public services through sustained investment funded by higher taxation.[69]

The opinions of the respondents can be categorised as follows: those who believe that the 2002 Budget and the

Comprehensive Spending Review was a reversion to 'Old Labour' principles and those who claim that the 2002 Budget and the Comprehensive Spending Review was a change of emphasis for New Labour but not necessarily a reversion to 'Old Labour' principles.

Regarding the question, 'Was the 2002 Budget and the Comprehensive Spending Review (on which the investment in the public services was contingent) a reversion to 'Old Labour' principles or not?' I follow the arguments outlined by Taylor and Jacobs, which assert that the 2002 Budget and the Comprehensive Spending Review was not a reversion to 'Old Labour' principles but a change in emphasis for New Labour. I support this view because I do not think that the term 'Old Labour' exists as a coherent ideological grouping in the Labour Party, therefore 'Old Labour principles' is an equally redundant concept. However, like Jacobs, I think it does demonstrate a change in emphasis and priority by New Labour. The issue of improving public services (as is stated above) is central to New Labour's second term but it appears that there was a belief, in some quarters, that public service improvement could be achieved by internal reform and without a significant amount of extra funding. Taylor suggests that this was the view of the 'Blairites' and that the 'Brownites' had always intended to change tack and invest substantially in public services. This is a plausible but ultimately impossible assumption to test because a government seldom discloses clear statements of such intent. In addition, like Giddens I would think that high levels of public spending were due to come after New Labour had successfully demonstrated that they could manage the economy and therefore, a surplus of funds was generated in the first two years of office when due to the pledge to keep to the previous Conservative Government's spending plans very little public money was spent. I think this was a politically prudent pledge to make and its successful completion has in part aided the Government's standing by casting away any notions (however unfair) that

Blair's Labour Government will fail to manage the economy like previous Labour Governments.

In the 2001 manifesto, Blair openly acknowledges that the 1997 manifesto and his first Labour Government made only modest promises.[70] The 2001 manifesto, as well as setting out ten broad goals to be reached by 2010, pledged to deliver five promises on the issues of economic stability, quality public services, a modernised welfare state, strengthening communities and British influence abroad.[71] Therefore one can posit the view that in economic terms the 2001 manifesto is more radical in what it pledges regarding investment in public services. Although the main historical point to note was the step change in economic thinking from the Pre-budget report of 1999 onwards.

In the latter half of New Labour's second term there have been few coherent declarations of what modernised social democracy and future New Labour governments should stand for. One reason for this lack of voice on philosophical issues is that New Labour, and Blair above all, has been preoccupied with foreign affairs throughout the course of the second term. The lead up, 'liberation' and bloody aftermath of the war in Iraq has consumed enormous amounts of intellectual and moral energy of the Government and Blair himself. Therefore it is unsurprising that little focus has been given to a restatement of their political philosophy after nearly two full terms in office.

During the period 2001-2004 the most notable attempt to outline ideas came from Blair in his speech to the Labour Party Conference in Brighton in 2004 where he spoke of his vision of the 'opportunity society':

'The 20th century traditional welfare state that did so much for so many has to be re-shaped as the opportunity society capable of liberation and advance every bit as substantial as the past but fitting the contours of the future. And this will be a progressive future as long as we remember that the reason for our struggle against injustice has always been to liberate the individual. The argument is not between those who do and those who do not love freedom. It is between the Conservatives who believe freedom requires only that Government stand back while the fittest and most privileged prosper. And we who understand, that freedom for the individual, for every individual, whatever their starting point in life, is best achieved through a just society and a strong community. In an opportunity society, as opposed to the old welfare state, government does not dictate; it empowers.'[72]

Blair was attempting to place 'opportunity', a recurrent New Labour theme, at the centre of his justification for reforming the public services. Opportunity can be understood as the principle that implies choice and individual liberty. It is quite possible that Blair was hoping to link a Labour value like opportunity to his agenda of market-led public service reforms. In one sense this is not controversial as New Labour is committed to raising standards and investment in public services that are for all citizens 'free at the point of delivery'. On the other hand even attempting to justify market-led reforms to sections of the Labour Party is controversial as some social democrats do not think markets should be encouraged to provide essential services as they could become more established and flourish and in turn pose a threat to high quality public provision. What is pertinent about the 'opportunity society' speech is that it came so late in the second term. This suggests that it was hoped it would provide fresh impetus for the public service reform agenda and grant Blair the opportunity of gaining ground with the Labour Party at the Party Conference, after a difficult summer when at one point he allegedly considered resigning. In addition, the attacks on the Conservatives' preoccupation with helping the privileged enabled Blair in essence to begin the 2005 general election campaign.

As the earlier quotation above from Martin Smith implied, the modernisers did not appear in the Labour Party in 1994 on Blair's victory as Party Leader. One claim to make is that 'modernisers' or as they are traditionally termed, 'revisionists' have always existed in political parties. However, meaningful revision usually occurs after notable societal and or economic change. Revisionists can on the other hand be agents of reform and in New Labour's case after 1994 they certainly were. For example, the modernisers proposed the redrafting of Clause IV of the Labour Party Constitution, which in effect repositioned the Party's aims and goals. Revisionists or modernisers have come to the forefront of political discourse at specific phases in history. Appropriate examples of previous modernisers or revisionists in the Labour Party are the Gaitskellite revisionists. As has been discussed in the third chapter, these individuals mapped out their brand of democratic socialism in the 1950s and one notable revisionist was able enough to produce a piece of political economy which would become the textbook of Gaitskellite revisionist socialism for the proceeding twenty years. If nothing more, that was Anthony Crosland's intellectual legacy and in producing *The Future of Socialism*[73] he cemented the revisionists position in the Labour Party and the Labour Movement.

New Labour's modernisers share similarities as well as differences with the Gaitskellite revisionists. One similarity between the groups is that in their specific eras they were committed to the idea that the world had changed significantly and therefore democratic socialism must also change and adapt. The New Labour modernisers assert that the world has changed and entered a time of increasing globalisation that affects the social, economic and geo-political activities of nation-states.[74] The Gaitskellite revisionists asserted that the nature of capitalism had changed due to a variety of factors including the technical change in the management of capitalism from owners to mangers, which in turn had affected the priorities of British socialism.[75] A second similarity is that both groups centred on the Labour leaderships of Gaitskell and Blair. Although the modernisers existed as a group under Kinnock's leadership when Blair himself was a key moderniser and the Gaitskellites were as much supporters of Gaitskell for the Party leadership whilst he was the Shadow Chancellor between 1951-1955. The similarity continues with regard to both Gaitskell and Blair demonstrating their boldness in attempting to raise issues of modernisation inside a deeply conservative institution such as the Labour Party. Modernisation or revisionism requires an atmosphere of open-mindedness and the freedom to dissent from popular perspectives. The personalities of Gaitskell and Blair permitted such atmospheres and this can be seen in their attempts to redraft Clause IV, the difference being Blair succeeded where Gaitskell failed. A further similarity with New Labour's modernisers and the Gaitskellite revisionists was in their commitment to change for the ability to win elections, form a government, and thus implement their ideas. The New Labour modernisers, especially Blair and Brown were new MPs at the 1983 General Election and were thrust into the deep-seated ideological battles for the Labour Party during the early to mid-1980s. They witnessed the defeat of the Labour Party three times as MPs before they won power in 1997. The Gaitskellites likewise witnessed the Labour Party lose the 1951, 1955 and 1959 General Elections before Harold Wilson's Labour Party won in 1963. A final main similarity between the New Labour modernisers and the Gaitskellite revisionists is that both groups are from the Labour right. The ideological journey of many of New Labour's modernisers is more dramatic than the Gaitskellites. For example, some such as Robin Cook, Jack Straw, John Prescott and Margaret Beckett were supporters of the Bennite New left. Others still, though fewer in number, were on the Labour right and would describe themselves as occupying the social democratic wing of the Party, such as Peter Mandelson and the late Donald Dewar. This brief summary of previous political commitments illustrate that individual political belief can shift to a greater or lesser extent. All of the aforementioned politicians could today be regarded as examples of New Labour and although they may differ on specific policies they would share the main thrust of New Labour's politics.[76]

Yet the differences between New Labour's modernisers and the Gaitskellite revisionists are also important. Firstly, by 1956, the Gaitskellites had a clearly articulated and coherent political and economic philosophy in *The Future of Socialism* whereas New Labour's modernisers have yet to produce a work of notable intellectual merit which sets out New Labour's political and economic philosophy. The absence of such a text makes the process of discerning the intellectual heritage of the modernisers quite difficult. One could say that Peter Mandelson and Roger Liddle's book *The Blair Revolution* comes closest to setting out New Labour's world view and its initial policy objectives before the general election of 1997, but it is definitely not a work of political economy or political philosophy. Another difference between the New Labour modernisers and the Gaitskellite revisionists is a purely practical issue, namely that the New Labour modernisers succeeded in gaining power and altering the political discourse of the Labour Party whereas, the Gaitskellite revisionists and later the Croslandites never completely dominated the ideas and policies of the 1964-1970 Wilson Labour Governments and the 1974-1979 Wilson-Callaghan Governments. It is fair to say that the 1974-1979 Labour Government contained Gaitskellites or Croslandite ministers who were exceptionally able men and women who included Crosland himself, Shirley Williams, Bill Rodgers and Roy Hattersley but they failed, unlike the New Labour modernisers to make their revisionism the dominant creed in the Labour Party.[77]

The modernisation process began in earnest as we noted in the previous chapter, under the leadership of Neil Kinnock in the form of the Policy Review of 1987-1989. After Kinnock's defeat John Smith became Labour Party leader and continued internal party reform, most notably by instituting One-Member One-Vote, which changed the way party members vote for issues and party candidates in elections. Smith's brief tenure was as a moderniser but was limited to party democracy and not to party policy and rhetoric. When Blair became leader after Smith's death in 1994, the 'ultra-modernisers'[78] as some commentators have termed them, seized the opportunity to further reform the Labour Party's policies, electioneering approach and its rhetoric beyond all previous manifestations of revision. With New Labour, the modernisers had modernised the Labour Party completely and up to the point where some traditional social democrats on the Labour right such as Roy Hattersley claimed that New Labour was, 'no longer my party'.[79] Therefore, by 1994 and certainly by 1997, the New Labour modernisers had established themselves as the new right-wing of the Labour Party. This is not to imply that to be a moderniser or revisionist in the Labour Party is to be exclusively from the Labour right because one could view the New left as revising the traditional or 'Old left' view of the ills of capitalism. In particular, the New left added the notions of meso-economic power of multinational corporations which was skilfully done by Stuart Holland in his 1973 work on the New Left's political economy, *The Socialist Challenge*.[80]

This chapter has attempted to provide an *intellectual* history of the Labour Party's most recent past and in doing so, has attempted to reveal some of the political influences and philosophical objectives of New Labour. It is the task of the next three chapters to analyse and discern New Labour's political philosophy from the commitments they hold to the triumpherate of traditional social democratic values: liberty, equality and community. Each chapter will begin with an examination of New Right ideas relating to each of the three values and then discuss various social democratic perspectives on each particular value and finally, an analysis will be presented of New Labour's specific philosophical commitment to each of the respective values discussed.

6

NEW LABOUR AND LIBERTY

Liberty is one of the three main values that define social democracy: liberty, equality and community. This chapter attempts to evaluate the role of liberty[1] in New Labour's political philosophy. The following three chapters take as their starting point, the historical implication that New Labour is a post-Thatcherite political organisation and because of this, has had to assert its social democratic values in light of the claimed intellectual hegemony in Britain of New Right[2] ideas and principles during the 1980s and 1990s. The first task of the chapter in light of this will be to discuss the New Right's view of liberty. The chapter's second task will be to develop the argument that New Labour's conception of liberty is in line with the traditional social democratic conception of liberty defined in the positive sense as well as the negative sense, whereas the ideas associated with the New Right affirm a strictly negative conception of liberty. The third and final task of the chapter is to suggest that New Labour's commitment to and its rhetoric of 'opportunity' and especially, 'opportunity for all' is evidence that New Labour holds a commitment to a positive conception of liberty. It is with the New Right's conception of liberty that the chapter begins.

The New Right View of Liberty

Discussing the New Right's view of liberty, Bosanquet states that:

'Freedom for the New Right is freedom from coercion. This is what has usually been called the negative concept of freedom: freedom from outside interference by human agencies.'[3]

Friedrich von Hayek who was arguably the leading New Right thinker maintained that freedom exists when an individual does not depend or is not subject to:

'...the arbitrary will of another.'[4]

Therefore, for an individual to be truly free he or she must be the author of their own actions and for that to happen he or she must not be coerced by others.[5] It is argued that these definitions of negative liberty are not inherently different conceptions but are all interrelated and are legitimate ways of expressing negative liberty. Bosanquet states that for negative libertarians freedom is essentially freedom from coercion. This can be understood as the main definition of negative liberty but, Hayek's belief that freedom can also be freedom from another individual's arbitrary will does not contradict the idea of being free from coercion, in fact it adds a second layer to the conception of negative liberty. Hayek's notion is still in line with the traditions of negative liberty inasmuch as it concerns only individual human coercion not coercion by economic or social forces. A possible criticism of this definition is that it opens up the debate over arbitrary and non-arbitrary will impacting on individual's lives. In addition, the idea that to be free a person must be the author of his or her own actions complements the first notion that freedom is the absence of coercion because according to the traditions of negative liberty, a person is not truly free if they are being coerced. If this is the case, one could add a third layer of reasoning to the definition of negative liberty by asserting that a person can only truly be the author of his or her own life if they are free from coercion. If they are forced to make life choices they are not truly the authors because their choices are being restricted and artificially influenced by threat of coercion.

A further belief which is derived from Hayek's notion that the absence of another person's arbitrary will on an individual's choices equates to freedom, is that 'unfreedom' or impositions on freedom only occur through individual human agency. For Hayek, an individual's freedom is infringed only by the unwanted, intentional actions of humans not through social or economic forces.[6] For example, according to Hayek's negative conception of liberty, the inability to afford accommodation due to poverty is not a constraint authored by another person but by the individual's economic status which is the result of the impersonal forces of the world. An individual is still free without accommodation because no human agency is present in coercing the individual's choice concerning where he or she will find shelter. It is from this simple philosophical commitment to a negative conception of liberty defined as the absence of human interference and coercion, that many policies and ideas of the New Right are based.

David Green suggests that Hayek's commitment to negative liberty, on his completion of *The Constitution of Liberty* in 1960, led him to develop an account of why liberty as individual freedom from coercion had failed to maintain widespread support and in particular the support of idealists.[7] Hayek identified three main reasons. Firstly, the failure to realise and appreciate the limits of human knowledge and by doing so, forgetting the sophistication and complexity of the social world. Social and economic institutions evolve through the history of civilisation and are not independently created by humans trying to solve problems in the abstract. Hayek argued that further attempts to order the social life of a nation would require significant government intervention and believed this tendency was wrong because it again fails to acknowledge the limitations of human knowledge, which should tell humanity that the social life of a nation is spontaneous not regulated and any means to regulate it will ultimately fail, and that such an attempt would impinge upon individual liberty and is therefore morally unacceptable. Green argues this point on pragmatic grounds, that impinging on individual liberty has negative effects for society in the long run:

'If force is used to restrict the freedom of ingenuity of individuals it undermines the mechanism which makes progress and adaptation to change possible - the free use of initiative. Reformers, in this view, should resort, not to interfering with the rules of spontaneous order, but to achieving their aims through private organisations.'[8]

The second main reason according to Hayek is the belief in social justice. For Hayek social justice requires big government and will be a threat to individual liberty. The third main reason is the danger of unlimited sovereignty. Hayek believes that democratic systems have strayed from their founding principle of granting individual liberty by limiting the power of government through devices such as the separation of powers, the rule of law, government under law, and the rules of judicial procedure.[9] The result is that democratic governments have the potential not to rule on behalf of the people but simply to rule over the people and are also influenced by specific and political interest groups. In particular, Samuel Brittan argues that Hayek believed that twentieth century Western democracy had:

'...degenerated into an unprincipled auction to satisfy rival organised groups who can never in the long run be appeased, because their demands are incompatible...Hayek endorses in a descriptive sense the American-inspired economic theory of politics, which analyses the political market in terms of competitive bidding for the citizen's vote, just as commercial businesses compete for the citizen's pound or dollar. But, unlike these theorists, he regards unprincipled vote competition and competitive lobbying as not merely defective – in the way that commercial markets can be, only more so – but inherently objectionable because they have nothing to do with justice.'[10]

Brittan suggests that Hayek views interest groups as a detrimental force in liberal democracies because government eventually concedes to the requests of a plethora of interests and the sum total of such concessions is that citizens are indirectly affected by the measures granted to the interest groups to which they do not belong.[11] This could take the form of financial costs through higher taxation on the individual citizen as a result of anti-poverty campaigners lobbying the government to redistribute more wealth to worse off groups or restrictions on the personal liberty of individual citizens due to a reduction in consumer choice at the supermarket because 'fair trade' campaigners had successfully persuaded the government to ban cheap products from certain developing nations until 'fair' labour laws were introduced. Thus, the individual citizen is more likely to experience a reduction in his or her liberty than an extension of it due to the nature of interest group bartering. This leads to the need to minimise the powers and remit of government so to safeguard individual liberty. This brief summary of Hayek's belief in a negative conception of liberty and the shortcomings of democratic systems, allows one to understand in part, the philosophical underpinnings of neo-liberalism and in turn, of aspects of the ideology during the Thatcher and Major years.

Thatcher states that although the Conservative Party for the majority of its history had been the party of free enterprise and had used electoral slogans such as, 'Britain Strong and Free' and 'Set the People Free'; it had in fact during the post war years:

'…merely pitched camp in the long march to the left.'[12]

Thatcher believed that each Labour Government moved the policies of the country further to the left and that the

Conservative Party, when returned to power, tinkered at reform but never reversed the left-ward drift. She describes this process as:

'The Tories loosened the corset of socialism; they never removed it.'[13]

Thatcher, as Prime Minister from 1979, saw it as her mission to reverse democratic socialism in all its forms.[14] She was intellectually influenced by Keith Joseph who came to be regarded as the most accomplished transmitter of New Right ideas from the mid-1970s onwards.[15] Freedom, for Thatcher, was explicitly linked to a specific attitude of government. She argued that government should establish a framework of stability within which individual families and businesses could pursue their own ambitions. The framework of stability included constitutional stability, the rule of law and economic stability through the management of sound money. Thatcher was adamant that government and state agencies should cease from interfering in the lives of individuals wherever possible.[16]

Social Democratic Views of Liberty

The New Right had a coherent conception of liberty, framed like the liberal theorists' conception in negative terms. Raymond Plant casts some light on the philosophical divergence between positive and negative conceptions of liberty:

'...the conception of liberty favoured by liberal theorists is a negative one... and rigorously independently of any particular view of the values and positive ends which liberty can serve. To define liberty in terms of the pursuit of particular ends such that individuals can only really be free if they are following values X, Y, Z would be a positive conception, presupposing a theory of human good and fulfilment and would thus be incompatible with the basic assumptions of liberal theory.'[17]

The social democratic conception had usually viewed liberty in a contrasting way, as an enabling agent, which guarantees freedom to pursue one's own ends, through the active hand of government. For example, by correcting the injustices of the free market economy through redistributive taxation and thus, securing more income to the worst off members of society therefore, enabling them to pursue their own goals. The precise role for New Labour was less about responding to the claimed intellectual hegemony of negative libertarian propositions as this task had begun in earnest from the early 1980s. As we noted in the fourth chapter thinkers and politicians such as Alec Nove, Raymond Plant, Bernard Crick, Bryan Gould and Roy Hattersley set out social democracy's version of liberty in positive as well as negative terms and connected this conception of liberty to other allied values such as equality. Therefore, New Labour's task is more about implementing policies that would connect a positive conception of liberty with the value of opportunity, thus linking the needs of individuals with the means to achieve their own version of the 'good life'.

However, framed in this way, the social democratic response to a negative conception of liberty; namely holding a commitment to the positive conception of liberty, appears to fade into it. Both political philosophies believe in, and want to promote liberty for individuals. This chapter argues that it is the term variables that are used which highlight the fundamental divide between these rival conceptions. Gerald C. MacCallum argues in his essay, *Negative and Positive Freedom*[18] that one cannot clearly distinguish between negative and positive conceptions of freedom. He argues that claims about freedom should be considered as a triadic relation of the form X is free from Y to do Z and that philosophers must recognise that different political groupings disagree over what they understand to be the ranges of the X, Y, Z variables.[19] Therefore, MacCallum believes one cannot adequately describe the philosophical differences in the debate over freedom as 'freedom from' and 'freedom to'. As he states that:

> 'Evidence of such failure or, alternatively, invitation to it is found in the simple but conventional characterisation of the differences between the two kinds of freedom as the difference between 'freedom from and freedom to' - a categorization suggesting that freedom could be either of two dyadic relations.'[20]

MacCallum suggests that it is more useful to assume that disagreement over negative and positive liberty is not to do with what freedom is but in part, with what counts as an obstacle to or interference with the freedom of persons in question.[21] He asserts that:

'The differences would be rooted in differing views on the ranges of term variables, - that is, on the ('true') identities of the agents whose freedom of such agents, or on the range of what such agents might or might not be free to do or become. Although perhaps not always obvious or dramatic, such differences could lead to vastly different accounts of when persons are free.'[22]

MacCallum then provides a three-point distinction between commitments to term variables of negative and positive conceptions of liberty. They are as follows:

1. Writers adhering to the concept of negative freedom hold that only the presence of something can render a person unfree; writers adhering to the concept of positive freedom hold that the absence of something may also render a person unfree.[23]
2. The former hold that a person is free to do (X) just in case nothing due to arrangements made by other

persons stops him from doing (X); the latter adopts no such restriction.[24]
3. The former hold that the agents whose freedom is in question (for example, 'persons', 'men') are, in effect, identifiable as Anglo-American law would identify 'natural' (as opposed to artificial) persons; the latter sometimes hold quite different views as to how these agents are to be identified.[25]

Plant expands on MacCallum's idea of freedom being a triadic relation:

'That is to say, freedom is a triadic relation in which we have to identify the agent (X), the preventing conditions which may be constraints, restrictions, interferences and barriers (Y) and actions or conditions of character and circumstance (Z) which the agent wishes to achieve or values.'[26]

New Labour's conception of positive liberty[27] could perhaps be expressed in the following schematic:

(X) Agent = Individuals and communities
(Y) Preventing conditions = lack of opportunities (e.g. poor education, material poverty, low sense of self-worth)
(Z) Actions or conditions of character/circumstance which the agent wishes to achieve or values = provision of opportunities so individuals and communities can follow their own conception of 'the good'

(X) Individuals and communities − (Y) Lack of opportunities − (Z) Provision of opportunities which enables individuals and communities to fulfil their conception of 'the good'.

Regarding the traditional social democrats in the Labour Party (those on the 'Old right'), it is fair to say that their schematic of liberty would be very similar if not identical to that of New Labour. However, liberty has been given different emphases in the Labour Party. The 'Old left' or Bevanite left believed that although reducing inequalities was important, socialism was centrally about ownership of the means of production and industrial democracy of the workers. Richard Crossman[28] who was arguably, the main 'Old left' intellectual stated that:

> 'The main task of socialism today is to prevent the concentration of power in the hands of either industrial management or the state bureaucracy - in brief to redistribute responsibility and so to enlarge freedom of choice.'[29]

Therefore, perhaps the following schematic could outline the difference in emphasis concerning their positive conception of liberty:

(X) Agent = Individuals (particularly industrial workers)
(Y) Preventing conditions = lack of opportunities (e.g. poor education, material poverty, low sense of self-worth) plus, the concentration of economic power by private management/state bureaucracies and the lack of industrial democracy
(Z) Actions or conditions of character/circumstance which the agent wishes to achieve or values = the same as New Labour's but in addition, the social ownership of industry and industrial democracy for workers.

(X) Individuals (particularly industrial workers) − (Y) lack of opportunities and the concentration of economic power − (Z) provision of opportunities which enables individuals to pursue their own conception of the good and the redistribution of economic power via industrial democracy enabling the working classes to manage their industries.

The 'New left' or Bennite left held a similar desire as the 'Old left' to redistribute economic power and assert worker's industrial democracy. As has been highlighted in the fourth chapter, the thesis of Stuart Holland set out in *The Socialist Challenge*[30] drew attention to the rise of meso-economic power, which had thwarted Keynesian demand management, and the goals of social democracy. In Foote's words, Holland thesis sought to provide:

'...a socialist remedy of state intervention through planning and public ownership. The modern state had not fully realised the changes which had taken place in international capitalism, undermining traditional Keynesian solutions by undermining national sovereignty on which these solutions were based.'[31]

Therefore, one can posit the view that a schematic setting out the 'New left' conception of liberty would be similar in emphasis to that of the 'Old left' schematic outlined above.

Hayek himself argues that the *liberal* idea of liberty was historically understood in negative terms.[32] In other words, freedom from coercion, freedom from the arbitrary power of other men and release from the ties which left the individual no choice but obedience to the orders of a superior to whom he was attached.[33] Furthermore, he noted that socialism had hijacked the meaning of freedom and altered it to mean freedom from necessity and as he clearly states:

'Freedom in this sense is, of course, merely another name for power or wealth.'[34]

Moreover, Hayek believed that socialists deliberately meant to bastardise the term 'liberty'. In fact, a fairer view would be to say that neo-liberals like Hayek were infuriated that the commitment to liberty could be convincingly argued in positive as well as negative terms and the pessimism which he presented in *The Road to Serfdom* demonstrated amply that the socialist arguments were being taken seriously by a significant amount of people.[35]

New Labour and 'Opportunity for All'

In New Labour's rhetoric, manifestoes and in the speeches of its main players the importance of freedom is not often mentioned. However, in his biography of Isaiah Berlin, Michael Ignatieff recalls a letter sent by Tony Blair to Berlin in October 1997. The letter raised the question, 'Wasn't it true that the limitations of negative liberty in Western societies had motivated generations of people to find some model of society that went beyond laissez-faire?' Blair continued that, 'positive liberty had its validity, whatever its depredations in the Soviet model.'[36] This suggests that Blair, to some extent, was concerned with philosophical commitments such as a commitment to positive liberty. One could argue that given the date of the letter being only five months after New Labour took office, Blair was perhaps searching for some philosophical idea to express New Labour's brand of social democracy. Nevertheless, Berlin was too ill to reply to Blair's letter and since then, New Labour has made little of the philosophical commitment to a positive conception of liberty.

As was noted in the fourth chapter, social democrats writing in the 1980s such as Roy Hattersley and Bryan Gould placed freedom at the centre of their account of social democracy. This was clearly a philosophical response to the New Right's usage of *freedom* in a purely negative sense. Regarding New Labour, there are no obvious reasons why the value of freedom is not often discussed, but one that is suggested here is that freedom is taken as an axiom of western democracies and especially as a principle that all British political parties advocate. In his famous essay entitled, *Two Concepts of Liberty*[37], Isaiah Berlin suggests that freedom is almost universally approved and because of this is open to many interpretations:

'Almost every moralist in human history has praised freedom. Like happiness and goodness, like nature and reality, the meaning of this term is so porous that there is little interpretation that it seems able to resist.'[38]

Freedom is taken as a given and so the next step for political parties is to define particular versions of freedom and connect them to policy proposals. In this sense, New Labour's belief in freedom is defined in terms of its commitment to a notion of pervasive opportunity or what is referred to as 'opportunity for all'.[39] Opportunity can be defined as a favourable or advantageous combination of circumstances, a prospect or a choice. Social democrats use 'opportunity' as an enabling agent to empower individuals especially those from disadvantaged backgrounds to improve the quality of their lives. A free society, for New Labour and other social democrats, is a society that provides opportunity for all. However, conservatives, liberals and neo-liberals could subscribe to equality of opportunity, which guarantees a level playing field for all citizens in relation to the law. Equal opportunity to make one's own decisions and to be free from coercion and outside interference is the brand of opportunity that neo-liberals advocate. New Labour's commitment to 'opportunity for all' is a 'thicker' and more pervasive version of equality of opportunity than that which is advocated by other political groups. However, New Labour must also express its commitment to 'opportunity for all' in terms of its other values otherwise the charge that it is no different from equality of opportunity will prove hard to dismiss. For example, one could argue that 'opportunity for all' is the practical outworking of New Labour's commitment to a positive conception of liberty and a 'priority' version of equality.[40]

Positive liberty builds upon the negative conception of liberty. It is not an absolute opposite like darkness is to light, but it is an extension of negative liberty like the desire for social equality is an extension of the achievement of political equality according to social democrats.[41] People who consider themselves to be positive libertarians do not deny the assertion of the negative libertarians that people should be set free from human interference in areas of life that are constraining for no apparent 'good', they extend the remit of liberty from being simply a notion of liberation from coercion to being a notion of empowerment for action. From intentional coercion by individuals to structural and indirect coercion by the free market and the lottery which is the distribution of life chances.[42] Positive liberty could be argued as being an extension of negative liberty in this sense. However, this position becomes complicated if one considers some observations on the two concepts of liberty made by Isaiah Berlin:

'The answer to the question 'Who governs me?' is logically distinct from the question 'How far does government interfere with me?' It is in this difference that the great contrast between the two concepts of negative and positive liberty, in the end, consists. For the 'positive' sense of liberty comes to light if we try to answer the question, not 'What am I free to do or be?' but 'By whom am I ruled?' or 'Who is to say what I am, and what I am not, to be or do?''[43]

Such questions as 'By whom am I ruled?' and 'Who is to say what I am?' indicate that when the two concepts of liberty are thoroughly examined, they are attempting to answer different questions about the condition of humanity. Therefore, the emphases that are placed on these questions will result in which concept of liberty one supports more vigorously. This in turn can lead to assumptions of the type of society one desires and the value one places on allied political concepts such as greater equality of outcome and community. Anthony Arblaster makes this point when he states that:

'...what distinguishes one political creed from another is often not so much the values to which they officially subscribe, which may very well be substantially the same, but the hierarchy of those values."[44]

An example of this proposition can be found in the contrasting politics of two liberal thinkers. Anthony Arblaster argues that liberalism differs from other political creeds because liberals place liberty at the top of their hierarchy of values.[45] Both T.H Green and Hayek can be classified as liberals because of their belief in the primacy of liberty, but they belong to different versions of liberalism. Green is a social liberal in the New Liberal tradition and Hayek a neo-liberal in the sense of classical liberalism. As we noted in chapter two Green advocates a positive and a negative conception of liberty and Hayek a purely negative conception of liberty.[46] Though both thinkers are liberals who believe in the primacy of the individual and hold individual liberty as their main political principle.[47] Green and Hayek support different conceptions of the 'good society' and value differently secondary principles, such as community.[48] Positive and negative liberty are not merely concepts of the left and right, in many ways this oversimplification is misleading and inaccurate. What the discussion of the two concepts does lead to is for individuals to decide what questions about society and human nature they desire to ask the most and what answers they value above others. Positive and negative liberty are political concepts that relate to other political values and other issues which people promote and neglect due to their own beliefs in the nature of humanity and in the type of society they want to create.

New Labour subscribes (like traditional social democrats) to the positive conception of liberty because it would assert that the answer to the question, 'By whom am I ruled?' is 'yourself and your community' and there begins the political journey of enabling all people to be as far as possible, and with respect to the well-being of the community, the authors of their own lives.[49] Thus, liberty becomes more than the condition of being free from unwarranted coercion and becomes liberty to choose one's own path and to fulfil the innate desire to have 'self-mastery' over one's own life. Liberty, for social democrats becomes an enabling agent in the political, social and economic spheres of life, rather than just the moral sphere and freedom from human interference as desired by negative libertarians. In the rhetoric of New Labour, 'opportunity' is the enabling agent, which empowers people to fulfil as much as possible, with respect to the well-being of the community, their own self-mastery.[50]

Therefore, the key for social democrats is that opportunity and positive liberty imply notions of social justice, government intervention and giving priority to the worst off members of society and raising them up to a sufficient minimum level. One can see that the principle of opportunity is charged with implicit social democratic ideas as the following quotations from Blair and Brown assert[51]:

'There is a *significant minority of people cut off, set apart* from the mainstream of society. Their lives are often characterised by *long-term unemployment, poverty, or lack of educational opportunities* and at times family instability, drug abuse and crime. This problem has got worse, not better.'[52]

'The new constitution of the Labour Party commits us *to seek the widest possible spread of wealth, power and opportunity.* I want to highlight *opportunity as a key value* in the new politics. Its importance has too often been neglected or distorted. For the Right, opportunity is characteristically presented as the freedom of individuals from the state. Yet for most people, *opportunities* are inseparable from society, in which *government action necessarily plays a large part.* The Left, by contrast, has in the past too readily *downplayed its duty to promote a wide range of opportunities for individuals to advance themselves and their families.* At worst, it has *stifled opportunity in the name of abstract equality. Gross inequalities continue to be handed down from generation to generation,* and the progressive Left must robustly *tackle the obstacles to true equality of opportunity*. But the promotion of equal opportunities does not imply dull uniformity in welfare provision and public services. Nor does the modern Left take a narrow view of opportunities: the arts and the creative industries should be part of our common culture.'[53]

'Stability provides the platform. But we cannot build a dynamic economy unless *we unleash the potential in everyone*. A welfare state that *thwarts the opportunities that we need*, will hold the economy back. A welfare state that *encourages work is not only fair but makes for greater dynamism in the economy*.'[54]

'I want a country in which people get on, do well, make a success of their lives. I have no time for the politics of envy. We need more successful entrepreneurs, not fewer of them. *But these life-chances should be for all the people*. And I want a society in which *ambition and compassion are seen as partners* not opposites - where we value public service as well as material wealth.'[55]

Stuart White suggests that there is an important difference of opinion regarding the interpretation of New Labour's value of opportunity and that these differences imply a division in New Labour's political philosophy. One of these differences is what White terms the:

'...division between 'leftists' and 'centrists' over the commitment to real opportunity: a philosophical division over exactly what this is a commitment to and, derivatively a division over exactly what policies are needed to satisfy it.'[56]

White asserts that there are 'leftists' and 'centrists' within the modernising faction of the Labour Party, and therefore, a philosophical division exists within New Labour. It is argued that Blair is the leading 'centrist' but a leading 'leftist' within New Labour is not presented. White's argument is simply that these two groups are divided over the commitment to 'real opportunity' and that the 'centrists' understand 'real opportunity' in meritocratic terms and the 'leftists' understand it in more egalitarian terms. This in turn, means they are divided over the correct policies to implement their versions of 'real opportunity' and in so doing implement their commitment to positive liberty.[57]

The argument then follows that the 'leftists' believe meritocracy permits unjust inequalities in 'real opportunity' which are due to brute luck or in other words, due to arbitrary differences in natural endowment and socio-economic factors.[58] White states that 'leftists':

'...believe that, in principle, policy ought to seek to mitigate for these undeserved brute luck inequalities.'[59]

Conversely, 'centrists' according to White's thesis, are conventional meritocrats who would be ambivalent towards income redistribution and would be opposed to higher taxes on merit beyond a 'reasonable' point.[60] Although White's thesis contains interesting observations about the possible tensions over different philosophical commitments in New Labour, there are however, two main problems. The first issue is empirical; namely, how does one discern whether individual New Labour politicians are 'centrists' or 'leftists' based on minimal source data? This is problematic and relies heavily on conjecture.[61]

The second shortcoming in White's thesis regarding 'real opportunity' for 'centrists' and 'leftists' is terminological. The term 'leftists' is acceptable and can be viewed as synonymous with the term social democrat but the term 'centrist' has no clear political implication. Perhaps, a more appropriate term and one that has roots in the traditions of British political philosophy is social liberal.[62] One can see this term as representing a position on the moderate left derived from the nineteenth century evolution of Liberalism. Social or New liberals occupied the liberal leftwing as opposed to the laissez-faire or Manchester liberals on the liberal rightwing. The latter can now be seen as the forefather of neo-liberalism.[63] The term social liberal, rather than centrist has a political tradition and is a brand of progressive left thinking, yet it is used differently from social democrat which has its traditions in the evolution of British socialism.[64] As was argued in chapter two, R.H Tawney is the crucial link in the intellectual heritage between New Liberalism and the Labour Party's social democracy. The New Liberalism of T.H Green, Hobhouse and Hobson overlaps with the ethical socialism of Tawney who is cited as an influence on the social democracy of Gaitskell, Blair and Brown.[65] The two traditions are intertwined and are not easily distinguishable. Therefore, as I stated above, the difference in political philosophy regarding 'real opportunity' between 'leftists' and 'centrists' as White describes them is one of emphasis and degree rather than conflicting political ends.[66]

The value of positive liberty is continued by New Labour in a similar mould as its traditional social democrat predecessors. New Labour, like the Croslandite social democrats of the 1960s and 1970s would adhere to the value of liberty expressed as a positive right to a set of political, social and economic entitlements. Although, perhaps there is a debate to be had here concerning the possible difference in the connection between the values of liberty and community by New Labour and the traditional social democrats in terms of the goods that positive freedom presupposes. One could argue that New Labour emphasise social reciprocity in exchange for certain state entitlements. An example of this is the *New Deal* programme whereby after six months of unconditional benefit whilst searching for employment, to continue to be eligible for benefits individuals have to take one of four options; an educational course; an organised job placement; work with an environmental project; or work with a charity or voluntary organisation. It is possible that the traditional social democrats of the mid-twentieth century would have continued to prioritise the citizen's right to entitlements regardless of any notion of social or communal reciprocity.[67]

Two important factors exist in the different conceptions of freedom between thinkers on the left and right. The first is the issue of obstacles that impede freedom and count as constraints on freedom. As has been discussed above, for thinkers on the right such as Hayek, only obstacles that are deliberately and intentionally imposed by human agency can restrict individual freedom. Conversely, thinkers on the left assert that any obstacles that are the result of human action or social and economic forces can constitute a restriction on individual freedom. For example, poverty would count as a restriction on freedom whether or not the individual in poverty was responsible for his state of affairs, and whether or not it had been imposed intentionally on him. Plant expands on this point when he argues that:

'The limitations on individual freedom are not just those imposed deliberately by the intentional actions of others and which the liberal tradition rightly wishes to resist and restrict, but also those limitations which are imposed by natural differences of birth and genetic inheritance, together with those which are the result of human action whether deliberate or not, in the field of family background, economic resources, welfare and education.'[68]

The second important factor in the discussion of the different conceptions of freedom is the issue of intentional and foreseeable consequences of individual actions. Hayek argues that in the operation of the market individuals bear no personal responsibility for the consequences of their actions because they are unintentional.[69] This means that the socialist notion of social justice (particularly with regard to the treatment of certain groups such as the worst off in society) and the correction of market injustice have no moral claim on the actions of individual decisions in the market.[70] Thinkers on the left generally assert that although an individual's actions may be unintentional their effects can at times be foreseeable. If they are foreseeable and they do in fact cause harm to others one can argue that they could have been prevented and therefore, the individual becomes responsible for the consequences of his or her own actions. As Plant states:

'In these ways it could be argued therefore, that the market can be made susceptible to a moral critique based upon some idea of social justice, and whatever difficulties there may be with this latter idea, these are not sufficient to abandon it.'[71]

As we have noted, New Labour's tool for implementing its belief in the value of positive liberty is the commitment to pervasive opportunity or 'opportunity for all' at various levels in the lives of individuals. The language of opportunity is New Labour's practical way of enunciating its conception of liberty; a liberty for individuals which crosses the moral, political, social, and economic spheres ensuring as far as possible, the widest choice of circumstances and options for every citizen.

7

NEW LABOUR AND EQUALITY

In the same way as the previous chapter on liberty, this chapter attempts to evaluate the value of equality in New Labour's political philosophy. The chapter will examine New Labour's approach in light of the claimed intellectual hegemony of New Right ideas and with regard to some traditional social democratic perspectives on equality. The first task will be to clarify the terminology surrounding different conceptions of equality in social democratic writing such as equality of opportunity, greater equality of outcome, equality of outcome and two ideas expressed by New Labour: 'equality of opportunity and fairness of outcome' and 'progressive universalism'. Then it will be argued that conceptions of equality can be better divided into sufficiency, priority and egalitarian conceptions. This is taken to be an essential task because it will be claimed that some social democratic commentators and writers misinterpret notions of greater equality of outcome and in doing so accuse New Labour of deserting traditional social democratic values. The second task will be a thorough discussion of New Right political thought on the issues surrounding equality. The third task of the chapter (following Derek Parfit's categorisation of different conceptions of equality) will be to suggest that traditional social democrats in the Labour Party, including those such as, and in the heritage of R.H. Tawney, Anthony Crosland and Roy Hattersley, hold priority and sufficiency conceptions of equality and not the strict egalitarian conception of equality. The fourth and final task will be to posit the thesis that New Labour believes in a version of equality which promotes conceptions of priority and sufficiency and which does not promote the strict egalitarian notion of equality and therefore, such traditional social democrats are philosophically very similar to New Labour social democrats regarding the value of equality. It is with the discussion of the terminology surrounding different conceptions of equality in social democratic writing that the chapter begins.

The Terminology of 'Equality' in Social Democratic Writing

It is apparent when discussing different versions of equality, particularly when discussing them in relation to social democratic ideas, that three versions are often outlined.[1] They are equality of opportunity, greater equality of outcome (sometimes called 'democratic equality'[2]) and equality of outcome. Equality of opportunity is a principle which social liberals, conservatives (both neo-liberals and liberal conservatives) and social democrats openly support. It is a principle, which maintains that each individual is to have equal access to jobs and positions such as holding public office. It includes equal treatment regardless of gender, race, class or religion and desires a society based on merit.[3] Equality of opportunity forbids nepotism and any form of preferential treatment and privilege of individuals and it attempts to guarantee the same starting point for all individuals. It is equality as non-discrimination.[4]

The principle of greater equality of outcome is held by social democrats and to a lesser extent by social liberals. It extends the principle of equality of opportunity to include issues determined by one's background, education, talents or abilities by mitigating against misfortune, genetic endowment and social injustice.[5] It attempts to redistribute incomes and wealth from the better off to the worst off and in doing so, reduce material and social inequalities within society. Political parties who hold a commitment to greater equality of outcome do so on the basis that many inequalities, such as differences in genetic endowment are arbitrary and therefore unfair and also because as a community, they believe individuals have a responsibility to help the disadvantaged further than merely guaranteeing equality of opportunity in the procedural non-discriminating sense, by securing to a certain extent greater equality of outcome.

The principle of equality of outcome (or complete equality of outcome) has been held by a small number of individuals and groups in the Labour Party such as George Bernard Shaw, the Marxist SDF and the Labour Marxists of the 1920s and 1930s. Marxist political economy asserts that with the ultimate collapse of capitalism, work will become a communal act for the benefit of the 'common good' and therefore, differences in wages and rewards will be irrelevant.

In addition to these three versions of equality, New Labour has espoused two ideas during its time in office, which claim to express its commitment to equality. These are 'equality of opportunity and fairness of outcome'[6] and 'progressive universalism'.[7] New Labour's idea of 'equality of opportunity and fairness of outcome' has been mainly used by Gordon Brown and his Treasury officials in the last few years. However, there does not appear to be a clear definition of the idea in Brown's speeches. One possible interpretation implies both a commitment to the procedural form of equality of opportunity and a commitment to guaranteeing outcomes so they do not fall below a minimum level. A policy example of this idea could be the *Minimum Income Guarantee* which is now the *Pensioner Credit*. New Labour's idea of 'progressive universalism' was most recently used by Brown in the 2003 Budget to describe the principle underpinning the new tax and benefit system. Progressive universalism, simply put, is the principle of providing nearly all citizens (apart from the very wealthy) with some form of financial support, but focusing more financial support on those who are in greatest need, when they are in greatest need. The Budget Report assert that:

'The new tax and benefit system puts into practise the principles of progressive universalism, with support for all, and more help for those who need it most, when they need it most.'

Yet the debate surrounding New Labour's commitment to equality is clouded further according to a conversation that Brown had with the former Liberal Democrat Leader Paddy Ashdown, in the lead up to the 1997 General Election:

'I have been trying to think of a single, central theme which expresses all our ideas and ties them all together. It would be wrong to call this an - *ism* - that sounds too ideological. I have decided that the central idea is 'equality of opportunity' – something you were talking about in your book Citizens' Britain. Like you, I have come to believe that we cannot engineer outcomes. What we must have is a Government that is prepared to intervene to provide equality of opportunity for all.'[8]

Therefore, Ashdown recounts in his memoirs that Brown was an advocate of equality opportunity and implied that this principle was central to his view of contemporary social democracy for New Labour. This raises some possible questions. Did Brown change his mind between his meeting with Ashdown in 1997 before the General Election and during his time in office when he outlined the principles of equality of opportunity and fairness of outcome and later progressive universalism? Is his account of equality of opportunity and fairness of outcome merely equality of opportunity in its traditional, procedural format? It is argued that the answer to the first question is that Brown changed his view of equality of opportunity as the central principle of New Labour's social democracy and the evidence of this is that his budgets have been substantially redistributive.

However, I believe that whilst the principles of equality of opportunity and equality of outcome are relatively clear, the principle of greater equality of outcome is open to various interpretations by different types of social democrats and this inevitably leads to significant confusion. In addition, New Labour's espousal of equality of opportunity and fairness of outcome appears to be ambiguous and therefore problematic when seeking philosophical commitments to concepts such as equality and the idea of progressive universalism is quite a new way for New Labour to describe its view of equality. It is partly for these reasons that in this chapter I prefer to follow the terminological distinction, but not all of the conclusions, set out by the political philosopher Derek Parfit in his article entitled *Equality and Priority*[9] and therefore distinguish between the following positions concerning the principle of equality: a commitment to raising people up to a particular level, where they have 'sufficient' resources to lead a satisfactory life; a commitment to always give priority to the worst off members in society; and a commitment to strict egalitarianism (in other words, the pursuit of abolishing all inequalities of income and wealth). These three positions can be respectively termed, the sufficiency conception of equality, the priority conception of equality, and the strict egalitarian conception of equality.[10]

New Right Ideas and Arguments Against Equality

Friedrich von Hayek's arguments[11] against a socialist[12] notion of equality[13] and therefore against the desire to reduce inequalities are directly linked to his notion of freedom. One of Hayek's main arguments is that poverty and income and wealth inequality do not imply a lack of freedom or cause 'unfreedom'.[14]

When studying Hayek's principles and his aversion to the socialist notion of equality one must remember that his critique in *The Road to Serfdom* was chiefly based on what he saw as the growth of socialism in Britain and abroad.

Although New Right thought did not come to dominate the ideological core of the Conservative Party until the 1980s, Robert Blake notes the effect of early New Right thought on the Conservative Party, after the publication of Hayek's book:

'It was essentially anti-socialist in its implications. The universities saw a notable revival of Conservative sympathies among undergraduates and to some extent among the dons too...The Labour Party had lost its monopoly of intellect and ideas.'[15]

This position is supported by Thatcher. She recounts the influence that Hayek's ideas had on her views and she implies that they made her views 'New Right' before it gained mainstream acceptance in the Conservative Party:

'(*The Road to Serfdom*)...provided crisp, clear analytical arguments against socialism, demonstrating how its economic theories were connected to the then depressing shortages of our daily lives...It left a permanent mark on my own political character, making me a long-term optimist for free enterprise and liberty and sustaining me through the bleak years of socialist supremacy in the 1960s and '70s.'[16]

Thus, a second argument against the socialist notion of equality is that it is contrary to classical liberalism and the values of the free-market[17](particularly stressing the importance of competition), limited government intervention[18] in the economy and in the lives of citizens and individualism[19](defined a the primacy of the individual and freedom from as much constraint as possible). Hayek's assault on collectivism, state planning, government intervention in the economy and redistributive taxation is what he viewed as being inherently socialist measures. Therefore, Hayek argued that there was a direct correlation between the growth of socialism on the one hand with the decline and abandonment of classical liberal ideas on the other:

'That socialism has displaced liberalism as the doctrine held by the great majority of progressives does not simply mean that people had forgotten the warnings of the great liberal thinkers of the past about the consequences of collectivism. It has happened because they were persuaded of the very opposite of what these men had predicted.'[20]

Furthermore, and quite clumsily, Hayek classed socialism regardless of its nature as being a monolithic ideology. Hayek saw democratic socialism and Marxist socialism linked through the idea of social justice. In that sense he viewed them as sharing some of the same 'ends'. However, he failed to differentiate between the 'means' involved in democratic socialism namely, democracy and gradual social change and the 'means' involved in Marxist socialism namely, violent revolution and totalitarianism. Moreover, Hayek implies that democratic socialism when taken to its natural conclusion, will lead to the antipathy of democratic freedom because of the pursuit of social justice:

'That democratic socialism, the great utopia of the last few generations, is not only unachievable, but that to strive for it produces something so utterly different that few of those who now wish it would be prepared to accept the consequences, many will not believe till the connection has been laid bare in all its aspects.'[21]

Hayek posits a third argument against the socialist notion of equality in a famous later book, *Law, Legislation and Liberty Vol.II: The Mirage of Social Justice*[22]. This time Hayek's rebuff is not solely based on the argument that better off individuals suffer an infringement of liberty when income is redistributed to the worst off, but simply on the grounds that social justice does not exist. The New Right following Hayek, believe that the concept of social justice is a mirage because no social injustice occurs through the transactions of the free market.[23] They reach this conclusion by asserting that injustice occurs only in the intentional violation of laws. For example, when a thief steals a wallet then an injustice is perpetrated on the victim of the theft. In the free market economy the New Right argue that no laws are violated and furthermore, that no injustice occurs even if individuals lose their jobs, or are rewarded in a disproportionate way because the operation of the market reflecting decisions by countless individuals does not intentionally cause injustice of any kind.

It is argued that the New Right is opposed to the socialist notion of equality which can be understood as the philosophical commitment to either the strict egalitarian conception of equality, the priority conception of equality or a generous sufficiency conception of equality. The means of implementing such commitments are the economic and social mechanisms of redistributive taxation, high public spending and a pervasive and enabling social welfare scheme. Therefore, does the New Right hold any conception of equality? It is argued in this chapter that the New Right holds a commitment to the sufficiency conception of equality because they believe that individuals should be paid a minimum income by the state to prevent complete destitution.[24] This however is an exceptionally limited and basic commitment to the sufficiency conception. Hayek's commitment to the sufficiency conception is radically different from other social democratic sufficiency conceptions for two reasons. Firstly, because Hayek draws the line in terms of what he thinks is morally 'sufficient' at are a far lower level than social democrats would accept. He states that the barest minimum to prevent destitution; in other words the smallest amount of state provision, which will prevent citizens from starving to death and prevent homelessness is all that is required and is all that is morally acceptable. Secondly, Hayek's commitment to the sufficiency conception is diffcrent because it is not based on a notion of social justice but on crude necessity and is therefore different in character to the type of commitment to the sufficiency conception of equality held by social democrats.

This raises a few questions and draws attention to some issues concerning the logic of Hayek's thought. One such question is 'Why does Hayek believe that the state should secure a basic minimum?' This question is problematic for Hayek to answer because the idea of a basic minimum requires a conception of what basic needs or absolute needs are and because he wants to say that many social concepts are subjective, how can a conception of basic needs escape this? A more practical issue, which highlights the inconsistencies in Hayek's thinking, refers to the implementation of a basic minimum. For a basic minimum to work it would have to be administered by a state bureaucracy and from what has been established in Hayekian thought so far, one could argue that Hayek should not in theory support a central state apparatus which acts as a distributor of resources, is expensive for taxpayers, through means testing is intrusive into the lives of some citizens and is a system which would be susceptible to being 'bid-up' by interest groups.

As the argument below will suggest, New Labour's sufficiency conception is substantially different to Hayek's conception as it is more generous because New Labour draws the line of sufficiency far higher than the New Right. Whereas the New Right seeks to provide merely enough to prevent homelessness and starvation, New Labour has substantially raised basic sufficiency entitlements.[25] New Labour's sufficiency conception of equality does not appear to imply a concern for relativities but is merely a more generous view of what the basic minimum should be than the one advocated by Hayek. In addition, New Labour's notion of equality also includes a commitment to the priority conception of equality. The priority conception means that even though individuals may have a modestly sufficient amount to survive, prioritarians want to go further and continually meet the needs of the worst off groups in society.[26] This is attempted regardless of whether these worst off groups have already been allocated basic 'sufficient' resources by the state.

Thus, to summarise the arguments against a socialist notion of equality by the New Right one can emphasise the following: that inequality and poverty does not constitute 'unfreedom' and attempting to redress relative poverty requires a coercion of the individual leading to a restriction of financial liberty among other things and large financial costs of implementing a system of equal rewards; social justice does not exist, it is a mirage and therefore any attempts to redistribute income and wealth on such grounds are morally illegitimate; the socialist notion of equality is false and contradicts the values of classical liberalism and thus should not be accepted. Bosanquet compresses these New Right arguments into two propositions. Firstly: there is no legitimate agenda for society on issues of distribution other than that of preventing poverty in an absolute sense; secondly: that the concept of relative poverty which is tied to the principle of greater equality is dangerous and illegitimate.[27]

Traditional Social Democratic Conceptions of Equality

R.H. Tawney is widely regarded as one of the most influential social democratic thinkers and his writings on equality have influenced many individuals within the Labour Party. Central to Tawney's belief in the principle of greater equality of outcome by reducing inequalities of income, wealth, opportunity and social status was his realisation that with greater equality comes greater individual liberty. Thus, one can assert that according to Tawney's logic greater equality brings greater freedom, which permits greater choice and ability to follow one's own path in life. Tawney asserts this, when he states that freedom means:

'...the ability to do, or to refrain from doing definite things, at a definite moment, in definite circumstances, or it means nothing all. The second question which arises, therefore, is not less simple. It is whether the range of alternatives open to ordinary men, and the capacity of the latter to follow their own preferences in choosing between them, have or have not been increased by measures correcting inequalities or neutralizing their effects. If an affirmative reply be given, liberty and equality can live as friends; if a negative one, they are condemned to be foes.'[28]

Interestingly Tawney realised the complexities of the term equality and the plethora of meanings that can be ascribed to it:

'It is obvious again, that the word 'Equality' poses more than one meaning, and that the controversies surrounding it arise partly, at least, because the same term is employed with different connotations.'[29]

In this chapter I argue that Tawney's belief in equality was not the strict egalitarian conception of equality which has traditionally found no support in the Labour Party save George Bernard Shaw[30], the Marxist SDF which left the Labour Party in 1901[31] and the Labour Marxists on the Labour left in the 1920s and 1930s.[32] Tawney's version of equality was composed of a generous sufficiency and a priority conception of equality. Unlike the liberal or neo-liberal who may hold to a sufficiency conception of equality in significantly watered down terms, the social democrat like Tawney asserts that society cannot become more free and fraternal if it is not becoming more economically and socially equal and that requires a type of equality which continually gives priority to those who are worst off. The following comments, especially the italicised comments, support this classification of Tawney's conception of equality:

'No one thinks it inequitable that, *when a reasonable provision has been made for all,* exceptional responsibilities should be compensated by exceptional rewards, as a recognition of the service performed and on inducement to perform it... What is repulsive is not that one man should earn more than others, for where community of environment, and a common education and habit of life, have bred a common tradition of respect and consideration these details of the counting-house are forgotten and ignored. *It is that some classes should be excluded from the heritage of civilization which others enjoy, and that the fact of human fellowship, which is ultimate and profound, should be obscured by economic contrasts, which are trivial and superficial.*'[33]

'Equality is to be sought, not by breaking into fragments the large incomes which are injurious both to those who receive them and to those who do not, but by securing that *an increasing proportion of the wealth which at present they absorb will be devoted to purposes of common advantage.*'[34]

Thus, Tawney was not a strict egalitarian who believed that all inequalities should be abolished but he did hold a commitment to giving all members of the community 'reasonable provision' or, what they needed, which can be viewed as a generous sufficiency conception of equality. Furthermore, it is argued that Tawney held a priority conception of equality because he felt that all classes of people should share in the wealth of the community and where this is not the case one should give priority to the poorest classes, namely the industrial working classes and thereby 'increasing the proportion of wealth... to the purposes of common advantage'. This language is not precisely outlining continual priority for the poorest but it is implying that an increasing amount of wealth from the rich must be used for the 'common advantage' and this phrase is a relative and communal term. In short this phrase is Tawney's parlance for giving priority, particularly through social spending,[35] to the poorest classes.

Other traditional social democrats such as Anthony Crosland and in more recent times Roy Hattersley have maintained that social democracy is centrally about a belief in greater equality of outcome between individuals and groups in society. As we noted in the third chapter, Crosland expressed the central tenet of social democracy when he said that:

'Socialism in our view, was basically about equality. By equality, we meant more than a meritocratic society of equal opportunities in which the greatest rewards would go to those with the most fortunate genetic endowment and family background; we adopted the 'strong' definition of equality – what Rawls has subsequently called the 'democratic' as opposed to the 'liberal' conception.'[36]

If traditional social democrats held a commitment to greater equality of outcome, in other words, the strict egalitarian conception, it specifically implies guaranteeing a constant narrowing of inequality of outcome. One of the issues then becomes what is defined as 'outcome'?[37] In the case of the traditional social democrats, it usually implied a narrowing of income inequality and wealth inequality.[38] As Crosland clearly states:

'Inequalities of wealth may be considered unjust, first if they stem from inherited property, and not from work. This offends against the principle that every citizen should have an equal chance of attaining the highest rewards, and confers a differential advantage related solely to the accident of birth, and not in any way the 'fruit of the man's own labour'. Secondly, large inequalities even of earned income may be thought unjust, either if they reflect not simply differences in ability but also differences in opportunity - if, that is to say, there is an artificial 'rent' element: or if they are so large that people think it unfair to single out the one quality of economic ability for so large a reward as compared with other personal attributes. Thirdly, injustice may arise if certain incomes are too generously treated by the tax system as compared with other similar incomes - if the basis of taxation, that is to say, is a poor measure of the taxable capacity of individuals.'[39]

Nonetheless, Crosland was also concerned with narrowing inequality in the educational system, in the distribution of property, in the distribution of resources in periods of need, and in the location of power in industry.[40] However, the most pertinent question to ask in this discussion concerning the allegation that New Labour and the traditional social democrats have different conceptions of equality, is 'Did the traditional social democrats actually ever hold the strict egalitarian conception of equality?' Traditional social democrats and those who would follow their brand of social democracy tend to criticise New Labour for abandoning the principle of greater equality of outcome or what Rawls termed 'democratic equality'. It is argued that New Labour's version of equality is similar to Crosland's version *in principle*. Both want to guarantee a 'sufficient' minimum amount of income to live off in the form of benefits and entitlements, both want to continually give priority to the very worst off and both want to reduce material and social inequalities by guaranteeing opportunities such as skills training and education therefore promoting their positive conception of liberty. The salient questions are as follows: 'Where did Crosland and where does New Labour 'draw the line' to decide what amount is 'sufficient' to live on? To whom amongst the worst off groups in society should immediate priority be given? How much income and wealth inequality is permissible in society?'

On these three issues it is argued that there are differences between the traditional social democrats and New Labour over emphases, policy prescriptions and expectations due to the different societies in which they were constructing their versions of social democracy at different period of time: Crosland in the 1950s and 1960s and New Labour in the early twenty-first century. Did the traditional social democrats not hold commitments to the priority and sufficiency conceptions of equality like New Labour? If the answers are 'no they never held the strict egalitarian conception of equality' and 'yes they held to the priority and sufficiency conceptions of equality like New Labour' then traditional social democrats like Hattersley are philosophically, far more similar to New Labour than they may think.

As the quotation above demonstrated, Crosland's brand of socialism was to him essentially about equality and the equality termed by John Rawls as 'democratic equality'. Rawls's position is what he termed 'justice as fairness' and it is comprised of his two principles of justice. The first principle is that each person is to have an equal right to the most extensive basic liberty compatible with a similar liberty for others. The second principle asserts that social and economic inequalities are to be arranged so that they are both reasonably expected to be to everyone's advantage and attached to positions and offices open to all.[41] In addition, Rawls argues that when the two principles conflict the first principle or the 'liberty principle' must take priority over the second or 'difference principle'.[42] Therefore, Rawls's infers that there will be social and economic inequalities in society and in certain circumstances they will be just providing they have complied with the difference principle. It is clear that Rawls is not advocating strict egalitarianism. What the difference principle does allude to is that Rawls is an advocate of the priority conception of equality, as he desires that all forms of inequalities be arranged:

'...to the greatest expected benefit of the least advantaged...'[43]

The pertinent question that follows is what type of prioritarian is Rawls? Rawls appears to be advocating that the theory of justice on which a society is based should constantly give priority to the least advantaged, and one can assume that principle would not be affected by a diminishing amount of inequality between the least advantaged group and for example, the average groups in that society. Therefore, if this is the case one can argue that Rawls's commitment to the priority conception of equality is a strict prioritarianism. It will be argued later in this chapter that New Labour hold a non-strict priority conception, which is subtly different from the type, held by Rawls. In general, Crosland's conception of equality appears to follow Rawls's and is similar to the conception held by New Labour but the particulars of the principle show a subtle difference.

Hattersley is a notable social democrat who argues for the principle of greater equality of outcome and berates New Labour for abandoning such a commitment when in fact in a recent interview he demonstrated this precise misinterpretation of the relationship between equality and liberty in answer to two of my questions:

> '*What is your main political philosophical value?* My basic political value is the pursuit of equality. In the knowledge that we're never going to achieve it up to the degree that I want to see. I don't only mean economic equality, I mean gender equality, racial equality, I mean equality before the law, I mean equal distribution of power as well as wealth. Is the commitment to greater equality an end in itself? The end in itself for social democracy is greater freedom. But I hold the view that freedom requires a redistribution of wealth and power and gives agency which makes freedom a reality. I don't think freedom is the absence of restraint, I think freedom is the ability to do things. A socialist view of freedom is ability to do what you chose to do.'[44]

Hattersley's answers are philosophically confused. He states that equality and the pursuit of greater equality of outcome is his main political principle thus making him an advocate of the strict egalitarian conception of equality. However, in the next question he says that the end for social democracy is freedom not equality and that people need to be more equal before they can exercise greater freedom. Therefore, if freedom is the ultimate principle then the answer to the initial question should be 'freedom' not the pursuit of equality or greater equality of outcome. In addition, this confirms the doubts raised earlier in the chapter that traditional social democrats are philosophically very similar to New Labour social democrats regarding equality and the general order of their political values, even if they detest New Labour's conservative rhetoric and overcautious approach to policy prescriptions.

New Labour's Conception of Equality

It is argued in this chapter that New Labour conceives a socialist notion of equality to consist of two different components neither of which is the strict egalitarian conception of equality. The first component is a commitment to raising people up to a particular level whereby they have 'enough' to lead a satisfactory life. One can refer to this (as is noted above) as the sufficiency version of equality. Of course, this is problematic because what is meant by the term 'enough'? What is 'sufficient'? There is no general understanding or consensus in British society about the minimum level one must have met before one can claim to lead a satisfactory life.[45] Nevertheless, the sufficiency conception of equality is understood as providing a sufficient level of income and services. Historically, this has been the job of the welfare state through a variety of welfare payments and entitlements. In one sense, this conception of equality is greater equality up to a sufficient level and then it permits individuals to earn incomes unreservedly. The *National Minimum Wage* is an example of the sufficiency conception of equality inasmuch as it regulates that labour is paid at a sufficient minimum level.[46]

The second component to New Labour's conception of equality is a commitment to giving financial priority to the worst off members in British society. This (as we have noted above) can be referred to as the priority conception of equality. It is perhaps worth pointing out that the priority conception of equality can have two strands or can be interpreted in two different ways. We can refer to them as strict and non-strict prioritarians. Strict prioritarians want to give priority to the worst off groups in society no matter how well off they are in absolute terms. For example, such members of the worst off groups could in fact (according to strict prioritarians) possess a relatively high level of disposable income, own their own homes, holiday abroad, possess a relatively high amount of savings and still would warrant financial priority given to them, because in relative terms they may still be one of the worst off groups in a given society.[47] Non-strict prioritarians also want to give priority to the worst off groups in society but they believe that giving priority becomes less important the better off the worst off groups become.[48] Thus, for example, if one of the two worst off groups in a society gradually became better off in absolute terms, non-strict prioritarians would gradually cease to give such a group priority status. An issue such as this rests on defining two questions. Firstly, who are the worst off groups in society? Secondly, at what level of resources does a government (which holds a commitment to the priority conception of equality) draw the line and ceases to give such groups financial priority? This chapter suggests that New Labour holds a commitment to the non-strict priority conception of equality.

For example, if New Labour managed to raise living standards throughout Britain to the point where everyone had a morally 'sufficient' level and there was no clear category of the neediest members because 75% of people lived comfortably and sufficiently (meaning that more than just their basic 'needs' were met and that they also had a 'reasonable' level of disposable income) and the remaining 25% were very wealthy, it would then appear, according to New Labour's commitment to the non-strict priority and the generous sufficiency conceptions of equality, that British social democracy no longer needed to hold a commitment to such conceptions of equality. Nevertheless, if New Labour held a commitment to equality in its strict egalitarian form then it would continue to campaign for greater equality between the 75% of British people who would be living in relative poverty (although all their basic 'needs' were met and they had the propensity to gain some of their financial 'wants') compared to the wealthy 25% of British people. Some traditional social democrats would claim to be egalitarians different from New Labour, but the question of whether they have reasoned through the extent to which they dismiss non-strict priority and generous sufficiency conceptions of equality and embrace the strict egalitarian conception of equality is not known. It is posited here, that many fewer would commit themselves to the strict egalitarian conception of equality if the distinction were fully realised.

Examples of the non-strict priority conception of equality by New Labour are the *Pensioner Guarantee* and *Working Families Tax Credit* programmes to the poorest pensioners and poorest families with children.[49] Other examples of New Labour's commitment to the priority conception of equality include its £580 million investment in *Surestart* for young children, nursery places for every four year old; £450 million in the *Children's Fund* for children's charities to spend; £5 billion investment in *The New Deal* for 18-25 year olds, *New Deal* for the over 25's; *New Deal Plus* for the over 50 year olds, *New Deal* for single mothers and for disabled people; also, *Action Teams* for jobs in the 2000 poorest areas; high levels of spending on secondary schools; and the *Connexions* programme for 11-25 year olds who fail to gain educational attainment and skills training.

As we have noted, the principle of equality as understood by traditional social democrats has proved to be the philosophical bone of contention for some who doubt New Labour's social democratic credentials. It is apparent that New Labour is quite vague about the principle of equality. Akin to this debate surrounding the principle of equality is the issue of whether New Labour favours an absolute, a relative or what is sometimes referred to as a rising absolute level of measuring poverty. In one sense, these two discussions are two sides of the same coin. Once again, New Labour appears to be sending out conflicting signals. Blair famously stated that the absolute level of poverty is what he considered important when questioned by Jeremy Paxman in an interview on the BBC's *Newsnight* and came close to advocating the neo-liberal trickle down theory.[50] Brown then confused the debate further when using relative measurements in outlining his strategy for combating child poverty and then subsequently announced figures showing a significant reduction in the absolute level of child poverty.

Evidence of New Labour's vagueness concerning the principle of equality is that on 18th March 1999, Blair gave the Beveridge Lecture at Toynbee Hall, London to mark the 750th anniversary of University College, Oxford. In the speech he set out the Government's desire to abolish child poverty by 2020, half it by 2010, reduce it by a quarter in 2004 and reduce it by 1.2 million in 2001.[51] However, on 11th April 2002, Brown announced that the Government had reduced child poverty by 0.5million (in relative terms), which was a reduction from 4.4 million in 1996-1997 to 3.9 million in 2000-2001. Therefore, the target was missed by 0.7million in relative terms but it was exceeded in absolute terms in a reduction of 1.5million. The Government initially used relative figures and then failed to meet the target so presented its findings in absolute terms.

It is also an ambiguity that some suggest goes right to the heart of New Labour, inasmuch as both Blair and Brown hold different versions of equality. This is purely conjecture and will perhaps only be definitively resolved well in to the future when memoirs are published. However, in a recent interview discussing New Labour's political ideas with a senior civil servant I was told that New Labour or at least the Treasury, holds to the Croslandite conception of equality but is applying that principle in a modern economic context.[52] The interviewee stated that the Treasury is applying greater equality of outcome through targeted tax credits, educational allowances and specific skills and education training opportunities such as *Surestart*, but also through the *Working Families Tax Credit* which has secured fairer outcomes to families with two children earning around £13,000 or half the national average earnings whereby they are roughly £3,500 better off per year. The interviewee informed me that was done not merely to make work pay, but to provide fairer outcomes and therefore greater equality of outcome for such low-income families.[53]

What is overtly clear amidst the ambiguity of New Labour's commitment to the principle of equality is that it contains an extra dimension. New Labour's version of equality includes investment in local communities and neighbourhoods.[54] *The New Deal For Communities* decentralises power to the community and democratises decision-making as to where government money should be spent. As Toynbee and Walker assert, *The New Deal For Communities*:

> '...was concentrated first on a score or more neighbourhoods of 1,000-4,000 people, offering £20-£50 million each for programmes that had to show they were genuinely grounded in the local community, pulling in every local service - school, health, social workers, police, housing departments and the Employment Service. They were free to try anything and to come up with local solutions to whatever seemed the worst local problems.'[55]

These measures are a product of the realisation that inequality is more than just the unequal rate of pay between individuals and that it includes inequalities in provision of social and public services from community to community and that neighbourhoods suffer from varying degrees of inequality of access to social goods such as public spaces, good schools, libraries and local amenities.[56]

New Labour's ambiguity over its version of equality is unfortunate but its emphasis on education, skills and opportunity at every stage of life is a pragmatic and electorally expedient response to the changing attitudes and demographics of British society. For example, the very high levels of income taxation during the Wilson-Callaghan Governments of 1974-1979 namely: a lower tax rate of 25%, a basic tax rate of 33%, a higher tax rate of 83% and a higher tax rate for unearned income of 98% would not be electorally feasible today. This is not to say that the British public opposes all forms of increased taxation. As in the 2002 Budget, the increase in taxation (notably through National Insurance Contributions) to invest vast sums of money in public services such as the National Health Service proved popular with the majority of the public (at the time of writing and based on available polling data).[57] Nor does this scepticism towards what can be termed traditional social democratic levels of direct taxation dismiss entirely the prospect of a higher tax band for the very highest earners in society. The Fabian Society's *Commission on Taxation and Citizenship*[58] recommended that a 50% tax band be created above a threshold of £100,000 pa in taxable income that would affect approximately 200,000 citizens. The Inland Revenue calculated that such a tax band would yield £2.9 billion in the year 2000-01 and it would be expected to rise by approximately £200 million per year over the next few years as more people enter the £100,000 income bracket.[59]

When evaluating New Labour and the commitment to equality one must consider that New Labour is not only a product of the globalised age but it is also a post-Thatcherite government trying to persuade a still sceptical electorate that a rise in taxation can deliver better public services. New Labour's social democracy has had to dwell in an intellectual climate which was, and to a certain extent still is, imbued with New Right ideas such as individualism, limited government intervention and a reticence towards redistribution of income and wealth. If what Hattersley says is correct, that a belief in greater equality of outcome (circa 1956[60]) is the definitive test to see if a political party is social democratic, then the British Communist party would count as social democratic whilst not even believing in and participating in democracy and New Labour, like the breakaway SDP of the early 1980s, would find no space to sit in the broad chambers of social democracy.

In this chapter it has been suggested that Tawney, Crosland, Hattersley and New Labour have advocated the principle of equality not as an end in itself but as a means to greater individual freedom and at times as a means to securing a more communal society. The argument is that social democrats in the Labour Party have always been committed to the priority conception of equality as well as holding a commitment to a generous sufficiency conception of equality. In addition, it has been maintained that only George Bernard Shaw, the Marxist Social Democratic Federation and the Labour Marxists of the 1920s and 1930s, ever claimed to hold a commitment to the strict egalitarian conception of equality in the Labour Party.

Finally, it has been suggested that ideas such as 'equality of opportunity and fairness of outcome' and 'progressive universalism' are ambiguous and that New Labour's conception of equality is better understood as a commitment to a non-strict prioritarianism and a generous sufficiency conception of equality.

8

NEW LABOUR, COMMUNITY AND DEMOCRACY

Once again, in the same way as the previous chapter on equality, this chapter attempts to evaluate the value of community in New Labour's political philosophy. The chapter will examine New Labour's approach in light of the claimed intellectual hegemony of New Right ideas and with regard to some traditional social democratic perspectives on community. The first task will be to outline the attitude of the New Right regarding the value of community and in particular, their antipathy towards it. The second task will be a thorough discussion of traditional social democratic conceptions of community from thinkers including R.H Tawney, Ramsay MacDonald and Anthony Crosland. The third task of the chapter will be to explain New Labour's communitarian social philosophy. A discussion of Amitai Etzioni's American communitarianism and the Christian socialist notion of community as 'fellowship' will be developed and it will be argued that these two elements are useful when attempting to understand New Labour's value of community. The fourth task of the chapter will be to discuss the issue of widening democracy within New Labour's communitarian framework. It will consider the implications surrounding New Labour's decentralisation programme; it will investigate how devolution affects the social democratic concern with equality and specifically, with equality of services across the nation; and it will comment upon New Labour's attitude towards the voluntary sector. It is with the discussion of the attitudes of New Right thinkers regarding the value of community that the chapter begins.

New Right Ideas and Arguments Against Community

John Kingdom argues that the principle of community is antipathetic for neo-liberals:

'The idea of an instinct towards a communal, mutually supportive life stands in direct contradiction to the state of nature envisioned by New Right liberals where the community, as a body with rules and ties, is a mere artefact created by contract to permit the operation of a more natural association – the market. For Adam Smith the instinct to barter was embedded deep within human nature and, in similar vein, Nozick argues that market activities come first, leading the state to sneak up on people, without even the need for a notional contract. Always, the joy of a good bargain comes before the instinct of fellowship.'[1]

What therefore does Hayek say about this political value? In short, a thorough discussion of the value of community does not appear in Hayek's political thought.[2] Hayek does not attack community nor propose methodological arguments against it because it does not overtly figure in his philosophy.[3] As a neo-liberal Hayek's concerns were set against the notion of social justice, the alleged growth in power of the central state and any movement or policies that would limit or restrict the autonomy of the individual. His enmity was focused towards the collectivist tendencies of socialism and the effects he believed they would have on the power of the state.[4] Therefore, this implies that Hayek would have been in opposition to state-level community action but not local-level community action. Of course it depends what one means by 'community action'. In this case I want to offer the definition that community action is more than the idea of *gesellschaft*[5], of contractual relationships and mere pragmatic association and can be understood more fully by the notion of *gemeinschaft* or fellowship based on shared values and beliefs. The argument posited here suggests that Hayek as a classical liberal would have resisted the movement to allow the state, and by that one is referring to the central government and its institutions, to suggest a conception of the good for its citizens to follow grounded in communal values, norms and beliefs, in other words a type of *gemeinschaft* advocated by communitarians. By implication Hayek was not against ideas surrounding local-level community, as it would not have directly alerted his concerns about the growing power of the state, which according to his thesis impinges upon individual liberty. In this sense Hayek is firmly a philosophical liberal and not a libertarian.[7] Therefore, as a liberal he placed the right of the individual ahead of the conception of the good life valued by communities and eschewed any communitarian strand of thought be it methodological or normative. Hayek would have regarded communitarian designs on state-level citizenship as moving politics on to the slippery slope towards totalitarianism.[8] In addition, Hayek would have categorically opposed any conception of social justice couched in terms of community obligation to worse off citizens or in terms of responsibility to other members of one's community based on an understanding of brotherhood or fellowship beyond the most basic social provision to prevent destitution.[9]

In summary, the collectivist leanings of the political value of community whether used as a justification for some form of socialist distributive justice, as an account of state-level citizenship or as a reason for advocating a certain conception of the good would have in turn, offended the individualism and the negative libertarianism which largely made up Hayek's neo-liberal philosophy.

In practical politics New Right governments in Britain under Thatcher and Major have commented little on the idea of community. In a phrase which summarised the zeitgeist of the political world occupied by the New Right, Thatcher famously declared that:

'...there is no such thing as society; only individuals and families...'

This statement has been understood not only as evidence of the New Right's ambivalence towards notions of community, social responsibility and 'brotherhood', but also as axiomatic for all strands of Conservative thought. This is incorrect, as the Conservative Party has long contained an account of community and social responsibility in its political thought. From perhaps the days of Disraeli, but certainly from the influence of the Fourth Party led by Lord Randolph Churchill under the banner of 'Tory Democracy', Conservatives have regarded social responsibility to the community at large, and especially to the worst off sections of society as part of their political mission statement. Although small in number, Churchill and his allies passed on a political heritage to Joseph Chamberlain, and in turn to his son and future Prime Minister Neville Chamberlain, which stretched in to the twentieth century. Greenleaf accurately portrays the influence of 'Tory Democracy' in the late nineteenth century on the Conservative Party:

'Of course, many of the ideas of Tory Democracy hardly aroused widespread support in Conservative circles. And, under the rather sceptical aegis of Lord Salisbury, perhaps little was to be anticipated, for his attitude was a sort of pale and negative Disraelism...Yet after Lord Randolph's departure the radical spirit continued strong as in the activities of bodies like the Tory Reform League.'[10]

Joseph Chamberlain was arguably the most radical Conservative politician of his generation in terms of his communitarian political outlook. He was originally a radical liberal prior to the growth of the New Liberalism that the

Liberal Party would embrace.[11] As Greenleaf notes, Chamberlain was:

> '...envisaging the formation of a new Radical party with an advanced programme to replace the old Liberalism, one capable of dealing with the social issues occasioned by the development of industrialization and democracy.'[12]

However, Chamberlain crossed the floor due to his disagreement with Gladstone's position on Irish Home Rule and he became a powerful voice for social reform on the Conservative benches. Greenleaf further recounts that Chamberlain's political beliefs required him to approach social problems from a state-centric position with the government working on behalf of the whole community.[13] He suggests that Chamberlain's radical Tory ideas of public duty and social enterprise focused at bettering the life of the worst off stands in stark contrast to the classical liberal attitude to the state.[14] This chapter suggests that the term 'communitarian conservatism' is appropriate when describing a specific kind of paternalistic conservatism that emphasises community responsibility and social duty and this is clearly a strand of thought within conservatism, which has been overshadowed since the mid-twentieth century[15] and especially since the early 1970s.

Social Democratic Conceptions of Community

R.H. Tawney has come to be regarded as the figurehead of ethical socialism in the history of the Labour Movement. Many members on opposite wings of the Labour Party have cited him as a guiding influence in the development of their political thought.[16] Within the Labour Movement Tawney's writings are synonymous with the value of community or as he often termed it, 'fellowship' but at first sight Tawney's writing on political thought can appear preoccupied with issues of inequality and the lack of liberty that poverty causes. It is because of this, that it is sometimes difficult to find any obvious and explicit discussion of community. However, once the reader has studied all of his major works including his *Commonplace Book*[17], it is clear that Tawney's socialism was his ideal of Christian fellowship. His attitude that all people are equal because the Creator God made them equal in moral worth and as ends in themselves, pervades his work. The following comment by Greenleaf exposes the theological order of his socialism:

'...Tawney's view of Socialism could never be one which primarily stressed efficiency, the symmetry of a perfect social machine, or even abundance. Rather its emphasis was inevitably spiritual or ethical, emphasizing instead a right order of social relationships based on human fellowship.'[18]

This quotation appropriately reveals Tawney's Christian understanding of socialism and thus his ideal of community or Christian fellowship. Equality or greater material and social equality were in a way, values that Tawney was campaigning for although he recognised that his actual socialist goal was greater individual liberty and a more communal society. Greenleaf regards Tawney's aim of granting greater individual liberty and encouraging a more fraternal society, as individuals being encouraged and enabled by the community to reach their own potential and become active citizens within a more egalitarian and ethical community:

'His ideal was fellowship, participating citizenship, a process of growing individual self-development in a richer and less privileged social environment than that which he criticised. He was concerned, not so much to build a tidy social system, as to release people's energies and potentialities in a proper nexus of social relationships based on genuine moral principle.'[19]

In a similar way to New Labour, Tawney saw reducing material and social inequalities as the most effective way of making society simultaneously more free and communal and in addition, the main vehicle that Tawney believed was capable of achieving his goals is the same social vehicle advocated by the New Labour social democrats, namely education. Greenleaf highlights two reasons, which underpinned Tawney's emphasis on learning:

'One was that diversities of schooling and its quality played a substantial role in sustaining the class distinctions Tawney criticized so vehemently. The other was that if society was to be transformed in the way Tawney desired it would involve a radical change of heart on the part of all sections of the community, a transformation of the acquisitive and competitive attitude into one characterized by fellowship, co-operation and mutual understanding so that an assertion of rights would be accommodated to a realisation of duties. And in respect of each consideration education was vital.'[20]

This chapter also contends that Tawney realised and advocated the opinion that none of his goals such as greater individual liberty and a more communal society could be achieved until British society reduced or perhaps ceased its acquisitiveness and selfish individualism, which characterised its type of capitalist political economy.[21] Tawney's subtext of socialism as fellowship is conveyed in this paragraph in the opening chapter of his acclaimed book, *Equality*:

'The equality which all these thinkers emphasize as desirable is not equality of capacity or attainment, but of circumstance, institutions, and manner of life. The inequality which they deplore is not inequality of personal gifts, but of the social and economic environment. They are concerned, not with a biological phenomenon, but with a spiritual relation and the conduct to be based on it. Their view, in short, is that because men are men, social institutions - property rights, and the organization of industry, and the system of public health and education - should be planned, as far as possible to emphasize and strengthen, not the class differences which divide, but the common humanity which unites them.'[22]

However, if R.H Tawney's principled commitment to community as his core political value can be most accurately understood as a commitment to Christian fellowship, then his contemporary and the Labour Party's first Prime Minister, Ramsay MacDonald conceived of his principled commitment to community in an altogether different way. Foote notes that Ramsay MacDonald's socialism was predicated upon a notion of community that was quasi-scientific and evolutionary:

'MacDonald counterposed the organic community of socialism to the present state of affairs, a community where the different functions would be co-ordinated and regulated in the interests of the whole. In such a community, true individuality would flourish as each person would be happily integrated in the advanced whole and would work for that whole. Just as in biology the individual cell has both a function and an individual existence through the totality, so in society the different classes and people would have a social function and an individual part to play in the whole.'[23]

MacDonald's communitarian socialism was based less on the traditional values of Christianity and more upon ideas of Darwinian evolutionary theory. He argued that socialism was centrally about the community as a whole not a crusade on behalf of a specific class or interest group such as the trade unions. MacDonald desired the Labour Party's socialism to raise the working class to be full citizens within the community. In his biography of MacDonald, David Marquand cites an article written by MacDonald in 1903, which makes this exact point:

'If the new Labour movement were simply an attempt of Trade Unionists to use their political power for purely sectional ends...it would be a menace to all the qualities that mark public life with distinction and honour...Trade Unionism in politics must identify itself with something higher and wider than Trade Union industrial demands. It must set those demands into a system of national well-being; the wage earner must become the citizen; the Union must become the guardian of economic justice.'[24]

The above quotation merely gives an impression, and a brief impression at that, of what MacDonald thought of the political value of community. It does indicate that it was an actively held principle that MacDonald derived from an ethical but non-Christian account of socialism. MacDonald and Tawney were important figures in the Labour Party during the Edwardian era and yet one can observe the differences in their conceptualisation of the principle of community. In some ways the first half of the twentieth century can be seen as a high watermark or zenith of communitarian socialism in the British Labour Movement and with that in mind it is argued that the second half of the twentieth century saw little further development of social democratic thought on a communitarian basis until the advent of New Labour. It is with the main thinker of British social democracy in the mid-century period that our discussion now turns.

In all of the twenty-five chapters of Anthony Crosland's seminal piece of social democratic writing *The Future of Socialism*, there is no single chapter on the principle of community. This chapter wants to develop the argument that there are three main reasons why the paradigmatic thinker of mid-twentieth century social democratic thought chose to omit one of the traditional values of social democracy from his writings.

Firstly, Crosland's work was preoccupied with constructing a brand of socialism based on the pursuit of greater economic and social equality. As was discussed in detail in the third chapter, Crosland was a Gaitskellite revisionist and during the 1950s the Gaitskellites were involved in the 'Great Debate' with the Bevanites in the Labour Party, over the direction and the philosophical approach that the Labour Party should take. Crosland, like the revisionists, believed that socialism was not about any specific act of policy such as nationalisation, but about political values and above all others he suggested that greater equality of outcome was the value that united socialists more than any other.[25] Therefore, it was Crosland's task to produce a textbook of revisionist socialist thought and one, which placed the political value of greater equality at its centre. This is the first reason why Crosland's writings were focussed primarily on equality and commented little if anything about the value of community.

Secondly, according to David Lipsey, Crosland was not a social democrat who deeply valued the principle of community because he could not see its contemporary relevance. The italics emphasise these points:

'On fraternity, Crosland is agnostic: "not because I think its content less important, *but simply because I find it impossible to reach a definite conclusion about its relevance in contemporary conditions.*" '[26]

'His earlier scepticism towards incomes policy - a policy originally associated with the Left of the Labour Party - turned to passionate support for it as a way of subordinating excessive individual claims to those of the community as a whole. *Yet this shift went only so far, for Crosland never lost his concern lest on excess of community spirit led to busybodying invasions of privacy and personal freedom.*'[27]

Third and finally, Crosland's era was one of liberalism and in particular, an era of liberalisation in the legal, social and personal spheres of life. The late 1950s–1970s witnessed social and moral changes that would have been unthinkable even during the years leading up to the Second World War.

Part of the absence of the notion of community, as has been inferred, is simply because it was the age of individual rights and the progressive left within the Labour Party believed this needed to be on the social agenda as Britain was an exceptionally socially conservative country, stratified by class, gender and mono-ethical traditions. Another factor relating to the absence of community in Crosland's writings was that his natural inclination was liberal not communitarian.[28] His social democracy, although his writings sometimes confuse it, was about granting greater individual freedom through greater material and social equality. Some social democrats desire both greater individual freedom and greater fraternity, but it is suggested here that Crosland was simply a liberal social democrat and thus was sceptical and at times rather suspicious of notions of community.

Crosland's perspective on community stands in stark contrast to Tony Wright's contemporary social democratic view of the value of community. To him social democracy means that:

' ...we are all in it together, that society is not to be understood (either morally or empirically) as merely a maelstrom of atomized individuals but as a moral community embedded in a dense fabric of social relationships and obligations and capable of framing common purposes. There is nothing monolithic, oppressive, or nostalgic about this.'[29]

It is with this contemporary social democratic notion of community that we move on to discuss its salience and its role in the political philosophy of New Labour.

New Labour's Conception of Community

Raymond Plant, Harry Lesser and Peter Taylor-Gooby suggest that the concept of 'community' suffers from widespread ambiguity in its meaning.[30] The vast range of descriptions that the term 'community' can be used to employ, amply supports this point:

'Conventionally the term is used to refer to locality; interest groups; a system of solidarity; a group with a sense of mutual significance; a group characterized by moral agreement, shared beliefs, shared authority, or ethnic integrity; a group marked by historical continuity and shared traditions; a group in which members meet in some kind of total fashion as opposed to meeting as members of certain roles, functions or occupational groups; and, finally, occupational, functional or partial communities.'[31]

Therefore, the crux of the issue for Plant, Lesser and Taylor-Gooby is to clarify the understanding of the term 'community'. Andrew Mason attempts this task by arguing that 'community' is better understood as two distinct concepts: the 'ordinary concept' and the 'moralized concept'. The ordinary concept takes an association of people to be different from a community of people.[32] Mason suggests that the ordinary concept is constituted by:

'…a group of people who share a range of values, a way of life, identify with the group and its practices and recognise each other as members of that group.'[33]

Mason defines a group as a collection of individuals that act or co-operate to fulfil their own aims or who share common interests.[34] He acknowledges that his description of the 'ordinary concept' of community does not outline necessary and sufficient conditions that qualify groups to be communities.[35] The 'moralized concept' contains the characteristics of the 'ordinary concept' but includes two extra components:

'First, there must be solidarity between its members. 'Solidarity' is a multiple ambiguous notion, but in the sense I intend it consists in mutual concern: minimally this means that members must give each other's interests some non-instrumental weight in their practical reasoning. Second, there must be no systematic exploitation or no systematic injustice.'[36]

From this brief distinction of two concepts of community, one can argue that Mason's 'ordinary concept' is a 'thin' concept of community as opposed to the 'moralized' concept which is a 'thick' concept of community. In other words, the 'ordinary concept' is specifically descriptive whereas the 'moralized conceptive' is inherently normative. The 'ordinary concept' attempts to explain a type of community that is more of an association of individuals in the form of groups. The explanation is based upon empirical assertions and to a lesser extent normative assertions and in the 'moralized concept'; the explanation is based mainly, although not exclusively, on normative assertions and includes an account of solidarity, which implies a closer ethical bond between members.

Community is one of the main philosophical values that defines New Labour and is indicative of its modernised social democracy.[37] This chapter argues that New Labour's concept of community can be understood by Mason's description of the 'ordinary' and 'moralized concept'; at times both a 'thin' and a 'thick' concept of community. The 'ordinary concept' is used by New Labour when they talk about local-level and regional-level community and when they suggest that decentralisation to the regions, including devolution, can enable groups of people with some shared goals and who are part of a specific geographic area within the nation, to determine the politics of their region to a greater extent. The 'moralized concept' is consistent with New Labour's communitarian citizenship which it advocates from the state-level. It wants all citizens to be motivated by their equal rights and responsibilities to each other. This implies a solidaristic ethic of reciprocity and mutual concern for others which is derived from the Christian socialist idea of community as 'fellowship'.[38] For example, the Labour

Party's new Clause IV desires the creation of a society of 'solidarity, tolerance and respect'. This is more than an association of individuals, or a group who share some values or who co-operate for their own specific interests. It conveys an ethical prescription that New Labour's social democracy wants to foster in all citizens.

As Plant, Lesser and Taylor-Gooby have noted, community is an ambiguous concept and one that can exist at different levels. For example, much of New Labour's belief in the value of community has been a commitment to community at the level of the state. It involves a communitarian conception of citizenship that emphasises responsibilities to the community as well as individual rights within that community. Another level of community is regional community. New Labour has shown interest in issues and problems within specific regions and the establishment of the Regional Development Agencies is evidence of this interest. Furthermore, the discussion about regional assemblies especially by the Deputy Prime Minister John Prescott highlights that regions in Britain are cultural, social and economic communities that may benefit from greater devolved power and a regional focus to solving problems and managing public services. A further level of community is local level community. New Labour promotes its conception of community at the local level through its financially decentralist program: the *New Deal for Communities*.[39]

The social philosophy of communitarianism, according to Avineri and de-Shalit, can be understood in two separate spheres. Firstly, it can be understood, interpreted and advocated on a philosophical level which draws on its methodological criticisms of liberalism and secondly, on an ethical level which critiques the normative consequences of a purely liberal society.[40] Thus, like the value of community, communitarianism can appear to be difficult to define and seem ambiguous. For example, Ruth Levitas notes that communitarianism as a social philosophy can be given varying inflections.[41] This chapter argues that one form of communitarianism, which helps to understand New Labour's interpretation of community, is contemporary American communitarianism.

Contemporary American communitarian thought has, according to some commentators, had an influence on New Labour and in particular, on the Prime Minister's political thought.[42] Amitai Etzioni is arguably the main figure in the contemporary American communitarian movement since the 1990s.[43] Whilst acknowledging the role of previous communitarian political theorists such as Charles Taylor[44], Michael Sandel[45] and Michael Walzer[46], especially throughout the 1980s, Etzioni states that they are different from the 'new communitarians' who are connected with *The Responsive Community: Rights and Responsibilities*[47] journal, and who are chiefly involved in:

'...the question of balance between individual rights and social responsibilities, between autonomy and the common good...'[48]

The type of communitarianism that Etzioni is advocating is a democratic campaigning communitarianism that seeks to address the imbalance between rights and responsibilities in American society.[49] It does not negate the role of the state or the market as two of the primary organs in society but it merely values the role of communities be they families, neighbourhoods, voluntary and religious organisations and, more generally, any groups that are bound together by shared values. This is very similar to New Labour's emphasis on cohesive communities. For example, in his Fabian Pamphlet, *The Third Way: Politics for the New Century*[50], Tony Blair outlined his belief in the value of communities in society. He argues that:

'Strong communities depend on shared values and a recognition of the rights and duties of citizenship - not just the duty to pay taxes and obey the law, but the obligation to bring up children as competent, responsible citizens, and to support those - such as teachers - who are employed by the state in the task. In the past we have tended to take such duties for granted. But where they are neglected, we should not hesitate to encourage and even enforce them, as we are seeking to do with initiatives such as our 'home-school contracts' between schools and parents.'[51]

Furthermore, Etzioni does not naively believe that all communities are morally equivalent or virtuous:

'Communities are not automatically or necessarily places of virtue. Many traditional communities that were homogenous, if not monolithic, were authoritarian and oppressive. And a community may lock into a set of values that one may find abhorrent, say an Afrikaaner village that legitimates an ideology of lynching.'[52]

This form of American communitarianism positions itself between the moral and philosophical divide that separates social conservatives and libertarians. Etzioni argues that social conservatives give moral primacy to social order in a similar way that libertarians give moral primacy to autonomy.[53] He asserts that the difference between communitarians and the social conservatives is that social conservatives are:

'...more order-focused and less concerned with autonomy as a primary virtue, have a much more pervasive and unitary normative agenda, and are more inclined to rely on the state than on the *moral voice* for the ultimate enforcement of values.'[54]

Regarding libertarians or individualists, Etzioni believes that they claim that because autonomy is the core virtue in western society it should never be negated or in any way impinged by a specific communal or social construction of 'the good'.[55] This is similar to neo-liberal philosophy of the Thatcher and Major Governments with their reticent attitude towards community, social cooperation and collective action. The neo-liberal philosophy gave political and moral primacy to the individual and was deliberately silent about the social responsibility of individuals. Driver and Martell suggest that communitarian political ideas provide New Labour with an alternative social philosophy to neo-liberalism.[56]

Etzioni outlines the typical libertarian frame of reference when defending their view of autonomy:

'Reference is typically made to legal rights and freedom from government. Special significance is attributed to individuals' rights to have their lives protected and to control and use their property.'[57]

In Britain, New Labour wanted to reclaim the social policy prescriptions consistent with a communitarian left approach to social theory as the communitarian instinct of the Labour Movement and of the majority of Labour MPs had diminished.[58] In the Labour Party a liberalism which emphasised personal individual rights rather than property rights had become the dominant approach to social theory and therefore, personal and communal responsibilities were relegated, if not completely discarded, in favour of individual rights.[59] New Labour's communitarian policies have included, tough sentencing for young offenders but with education and rehabilitation, teenage curfews in violent neighbourhoods but with government funded support for youth projects. In addition, welfare to work schemes which give the individual the right of state benefits for a fixed period of time and expects the individual to take responsibility for his or her own future through one of several options, ranging from further training or education, voluntary work, an environmental project or an organised job placement.[60]

In addition, Etzioni asserts that contemporary communitarians recognise the need for an updated philosophical map because the terms, right and left, conservative and liberal are now often inappropriate in contemporary discussions[61]:

'We see at one extreme Authoritarians (such as the Moral Majority and Liberty Bell). They urge the imposition on all others of moral positions they believe in, from prayer in schools to forcing women to stay in the kitchen. At the other end we see Radical Individualists (libertarians such as the intellectuals at the Cato Institute; civil libertarians, especially the American Civil Liberties Union; and laissez-faire conservatives), who believe that if individuals are left on their own to pursue their choices, rights and self-interests, all will be well. We suggest that free individuals require a community, which backs them up against encroachment by the state and sustains morality by drawing on the gentle prodding of kin, friends and neighbours, and other community members, rather than building on government controls or fear of authorities.'[62]

Etzioni states that his brand of communitarianism is neither conservative nor authoritarian because he is committed to gender equality[63] and non-coercive methods of social control.[64] For example, some of Etzioni's reforms include an increase in unpaid work such as bringing up children and caring for the elderly[65], 'peer marriage' whereby both husband and wife have equal rights and duties and where the division of labour is a personal matter to settle[66], corporations should provide paid family leave for one year and be required to keep a job open for a parent for two additional years.[67] Furthermore, that an array of public and social services be decentralised to communities carried out by voluntary not for profit organisations as the third sector can often have a more responsive and tailor-made approach to the needs of specific communities as well as saving public money.[68] These suggestions are ideas that many social democrats would welcome and the combination of greater social responsibility by large corporations and the state funding of unpaid care, as well as issues of greater women's rights in conjunction with childcare are certainly contemporary issues for social democrats to campaign upon.

Critics of American communitarianism such as Levitas, unfairly characterises Etzioni as a conservative because he offers the view that ideally speaking, two parent families are better placed to bring up children than one-parent families and therefore marriage should be encouraged.[69] Nowhere does Etzioni give moral primacy to any religious position on marriage, but he asserts that the children of married parents are less likely to experience educational and social problems than children of unmarried, divorced or step parents.[70] In this discussion Etzioni's position could be characterised as utilitarian and pragmatic because he believes that two parents can share the burden of bringing up children. Therefore, to categorise his brand of communitarianism as conservative is clearly an egregious misjudgement on Levitas's behalf. However, Levitas fairly argues that social and moral pressure to conform to the community's values is to an extent coercive and that it does have social ramifications. These range from disapproval to ostracism which intends to punish the transgressor and act as a deterrent to prevent future transgressions. Etzioni should concede that his brand of communitarianism does legitimise forms of coercion:

'To argue that social pressure of this kind, including ostracism, is not coercive actually undermines Etzioni's own argument. If communities are to rely on moral pressure to maintain social order, they can do so only if these pressures have some coercive effects over potential dissidents. This then raises the question of who has the power to impose their standards, as well as the difficulties of ensuring just, equitable and accountable implementation through informal mechanisms.'[71]

Nonetheless, what is morally wrong with this approach? Etzioni is incorrect to deny this type of coercion but Levitas is incorrect to equate it with authoritarianism. Social disapproval and even mild forms of ostracism occur at every stage of social life in societies. From the rowdy bully who is not invited to a child's party to the alcoholic father who gets drunk in front of his family and rows with anyone and is regarded with little respect by neighbours, colleagues or friends. These measures can be used as forms of social coercion but it is the phrase 'coercion', which is politically loaded, and one that frightens those who do not regard their behaviour as in any way 'coercive'.

This chapter argues that New Labour has rediscovered the traditional social democratic value of community and that it can be understood in part, by the Christian socialist principle of community as 'fellowship' that senior New Labour politicians including Blair, Straw, Brown and Blunkett would advocate[72] and, in part, by the contemporary American communitarian movement. José Harris comments that New Labour's ideas surrounding the value of community are akin to those of the Labour Party before the Second World War and that those similar conceptions of 'fraternity' and fellowship were lost during mid-twentieth century social democracy. She argues that:

'The Edwardian concern with 'duty and citizenship', largely sidelined by the technocratic culture of the mid-century, resonates strongly through many New Labour documents, as do Edwardian ideas about reciprocal relationships between welfare and work, punishment and fraud. Although ideas about what constitutes virtue have changed beyond recognition, early Labourites would certainly have endorsed the New Labour view that policies should be 'ethical' and citizens 'virtuous'.'[73]

This is an important point as it supports the argument outlined earlier in the chapter, namely, that whereas the value of community was a key component in British social democracy in the first half of the twentieth century and especially in the Edwardian era derived from sources such as MacDonald and Tawney, it was largely forgotten in the second half of the twentieth century. This was because social democratic thought was dominated by an ethos of personal and social individualism. In addition, the main economic concern for social democrats was the position of the individual worker and the inequalities he suffered and what the remedies were for reducing this wage inequality. The individual ethos in the social realm was related to extending rights to women in the workplace, protecting the rights of the disabled and citizens of ethnic origins, de-stigmatising the homosexual lifestyle, as well as changing the laws against homosexual behaviour. All of these issues, which are often categorised as part of the drift into the 'permissive society' are associated with the British left, the Labour Party and with a preference towards a liberal, not a communitarian social philosophy. For the Croslandite revisionists of the late 1950s to the 1970s the philosophical value of community was hardly mentioned within the gamut of social democratic ideas. The value of greater equality took centre-stage and consumed the philosophical discussion surrounding the principles of social democracy until New Labour social democrats reconnected it to their vision of modern social democracy framed in communitarian terms.

Democracy and Citizenship

As was stated above, New Labour's communitarian account of citizenship includes local, regional and state-level ideas. Greater democratisation through the decentralisation of power from the political centre has been a key idea of New Labour's citizenship agenda at the regional-level. This includes decentralisation of power to the regions of England through the establishment of the Regional Development Agencies with the idea of eventual regional assemblies for those regions who desire it. It also includes types of devolution for Scotland, Wales, Northern Ireland and London. Therefore, it is not surprising that New Labour's constitutional modernisation and in particular, the devolution of power to the regions is seen by some Labour commentators as the most radical reform of the British constitution for nearly two centuries.[74] Others suggest that it is New Labour's most significant reform whilst in power.[75] New Labour inherited the constitutional reform programme from John Smith's leadership, but to view them as mere pragmatists to win electoral votes is inaccurate, especially when only 51% of those who voted in the Welsh referendum opted for the creation of the Welsh Assembly in 1997 and therefore it cannot be classed as vote-hunting as it was not an obvious vote-winner. Thus, a commitment to decentralisation of power and in particular, to the policy of devolution exists in Blair's Government.

The purpose of decentralisation is that it claims to open up central government to the regions and in the case of Wales to a principality. It also claims to increase the democratisation of the political decision-making process. This democratisation enables citizens to have a greater say in the policies that affect their lives at a regional level, as well as at local level via borough and city council elections and at the national level through general elections. Therefore, philosophically, the motivation behind decentralisation for advocates of such an approach is twofold. From an individual standpoint it intends to increase individual liberty by granting the individual citizen the right to vote or to protest against a wider range of issues on the regional level of government. From a collective standpoint it can enable groups of citizens with some shared goals and who are part of a specific geographic region within the nation, to determine the politics of their region in a way consistent with their shared goals. Under Mason's definition this collective reason for decentralisation is an example of the 'ordinary concept' of community.

A possible criticism of Labour's approach to decentralisation is that it does not have a coherent philosophy of the state.[76] At best one could argue that New Labour's communitarian social philosophy believes that communities whether they are regions of individuals with shared cultural interests and values or whether they are cities have the right to exercise their democratic will as far as practically possible. Allied to this point is the notion that different communities desire different legislative solutions for certain issues and this is where the Government gets into difficulty because the plurality of demands and needs is ultimately incommensurable with the universal application of certain principles, such as the principle of equality of services across the nation.[77]

David Blunkett highlights this traditional criticism of the decentralisation of power within the nation state for social democrats committed to a conception of equality:

'That is whether empowerment of communities and the devolution of power to people in their localities will lead to inequality: to differences in outcomes that will violate our core principles of social justice for all. In other words, different communities will do things differently.'[78]

Blunkett argues that social democrats need to connect their belief in the value of community and decentralisation of power with social justice.[79] He believes that when decentralised power is established and communities take a significant role social justice is enhanced but he suggests that some inequalities such as the unfair distribution of life chances, community assets and high levels of crime and anti-social behaviour will not be permitted.[80] However, when investigating how devolution affects the social democratic concern with equality and specifically, with equality of services across the nation one has to raise the point that New Labour have not appeared to put in place any counter-measure to prevent such inequalities from arising. For example, primary and secondary education and health services have not been significantly affected by devolution but, the Scottish Parliament and Welsh Assembly have abolished tuition fees for university students whereas they apply in England. This is a form of inequality of service in the university sector for English students.

Another example is the free bus pass for all Welsh pensioners granted by the Welsh Assembly whereas English pensioners receive no such entitlement. Again this is a discrepancy in equality of service in public transport for a specific group of citizens. Therefore, New Labour's attitude to decentralisation and in particular to devolution has implications on its commitment to equality of services and entitlements, and perhaps they are less concerned about the inequalities across the nation regarding free bus passes for pensioners in Wales and the free higher education for students in Scotland, than with other substantive welfare entitlements and public services.

Another issue in the process of devolution and the decentralisation of power has been the diverse range of electoral systems put in place by the different electoral bodies. The Additional Member System of proportional representation is used for elections to the Scottish Parliament, the Welsh Assembly and the Greater London Assembly. The Single Transferable Vote is used for elections to the Northern Ireland Assembly, elections to the European Parliament use Regional Lists currently organised by the political parties and the London Mayoral elections use the non-proportional Supplementary Vote system. Such a diversification of electoral systems is indicative of giving individual citizens and regional communities greater autonomy over political decisions. A plurality of outcomes whether it is political, electoral or economic in nature is part of the general effect of decentralisation of power.

New Labour's account of communitarian citizenship also contains a role for the voluntary sector. In a speech to the NCVO's Annual Conference in 2000, Gordon Brown linked the act of volunteering with value of community:

'Your efforts represent society at work, compassion in action, community at its best – as someone once said, making the word 'neighbour' not just a geographical term but an ethical term as well.'[81]

The voluntary sector comprising of charities and not-for-profit organisations is a central pillar of civil society and can be understood as the third of three sectors in society along with the state and the market. The voluntary sector is multifarious in purpose and in method, yet five specific attributes can be listed which characterises the role of the voluntary sector. The first is that charities usually begin and many of them continue as community based initiatives. Unlike the state whose primary concern has been universal provision of services, and the private sector whose *raison d'etre* is to make profit, the voluntary sector is community focused. Connected to this approach is the advantage of local knowledge. Services provided can be tailor-made to meet the needs of a specific community. The state as the central distributional centre often lacks sophistication in shaping services to meet local requirements. Therefore, because the voluntary sector is community based and has local knowledge it must demonstrate a greater capacity for innovation because people have different needs and these needs change. This is a situation that the state also finds itself in as attitudes and lifestyles change, but the voluntary sector often appears to be more responsive to the idiosyncrasies of community life because they are led by local citizens who understand the changing needs of their fellow citizens. In the market, private companies are usually innovative due to the pressure of competition and the risk of losing customers who demand a diverse range of products and services. A further attribute of the voluntary sector is the greater degree of trust that the voluntary sector in all its forms is held in compared to the reputations of politicians looking for popularity and private businessmen maximising profit. Finally, the voluntary sector is less dominated by producer interests, as the mainstay of its labour is voluntary. Individuals are not concerned about maximising either their pay, working conditions or pension prospects. Therefore, the delivery of the services that are provided is free from these 'professional' issues. People volunteer for many different reasons but mainly do so due to a sense of 'community spirit' or altruism towards neighbours and community members.

It appear that New Labour are aware of the attributes of the voluntary sector as well as the shortcomings that the state and the market have in providing certain local, community based services that are constantly changing and that require levels of trust and responsiveness. In the same speech Brown argues that both 'Old Labour' and the New Right had wrong relationships with the voluntary sector but that New Labour more fully understands the ethic of partnership that is required between the state, the market and the voluntary sector:

> 'In the past, voluntary organisations have been caught in the middle of an unnecessary political fight. Parts of the Left saw the voluntary sector, as a threat to the things government should be doing... The Right, for its part, used the voluntary sector to relieve Government of Government's proper responsibilities. The New Right seeking to substitute charitable action for the state. Democratically elected government does have a responsibility to ensure the public interest is advanced, to ensure basic rights are upheld for everyone, to guarantee that where people vote democratically that a service must be provided. But government must recognise that it does not have a solution to every problem, that it must work with the grain of people, and that the advancement of the public interest does not always require public control...The way forward is government and charities, working in partnership based on mutual respect, a recognition that the voluntary sector is not a cut-price alternative to statutory provision, nor a way of ducking the responsibilities of families, including the extended family or society.'[82]

However, New Labour's relationship with the voluntary sector and its desire to permit charitable and not-for-profit organisations to run certain services where they feel the state is less equipped to do so raises some problems. Firstly, the voluntary sector is part of civil society and is usually seen as autonomous and independent of government. Yet the closer its relationship with government the more likely its reputation for being independent, citizen-led, and perhaps its efficacy, will be called into question.[83] Secondly, some charities have grown to be international in scope and this sometimes means that they compete with government in the public realm. Dahrendorf suggests that:

'In a fundamental sense, all charity is local. Time and money voluntarily given are for the most part given to do things for particular people in particular places. However, if local initiatives are successful they have a tendency to grow....Some charities are very big indeed, like Save the Children or Oxfam, to say nothing of the Red Cross. Their bigness alone propels them into the public realm as important actors which in some ways compete with government. They become as it were Quagos, quasi-governmental organisations.'

Dahrendorf points to the need for rules to be drawn up to regulate the relationship between the state and the voluntary sector and notes that this has been done in the form of the 'Compact on Relations between Government and the Voluntary and Community Sector in England'. In addition, the Treasury's cross-cutting review of the role of the voluntary sector in delivering public services sought to set out the nature of the relationship between the Government and the voluntary sector, its aims and its rules.[84] Although, the representatives from the voluntary sector have been involved in the planning of the cross-cutting review some problems such as the balance of financial risk set towards the voluntary sector; the continued pressure to provide services at a price that does not reflect the full cost; and, the lack of stability in funding relationships which can leave organisations financially vulnerable are salient issues which still need to be resolved.[85]

New Labour's communitarianism is best understood in the terms that people as individuals, have rights because they are citizens and their citizenship guarantees them specific political, economic, social and legal rights. However, citizens have to fulfil individual responsibilities as part of their citizenship within the community. For example, a communitarian left account may suggest that people as citizens have responsibilities to the state in keeping the law, to their families and to their communities to take a role in improving the quality of life where they live. For example, this could be achieved through active vigilance against crime and anti-social behaviour and through mutual help and voluntarism to those in their communities who need support. According to Blair and other leading communitarians in New Labour, the Labour Party had been for too long the party of liberal rights for all, without expecting and expressing the responsibilities individuals have as citizens.[86]

Many Labour MPs would perhaps still describe themselves as liberals not communitarians, but the debate is not as simplistic as the liberal social democrats versus communitarian social democrats because most people believe in liberal rights and in communitarian responsibilities.[87] It is in fact, not a conflicting dichotomous relationship but it can be a useful way to distinguish the social philosophy of individuals, political groups and political factions. Perhaps it is more accurate to say that many Labour MPs would regard themselves as more liberal than communitarian or even as 'liberal communitarians' or as 'communitarian liberals' rather than as exclusively labelling themselves as a liberal or as a communitarian.[88] One could suggest this is a false debate in setting up an irreconcilable social cleavage because no liberal would disregard the importance of community and no communitarian would disregard the importance of the individual. There may well be a grain of truth to such an evaluation, however, the discussion is about emphasis and it does represent a clear difference in social theory and this same divide on social and moral issues can be noted in the Labour Party.

Nevertheless, the centre of gravity surrounding the social thought of the Labour Party has returned to the communitarian standpoint. One could say that New Labour's re-emphasis on the value of community within social democracy is echoing R.H. Tawney's form of Christian socialism that sees other political values not as ends in themselves but as means of achieving a more ethical and fraternal society.[89] New Labour has not imported a new value in to its modernised social democracy, but rediscovered a traditional social democratic value that has not been given much attention since the Edwardian era.

9

CONCLUSION

The first half of the book attempted to chart the *intellectual* history of the Labour Party from its nineteenth century origins up until 2004 simultaneously situating New Labour within this *intellectual* history. The second half of the book sought to analyse the three traditional values of social democracy and examine what New Labour's interpretation of liberty, equality and community actually is, if it is anything at all. The purpose of the conclusion therefore, is to summarise the main findings of the book and specifically, to highlight the nature of New Labour's political philosophy.

In one sense the Gaitskellite revisionists can be understood as the grandparents of New Labour. In chapter 3 it was suggested that there are similarities in the premierships of Gaitskell and Blair. If the Gaitskellites and their revisionist right descendents of the 1970s are the founding generation of social democratic revisionism then the SDP are New Labour's parents. Policy prescriptions aside, the SDP of 1981 provided New Labour with an intellectual inheritance of markets, liberty, pro-europeanism and a scepticism for the inherent value of trade unions in the policy-making process. It is also worth noting the ambivalence of the SDP towards the principle of equality, this is also a fair criticism of New Labour and the Blairites in particular. The genealogy does not cohere neatly because New Labour is a product of people who remained inside the Labour Party unlike the Gang of Four. Also, New Labour is a more complex and broad political organisation with at least two competing tendencies vying for power and possibly different versions of social democracy. Furthermore, New Labour is a government and has had to face different issues that have affected their politics unlike the SDP. With these considerations in place one can see how New Labour is part of an intellectual history within the Labour Party that reaches back as far as the 'Great Debate' of the 1950s and 1960s and includes the formation of the break away SDP from the Labour Party in 1981.

Chapter 5 which focused on the recent *intellectual* history of New Labour also raised three research questions that I believe have been important in shaping the contemporary outlook of New Labour. The first question was: 'How far is the contrast between 'Old Labour' and New Labour a rhetorical one and how real is that distinction?' The second question was: 'What is your view of the influence of the New Democrats on New Labour?' The third question was: 'Was the 2002 Budget and the Comprehensive Spending Review (on which the investment in public services was contingent) a reversion to 'Old Labour' principles or not?'

I have argued, similarly to Taylor, Jacobs and Kinnock, that as a method of distinguishing different ideological groups in the Labour Party the Old Labour/New Labour distinction is an inaccurate formula. I have argued that there are historic distinctions in the Labour Party that are largely due to different accounts of political economy and different interpretations of social democratic values. I do not accept the view that the Old Labour/New Labour distinction is broadly accurate. I do not think 'Old Labour' is, or ever has been a single, coherent ideological grouping in the Labour Party and thus, the distinction is not accurate in terms of differentiating ideas and policy. I do think that the distinction is more about rhetoric and political tactics. I have argued that New Labour was attempting to demonstrate that they were not the 'Old right' or the 'Old left' or the 'New left' of the Labour Party but an ideologically moderate and significantly reformed social democratic party. In other words, the new right-wing of the Labour Party.

I have asserted, like all of the respondents bar Kinnock, that the New Democrats have in some way influenced New Labour particularly in terms of political tactics, presentation and rhetoric. In particular, I posit the view advocated by Jacobs, that the New Democrats taught New Labour how to use the media to get its message out and by introducing it to electioneering techniques such as 'triangulation', which enabled them to appear to be moderately left as well as right on issues at the same time. However, like Taylor, Jacobs, Kinnock and Radice, I have argued that the New Democrats influence on New Labour ideas and policy is at best negligible and at worst absent.

I have argued similarly to Taylor and Jacobs that the 2002 Budget and the Comprehensive Spending Review were not a reversion to 'Old Labour' principles but a change in emphasis for New Labour because I support the view which states that 'Old Labour' has never existed as a coherent ideological grouping in the Labour Party. However, I did suggest, as did Jacobs, that it demonstrates a change in emphasis and priority by New Labour. Like Taylor, I am persuaded that in some quarters of New Labour (notably the Brownites) high levels of public spending were expected after they had successfully demonstrated that Labour could competently manage the economy in its first two years.

The second half of the book sought to analyse the political values of liberty, equality and community with reference to New Right ideas, various social democratic perspectives and an evaluation of New Labour's philosophical interpretation of each of the respective values.

In chapter 6, I followed the argument of Gerald C. MacCallum which states that it is the term variables that are used which highlight the fundamental divide between rival conceptions of liberty and that claims about freedom should be considered as a triadic relation of the form X is free from Y to do Z. Also, it must be recognised that different political groupings disagree over what they understand to be the ranges of the X, Y, Z variables. In addition, I argued that the principle of positive liberty is continued by New

Labour in a similar mould as its traditional social democrat predecessors and that New Labour, like the Croslandite social democrats of the 1960s and 1970s, would adhere to the value of liberty expressed as a positive right to a set of political, social and economic entitlements. However, I noted that New Labour emphasise social reciprocity in exchange for certain state entitlements. I further argued that New Labour's tool for implementing its belief in the principle of positive liberty is the commitment to pervasive opportunity or 'opportunity for all' at various levels in the lives of individuals. The language of opportunity is New Labour's practical way of enunciating its conception of liberty; a liberty for individuals that crosses moral, political, social, and economic spheres ensuring, as far as possible, the widest choice of circumstances and options for every citizen.

In chapter 7, I claimed that Tawney, Crosland, Hattersley and New Labour have advocated the principle of equality not as an end in itself but as a means to greater individual freedom and at times as a means to securing a more communal society. I argued that social democrats in the Labour Party have always been committed to the priority conception of equality as well as holding a commitment to a generous sufficiency conception of equality and that only George Bernard Shaw, the Marxist Social Democratic Federation and the Labour Marxists of the 1920s and 1930s, ever claimed to hold a commitment to the strict egalitarian conception of equality in the Labour Party.
I have concluded that New Labour is quite vague about the principle of equality and its commitment to an absolute, a relative or what is sometimes referred to as a rising absolute level of measuring poverty is equally ambiguous. I followed Derek Parfit's terminological distinctions (but not all of his conclusions) concerning different commitments to equality: namely, the sufficiency conception of equality, the priority conception of equality, and the strict egalitarian conception of equality. I suggested that New Labour's conception of equality has two components. The first component is a

commitment to raising people up to a particular level whereby they have 'enough' to lead a satisfactory life: namely a generous sufficiency conception of equality. New Labour's *National Minimum Wage* is one example of the sufficiency conception of equality inasmuch as it regulates for labour to be paid at a sufficient minimum level. The second component to New Labour's conception of equality is a commitment to giving financial priority to the worst off members in British society: namely, the priority conception of equality. As Parfit stated that egalitarians could be separated by strict and non-strict commitments to equality, I proposed the strict and non-strict distinction for different types of prioritarians. Strict prioritarians, like Rawls want to give priority to the worst off groups in society no matter how well off they become in absolute terms. New Labour is a government that practices non-strict prioritarianism. They also want to give priority to the worst off groups in society but they believe that giving priority becomes less important the better off the worst off groups become. Examples of the non-strict priority conception of equality by New Labour are the Chancellor's *Pensioner Guarantee* and *Working Families Tax Credit* programmes to the poorest pensioners and poorest families with children. Furthermore, New Labour's version of equality contains an extra dimension. New Labour's version of equality includes investment in local communities and neighbourhoods. *The New Deal For Communities* is an appropriate example of a programme that decentralises power to communities and democratises decision-making as to how Government money should be spent.

In chapter 8, I argued that New Labour has rediscovered the traditional social democratic value of community and that it can be understood in part, by the Christian socialist principle of community as 'fellowship' and, in part, by the contemporary American communitarian movement. I follow Andrew Mason's argument that community is better understood as two distinct concepts: the 'ordinary concept' and the 'moralized concept'. The 'ordinary concept' is used by New Labour when they talk about local-level and regional-level community and when they suggest that decentralisation to the regions, including devolution, can enable groups of people with some shared goals and who are part of a specific geographic area within the nation, to determine the politics of their region to a greater extent. The 'moralized concept' is consistent with New Labour's communitarian citizenship which it advocates from the state-level. It wants all citizens to be motivated by their equal rights and responsibilities to each other. This implies a solidaristic ethic of reciprocity and mutual concern for others that is derived from the Christian socialist idea of community as 'fellowship'. Furthermore, I suggest that New Labour's belief in the value of community has been a commitment to community at the level of the state in the form of a communitarian conception of citizenship; at the regional-level in its interest in regional assemblies notably through John Prescott and with the establishment of the Regional Development Agencies; and at local-level where New Labour promotes its conception of community through its financially decentralist programme *The New Deal for Communities*. Also, I maintain that the issue of widening democracy is a feature of New Labour's communitarian framework and that a principled commitment to the decentralisation of power and in particular, to the policy of devolution exists in Blair's Government. Philosophically, I noted that the motivation behind decentralisation is that it intends to increase individual liberty by granting the individual citizen the right to vote or to protest against a wider range of issues on the regional level of government and collectively it enables groups of citizens with some shared goals and who are part of a specific geographic region within the nation, to determine the politics of their region in a way consistent with their shared goals. Finally, I argued that the centre of gravity surrounding the social thought of the Labour Party has returned to the communitarian standpoint after a generation of liberal influence.

To conclude, the central argument of the book it that New Labour is a revisionist social democratic government that believes in a positive as well as a negative conception of liberty, holds to non-strict prioritarian and generous sufficiency conceptions of equality, and advocates a belief in state-level, regional-level and local-level community in the form of a communitarian social philosophy. New Labour does not posses one, single cogent political philosophy. In places their philosophical commitments are ambiguous as with the principle of equality. Elsewhere they have reintroduced social democratic principles such as community and have placed their communitarian social philosophy at the front of the ideological battle with the neo-liberals who maintain their focus on individualism. Furthermore, it appears that New Labour is becoming more vulnerable to divergence from within as the circle of advisors and loyal politicians in the Blairite and Brownite camps dual over different policy proposals and emphases. Perhaps it is just a matter of time before a clear counter-philosophy appears to challenge New Labour from a different social democratic perspective. Until then New Labour remains the dominant revisionist social democratic force in British politics.

NOTES

Chapter 1

1. See, Marquand, David., 'The blair paradox', Prospect, May 1998, p.19 and Hattersley, Roy., 'It's no longer my party', Observer, Sunday 24th June 2001.
2. See, Freeden, Michael., 'The ideology of new labour', Political Quarterly, 1999, pp.48-50.
3. Between 1995-1996 New Labour attempted to define itself in terms of the idea of 'Stakeholding' and between 1998-2000 (although it is hard to find a clear cut off date) the Prime Minister suggested that his politics were 'Third Way' politics. It is arguable that from 2000-2004 no coherent description of New Labour's politics has been offered.
4. There are some book length studies of New Labour but they tend to focus on how New Labour emerged or an aspect of New Labour policy and are not studies of New Labour's political philosophy. These include Cronin, James., <u>New Labour's Pasts</u>, London, Pearson Longman, 2004, Finlayson, Alan., <u>The Making of New Labour</u>, London, Lawrence and Wishart, 2003, Mullard, Maurice., <u>New Labour, New Thinking</u>, Huntington, Nova Science Publishers, 2000, (Eds.), Ludlam, Steve., and Smith, Martin., <u>Governing as New Labour</u>, Basingstoke, Palgrave Macmillan, 2004. For a brief survey of New Labour's political thought see Beech, Matt., 'New labour' in (Eds.), Plant, Raymond., Beech, Matt., Hickson, Kevin., <u>The Struggle for Labour's Soul: Understanding Labour's Political Thought Since 1945</u>, London, Routledge, 2004.
5. Driver, Stephen., Martell, Luke., <u>New Labour: Politics After Thatcherism</u>, Cambridge, Polity Press, 1999.

Chapter 2

1. MacIntyre, Alasdair., 'A mistake in causality in social science' in Laslett, P., Runciman, W.G., (Eds.), <u>Philosophy, Politics and Society</u>, Oxford, Basil Blackwell, 1964, pp.48-70.
2. The issue of the 'free borough' concerns the universal right to vote for all working class men in specific boroughs such as Preston. However, after the Great Reform Act of 1832 this meant that male citizens in such boroughs without property were not permitted to vote. For these individuals the Great Reform Act of 1832 proved to be a democratic deficit.

3. Greenleaf, William., The British Political Tradition Volume II: The Ideological Heritage, London, Methuen, 1983, p.213.
4. Greenleaf: The British Political Tradition, p.213.
5. Greenleaf: The British Political Tradition, p.201.
6. Pelling, Henry., The Origins of The Labour Party 1880-1900, Oxford, Clarendon Press, 1965, p.2.
7. Pelling: The Origins of the Labour Party, p.3.
8. See, Beer, Samuel., Modern British Politics, London, Faber & Faber, 1969, pp.254-255.
9. For a further understanding of New Liberalism see, Carter, Matt., T.H. Green and the Development of Ethical Socialism, Exeter, Imprint Academic, 2003, Clarke, Peter., Liberals and Social Democrats, Cambridge, Cambridge University Press, 1978, Collini, Stefan., Liberalism and Sociology: L.T. Hobhouse and Political Argument in England 1880-1914, Cambridge, Cambridge University Press, 1979, Freeden, Michael., The New Liberalism: An Ideology of Social Reform, Oxford, Clarendon Press, 1978, and Searle, Geoffrey., The Liberal Party: Triumph and Disintegration 1886-1929, Basingstoke, Macmillan, 1992.
10. Vincent, Andrew., Plant, Raymond., Philosophy, Politics and Citizenship: The Life and Thought of the British Idealists, Oxford, Basil Blackwell, 1984, pp.43-44.
11. T.H. Green's most famous and influential work was the posthumously published Prolegomena to Ethics. See, Green, Thomas., Prolegomena to Ethics, Oxford, Clarendon Press, 1906.
12. Greenleaf: The British Political Tradition, p.155.
13. Masterman, Charles., (Ed.), The Heart of the Empire: Discussion of Problems of Modern City Life in England, London, T. Fisher Unwin, 1901.
14. Masterman, Charles., (Ed.), The Condition of England, London, Methuen, 1909.
15. Hobhouse, Leonard., Liberalism, London, Thornton Butterworth, 1911.
16. Greenleaf: The British Political Tradition, p.165.
17. Hobson, John., Imperialism: A Study, London, James Nisbet, 1902.
18. For more on the New Liberal principle of community responsibility see, Carter: T.H. Green and the Development of Ethical Socialism, pp.27-32.
19. Locke did believe in natural law, which he insisted was God given, and one would assume that Locke's belief in natural law would include an account of social morality and social responsibility. However, the Classical Liberals merely interpreted Locke's emphasis on personal morality and responsibility.

20. Marquand, David., The Progressive Dilemma, London, William Heinemann, 1992, p.16.
21. Marquand: The Progressive Dilemma, p.15.
22. For an informed history of the TUC see, Clegg, Hugh., et al, A History of British Trade Unionism since 1889, Vol.1, Oxford, Clarendon Press, 1964, Clegg, Hugh., A History of British Trade Unionism since 1889, vol.2, Oxford, Clarendon Press, 1985, Pelling, Henry., A History of British Trade Unionism, London, Macmillan, 1963, Roberts, Benjamin., The Trades Union Congress 1868-1921, London, Allen & Unwin, 1958.
23. Pelling: The Origins of The Labour Party, p.4.
24. Pelling: The Origins of The Labour Party, p.13.
25. To gain a fuller understanding of the conflicting socialist philosophies of the Eisenachers and the Lasallians see, Marx, Karl., Critique of the Gotha Programme, Peking, Foreign Languages, 1972.
26. Hook, Sidney., 'Introduction to Evolutionary Socialism' in Bernstein, Eduard., Evolutionary Socialism, New York, Shocken Books, 1961, p.11.
27. Pelling: The Origins of The Labour Party, p.60.
28. Further historical information on the Social Democratic Federation can be found in, Hyndman, Henry., The Record of an Adventurous Life, London, Macmillan, 1911.
29. Foote, Geoffrey., The Labour Party's Political Thought, London, Croom Helm, 1997, p.23.
30. Foote: The Labour Party's Political Thought, p.24.
31. Foote: The Labour Party's Political Thought, p.23.
32. Foote: The Labour Party's Political Thought, p.23.
33. Histories of the Fabian Society and Fabian socialism can be examined in, Cole, Margaret., The Story of Fabian Socialism, London, Heinemann, 1961, McBriar, Alan., Fabian Socialism and English Politics, Cambridge, Cambridge University Press, 1963, Pease, Edward., History of the Fabian Society, London, Fifield, 1916.
34. Foote: The Labour Party's Political Thought, p.30.
35. Foote: The Labour Party's Political Thought, p.32.
36. Pelling: The Origins of The Labour Party, pp.74-75.
37. Shaw, George., Fabian Essays in Socialism, London, Fabian Society, 1889.
38. Accounts of the ILP can be seen in biographies of Keir Hardie in chapters 4-5 of Morgan, Kenneth., Keir Hardie: Radical and Socialist, London, Weidenfield and Nicholson, 1975, in chapter 3 of MacLean, Iain., Keir Hardie, London, Allen Lane, 1975, in chapters 6-8 of Reid, Fred., Keir Hardie: The Making of a Socialist, London, Croom Helm, 1978, and in chapters 6-7 of

Moore, Roger., <u>The Emergence of the Labour Party 1880-1924</u>, London, Hodder and Stoughton, 1978.
39. In 1906, the Labour Representation Committee changed its name to the Labour Party.
40. Labour Party, <u>Programme for the Future</u>, London, 1918.
41. Drucker, Henry., <u>Doctrine and Ethos in the Labour Party</u>, London, Allen & Unwin, 1979, p.25.
42. Labour Party, <u>Programme for the Future</u>.
43. Labour Party, <u>Labour and the New Social Order</u>, London, 1918.
44. Labour Party, <u>Labour and the New Social Order</u>.
45. Bernstein: <u>Evolutionary Socialism</u>.
46. Bernstein: <u>Evolutionary Socialism</u>, pp. 6-7.
47. Bernstein: <u>Evolutionary Socialism</u>, p.7.
48. Bernstein: <u>Evolutionary Socialism</u>, p.145.
49. Hook: 'Introduction to evolutionary socialism', p.xiii.
50. Hook: 'Introduction to evolutionary socialism', p.xxix.
51. Hook: 'Introduction to evolutionary socialism', p.xxix.
52. Foote: <u>The Labour Party's Political Thought</u>, pp.105-106.
53. Cole, George., <u>The World of Labour: A Discussion of the Present and Future of Trade Unionism</u>, London, G.Bell & Son, 1928.
54. Foote: <u>The Labour Party's Political Thought</u>, p.107.
55. Foote: <u>The Labour Party's Political Thought</u>, p.107.
56. Cole, George., 'A short history of the British working-class movement, vol. III', in Haseler, Stephen., <u>The Gaitskellites</u>, London, Macmillan, 1969, p.1.
57. Crossman, Richard., 'Towards a new philosophy of socialism', in <u>Planning for Freedom: Essays in Socialism</u>, London, Hamish Hamilton, 1965, p.39.
58. Carter: <u>T.H. Green and the Development of Ethical Socialism</u>, pp.168-171.
59. Carter: <u>T.H. Green and the Development of Ethical Socialism</u>, p.168.
60. In fact Holland and Gore (to an extent), held orthodox Christian beliefs like Tawney and this inspired their political ideas which were ideas advocated by Green even though he did not share their commitment to the Christian faith. Green did share the view that humans were spiritual and should approach humanity in a spiritual as well as physical way, but he did not advocate the centrality of faith in Jesus Christ as Saviour and Lord and thus did not accept Christ's necessity as mediator between humanity and the Creator God. See, Carter: <u>T.H. Green and the Development of Ethical Socialism</u>, pp.107-122.
61. Carter: <u>T.H. Green and the Development of Ethical Socialism</u>, p.171.

62. Carter: T.H. Green and the Development of Ethical Socialism, p.183.
63. Carter: T.H. Green and the Development of Ethical Socialism, p.183.
64. Tawney, Richard., The Acquisitive Society, London, G. Bell & Son, 1921.
65. Foote: The Labour Party's Political Thought, p.74.
66. Tawney: The Acquisitive Society, pp.80-87.
67. Tawney: The Acquisitive Society, p.32.
68. Foote: The Labour Party's Political Thought, p.74.
69. Winter, Jay., Joslin, David., (Eds.), R.H. Tawney's Commonplace Book, Cambridge, Cambridge University Press, 1972, p.67.
70. Strachey, John., The Coming Struggle for Power, London, The Modern Library, 1932.
71. Strachey, John., The Menace of Fascism, London, The American League Against War and Fascism, 1933.
72. Strachey, John., The Nature of Capitalist Crisis, London, Victor Gollancz, 1935.
73. Thomas, Hugh., John Strachey, London, Eyre Methuen, 1973, p.131.
74. Thomas: John Strachey, p.131.
75. Strachey: The Coming Struggle for Power, p.245.
76. Thomas: John Strachey, p.129.
77. Thomas: John Strachey, p.138.
78. Foote: The Labour Party's Political Thought, p.205.
79. Foote: The Labour Party's Political Thought, p.150.
80. Laski, Harold., A Grammar of Politics, London, Allen & Unwin, 1925.
81. Laski, Harold., The State in Theory and Practice, London, Allen & Unwin, 1935.
82. Laski: The State in Theory and Politics, p.331.
83. Crossman: 'Towards a new philosophy of socialism', p.39.
84. Keynes, John, Maynard., The General Theory of Employment, Interest and Money, London, Macmillan, 1936.
85. Skidelsky, Robert., John Maynard Keynes: Fighting For Britain 1937-1946, Basingstoke, Macmillan, 2000, p.19.
86. Foote: The Labour Party's Political Thought, p.140.
87. Foote: The Labour Party's Political Thought, p.162.
88. Durbin, Elizabeth., New Jerusalems: The Labour Party and the Economics of Democratic Socialism, London, Routledge & Keegan Paul, 1985, pp.81-82.
89. White Paper on Unemployment, London, HMSO, 1944.
90. White Paper on Unemployment, London, HMSO, 1944.

91. Marquand, David., 'Moralists and hedonists' in, Marquand, D., Seldon, A., (Eds.), <u>The Ideas That Shaped Post-War Britain</u>, London, Fontana, 1996, p.7.
92. Marquand: 'Moralists and hedonists' p.7.
93. Przeworski, Adam., <u>Capitalism and Social Democracy</u>, Cambridge, Cambridge University Press, 1985, p.207.
94. Przeworski: <u>Capitalism and Social Democracy,</u> p.209.
95. For a detailed study see, Gamble, Andrew., Walkland, Stuart., <u>The British Party System and Economic Policy 1945-1983</u>, Oxford, Clarendon, 1984.

Chapter 3

1. See Haseler, Stephen., <u>The Gaitskellites</u>, London, Macmillan, 1969, p.2.
2. Drucker, Henry., <u>Doctrine and Ethos in the Labour Party</u>, London, George Allen & Unwin, 1979, p.1.
3. Crossman, Richard., 'Towards a new philosophy of socialism', in <u>Planning for Freedom</u>, London, Hamish Hamilton, 1965, p.36.
4. The year 1995 witnessed Tony Blair succeeding where Hugh Gaitskell had previously failed, to lead a campaign to redraft Clause IV. Clause IV was the Party's commitment to the common ownership of the means of production and in policy-making circles that meant nationalisation. By redrafting this part of the Constitution Blair released the Party from the theological grip that state ownership had upon the psyche of the Labour Party. Members on a ballot of 63% to 37% changed the Party's commitment to a fundamental tenet of post World War One democratic socialism.
5. Brivati, Brian., <u>Hugh Gaitskell</u>, London, Richard Cohen Books, 1997, pp.180-181.
6. The analysis is based not entirely on the Bevanite left and Gaitskellite right, as this is believed to be partly problematic as different MPs moved into different camps on particular issues. However, one accepts that the Labour Party is a broad church and houses people on different political wings. This section of the chapter distinguishes merely three positions of which the author has neither the time nor the empirical evidence to thoroughly evaluate. For more on the ideological groupings in the Labour Party after 1945 see 'Introduction' in Plant, Raymond, Beech, Matt and Hickson, Kevin, <u>The Struggle for Labour's Soul</u>, pp.1-4.
7. See Brivati: <u>Hugh Gaitskell</u>, p.184.

8. Haseler: The Gaitskellites, p.9.
9. Brivati: Hugh Gaitskell, pp.173-174.
10. As a point of information, the author uses the terms 'Bevanites', those on the 'ends' side of the Great Debate and the 'left-wing' interchangeably. As it is understood that the left-wing in the 1950s and early 1960s were followers of Aneurin Bevan and philosophically traditional socialists arguing that the Party's commitment to nationalisation laid down in Clause IV of the Constitution was a socialist end in itself and not merely a means to achieve socialist ends.
11. The term 'Gaitskellites', is used synonymously with the phrase those on the 'means' side of the Great Debate and the term 'revisionists'.
12. Bevan, Aneurin., In Place of Fear, London, William Heinemann, 1952.
13. Brivati: Hugh Gaitskell, p.166.
14. Crossman: 'Towards a new philosophy of socialism'.
15. Crossman: 'Towards a new philosophy of socialism', p.57.
16. Crossman, Richard., 'Planning for freedom', in Planning for Freedom: Essays in Socialism, pp.59-85.
17. Crossman, Richard., 'The affluent society', in Planning for Freedom: Essays in Socialism, pp.86-112.
18. As a point of information, the Gaitskellites were on the right-wing of the Labour Party but not all right-wing MPs were revisionists. See chapter 1, Crosland, Anthony., The Conservative Enemy, London, Jonathan Cape, 1963
19. Crosland, Anthony., Socialism Now and Other Essays, London, Jonathan Cape, 1974.
20. Crosland: Socialism Now and Other Essays, p.15.
21. Interview with the BBC's General Election Round-up 9th October 1959.
22. Williams, Phillip., Hugh Gaitskell: A Political Biography, London, Jonathan Cape, 1979, p.546.
23. Crosland: Socialism Now and Others Essays, p.17.
24. Crosland, Anthony., The Future of Socialism, London, Jonathan Cape, 1956, p.56.
25. Crosland: The Future of Socialism, p.57.
26. Crosland: The Future of Socialism.
27. Crosland: The Future of Socialism, p.59.
28. Crosland, Anthony., The Conservative Enemy, London, Jonathan Cape, 1962.
29. Foote, Geoffrey., The Labour Party's Political Thought, London, Croom Helm, 1997, p.212.
30. Crosland: The Future of Socialism.
31. Crosland: Socialism Now and Other Essays, p.15.

32. Crosland: <u>Socialism Now and Other Essays</u>, p.18.
33. Crosland: <u>Socialism Now and Other Essays</u>, p.44.
34. Crosland: <u>Socialism Now and Other Essays</u>, p.45.
35. Williams: <u>Hugh Gaitskell</u>, pp.546-549.
36. The informal name given to Gaitskell's revised version of Clause IV.
37. Williams: <u>Hugh Gaitskell</u>, p.570.
38. Williams: <u>Hugh Gaitskell</u>, p.572.
39. Williams: <u>Hugh Gaitskell</u>, p.574.
40. Hall, Stuart., <u>Breakthrough</u>, London, Combined Universities CND, 1958.
41. Foote: <u>The Labour Party's Political Thought</u>, p.286.
42. See, Healey, Denis., <u>The Time of My Life</u>, London, Penguin, 1990, pp.234-248.
43. Skidelsky, Robert., <u>John Maynard Keynes: Fighting For Britain 1937-1946</u>, p.499.
44. Skidelsky: <u>John Maynard Keynes</u>.
45. Skidelsky: <u>John Maynard Keynes</u>, p.500.
46. Skidelsky: <u>John Maynard Keynes</u>, p.500.
47. Skidelsky: <u>John Maynard Keynes</u>, p.503.
48. Skidelsky: <u>John Maynard Keynes</u>, p.503.
49. Skidelsky: <u>John Maynard Keynes</u>, p.503.
50. Skidelsky: <u>John Maynard Keynes</u>, p.504.
51. Skidelsky: <u>John Maynard Keynes</u>, p.504.
52. Skidelsky: <u>John Maynard Keynes</u>, p.504.
53. Skidelsky: <u>John Maynard Keynes</u>, p.504.
54. Gamble, Andrew., <u>The Free Economy and the Strong State: The Politics of Thatcherism</u>, Basingstoke, Macmillan, 1988, p.3.
55. Gamble: <u>The Free Economy and the Strong State</u>, p.4.
56. Gamble: <u>The Free Economy and the Strong State</u>, p.19.
57. A discussion of the political philosophy of the New Right is provided in the first section of chapters 6-8 on the respective issues of liberty, equality and community.
58. However, it should be noted that during Thatcher's first term her Cabinet also contained several prominent one-nation conservatives or 'wets' as she termed them, and the first privatisation initiative did not begin until after the 1983 General Election. Therefore, the 1979 General Election was an election of a New Right Conservative Government but only up to a point.
59. Gamble: <u>The Free Economy and the Strong State</u>, p.28.
60. Hoover, Kenneth., Plant, Raymond., <u>Conservative Capitalism in Britain and the United States: A Critical Appraisal</u>, London, Routledge, 1989.
61. Hoover and Plant: <u>Conservative Capitalism and the United States</u>, p.76.

62. For this type of analysis see, Gamble: <u>The Free Economy and the Strong State</u>, pp.27-60 and Hoover and Plant: <u>Conservative Capitalism in Britain and the United States</u>, pp.76-90.
63. Plant, Raymond., 'Social democracy', in Marquand, David., Seldon, Anthony., (Eds.), <u>The Ideas That Shaped Post-War Britain</u>, p.176.
64. Plant: 'Social democracy', p.177.
65. Plant: 'Social democracy', p.177.
66. Plant: 'Social democracy', p.178.
67. Plant: 'Social democracy', p.179.
68. Plant: 'Social democracy', pp.181-182.

Chapter 4

1. For a fuller understanding of the works of these New left writers see, Hall, Stuart., <u>Breakthrough</u>, London, Universities CND, 1958, and <u>NATO and the Alliance</u>, London, CND, 1961, Williams, Raymond., <u>Culture and Society</u>, London, Chatto & Windus, 1958, and <u>The Long Revolution</u>, London, Chatto & Windus, 1961.
2. Thompson, Edward., (Ed.), <u>Out of Apathy</u>, London, Stevens & Sons, 1960, and <u>The Making of the English Working Class</u>, London, Gollancz, 1963.
3. This dissident communist thought was triggered by some British Communist Party members' disillusionment and disgust at the authoritarianism of Soviet Communism, particularly in light of the crushing of the 1956 Hungarian Revolution.
4. From 1960-1962 Thompson, Hall and Williams sat on the editorial board of the <u>New Left Review</u> but between 1962-1963 the editorial board was replaced (an event still shrouded in some mystery), and a new board was led by Perry Anderson. See, Foote, Geoffrey., <u>The Labour Party's Political Thought</u>, Basingstoke, Macmillan, 1997, pp.280-293.
5. Holland, Stuart., <u>The Socialist Challenge</u>, London, Quartet Books, 1973.
6. Kogan, David., Kogan, Maurice., <u>The Battle for the Labour Party</u>, Glasgow, Fontana Paperbacks, 1982, p.11.
7. Kogan and Kogan: <u>The Battle for the Labour Party</u>, p.11.
8. Benn, Tony., <u>Arguments for Socialism</u>, London, Jonathan Cape, 1979.
9. Benn, Tony., <u>Arguments for Democracy</u>, London, Jonathan Cape, 1981.
10. Foote: <u>The Labour Party's Political Thought</u>, pp.307-308.
11. Holland: <u>The Socialist Challenge</u>, p.9.
12. Holland: <u>The Socialist Challenge</u>, p.15.

13. For more on Holland's policy suggestions see Holland: The Socialist Challenge, pp.142-176.
14. Benn: Arguments for Democracy, pp.xi-xii.
15. Therefore, Benn does suggest that he desires greater economic and social equality for British citizens and he wants to empower citizens to participate in civic life more fully but he also desires radical democratisation of British institutions. However, there is confusion over his 'end goals' for socialism. Does he desire the radical democratisation of British institutions and civic life as an end in itself or as a means for greater equality and fuller citizenship? The chapter contends that Benn's arguments do not make this distinction clear and therefore, his brand of socialism is not thoroughly conceptualised.
16. Kogan and Kogan: The Battle for the Labour Party, p.14.
17. Kogan and Kogan: The Battle for the Labour Party, p.11.
18. The Old left and the New left positions are different in approach but less different in ends.
19. Kogan and Kogan: The Battle for the Labour Party, p.12.
20. The Bennite left's policy prescriptions were most famously outlined in a collection of Tony Benn's speeches and articles, see, Benn: Arguments for Socialism.
21. Shaw, Eric., Discipline and Discord in the Labour Party, Manchester, Manchester University Press, 1988, p.207.
22. For a thorough examination of the history of the SDP see, Crewe, Ivor., King, Anthony., SDP: The Birth, Life and Death of the Social Democratic Party, Oxford, Oxford University Press, 1996.
23. For the New left critique of Crosland's revisionist thesis see, Holland: The Socialist Challenge, however, there has been no single work produced by a neo-liberal thinker specifically concerned with critiquing Crosland's brand of social democracy.
24. Crick, Bernard., Socialist Values and Time, London, Fabian Society, Tract 495, 1984.
25. Kogan and Kogan: The Battle for the Labour Party, p.69.
26. Owen, David., Face The Future, Oxford, Oxford University Press, 1981.
27. Owen: Face the Future, p.19.
28. Owen: Face the Future, p.27.
29. Owen: Face the Future, pp.3-4.
30. Owen: Face the Future, p.4.
31. Tawney, Richard., Equality, London, G, Bell & Son, 1931.
32. Therefore his desire for greater equality was related to other principles such as community and liberty and a specific account of Christian morality. It is claimed in chapter 7 that Tawney did not advocate equality as an end in itself.

33. Owen: Face The Future, p.4.
34. Owen: Face the Future, p.1.
35. Owen: Face the Future.
36. The Rank and File Mobilising Committee was formed in 1980 by the merger of the Militant Tendency and the Socialist Campaign for Labour Victory.
37. Kogan and Kogan: The Battle for the Labour Party, pp.15-16.
38. Healey, Denis., The Time of My Life, London, Penguin, 1989, p.473.
39. Healey: The Time of My Life, p.474.
40. Healey: The Time of My Life, p.474.
41. Healey: The Time of My Life, p.480.
42. I take David Owen's book, Face the Future, as the main statement of the SDP's political ideas.
43. Healey: The Time of My Life, p.480.
44. Jefferys, Kevin., The Labour Party Since 1945, Basingstoke, Macmillan, 1993, p.110.
45. Kogan and Kogan: The Battle for the Labour Party, p.106.
46. Jefferys: The Labour Party Since 1945, p.109.
47. Mitchell, Austin., Four Years In The Death Of The Labour Party, London, Methuen, 1983, p.27.
48. Mitchell: Four Years In The Death of The Labour Party, pp.26-28.
49. As a point of information several other notable academics and politicians contributed to the debate about social democratic ideas and values during this period and their work could also have been discussed if space allowed. See Estrin, Saul., Le Grand, Julian., (Eds.), Market Socialism, Oxford, Clarendon Press, 1989, Radice, Giles., Labour's Path To Power, London, Macmillan, 1989 and Mitchell, Austin., Competitive Socialism, London, Unwin Hyman, 1989.
50. In my opinion these five individuals significantly influenced the revitalisation of social democracy in the Labour Party in the post-1983 period. Time and space dictates that a study cannot examine the work of every economist, philosopher and politician who commented on the Labour Party's need to rediscover its social democratic approach.
51. Foote: The Labour Party's Political Thought, p.324.
52. Nove, Alexander., The Economics of Feasible Socialism, London, Allen & Unwin, 1983.
53. Foote: The Labour Party's Political Thought, p.325.
54. Nove: The Economics of Feasible Socialism, p.101.
55. Plant, Raymond., Equality, Markets and the State, Fabian Tract 494, London, Fabian Society, 1984, p.13.
56. Plant: Equality, Markets and the State, pp.2-5.

57. Plant: <u>Equality, Markets and the State</u>, pp.6-10.
58. Plant: <u>Equality, Markets and the State</u>, p.13.
59. Plant: <u>Equality, Markets and the State</u>, pp.14-16.
60. Plant: <u>Equality, Markets and the State</u>, pp.24-28. Rawls's view of equality and especially his ideas concerning what inequalities are justified and why they are legitimately justified are more fully discussed in chapter 7 of the book.
61. Plant, Raymond., <u>Citizenship, Rights and Socialism</u>, London, Fabian Society, Tract 531.
62. Plant: <u>Citizenship, Rights and Socialism</u>, p.1.
63. Plant: <u>Citizenship, Rights and Socialism</u>, pp.14-15.
64. Plant: <u>Citizenship, Rights and Socialism</u>, pp.1-3.
65. Plant: <u>Citizenship, Rights and Socialism</u>, pp.16-20.
66. Plant: <u>Citizenship, Rights and Socialism</u>, p.10.
67. Plant: <u>Citizenship, Rights and Socialism</u>, p.19.
68. Crick: <u>Socialist Values and Time</u>, p.1.
69. Crick: <u>Socialist Values and Time</u>, p.13.
70. Crick: <u>Socialist Values and Time</u>, p.13.
71. Crick: <u>Socialist Values and Time</u>, p.21.
72. Crick: <u>Socialist Values and Time</u>, p.16.
73. Crick: <u>Socialist Values and Time</u>, p.14.
74. Crick: <u>Socialist Values and Time</u>, p.23.
75. Hattersley, Roy., <u>Choose Freedom</u>, London, Michael Joseph, 1987.
76. Hattersley: <u>Choose Freedom</u>, p.6.
77. Hattersley: <u>Choose Freedom</u>, pp.24-25.
78. Hattersley: <u>Choose Freedom</u>, pp.14-15.
79. Hattersley: <u>Choose Freedom</u>, pp.16-17.
80. Hattersley: <u>Choose Freedom</u>, pp.17-18.
81. Hattersley: <u>Choose Freedom</u>, p.21.
82. Hattersley: <u>Choose Freedom</u>, p.150.
83. Hattersley: <u>Choose Freedom</u>, p.189.
84. Hattersley: <u>Choose Freedom</u>, p.190.
85. Hattersley: <u>Choose Freedom</u>, p.254.
86. Foote: <u>The Labour Party's Political Thought</u>, p.332.
87. Gould, Bryan., <u>Socialism and Freedom</u>, Basingstoke, Macmillan, 1985.
88. Gould: <u>Socialism and Freedom</u>, p.21.
89. Gould: <u>Socialism and Freedom</u>, p.56.
90. Gould, Bryan., <u>A Future For Socialism</u>, London, Jonathan Cape, 1989.
91. All statistics are taken from, Butler, David., Kavanagh, Dennis., <u>The British General Election of 1992</u>, Basingstoke, Macmillan, 1992, pp.284-285.

92. Butler and Kavanagh: <u>The British General Election of 1992</u>, pp.284-285.
93. Labour Party, <u>Aims and Values</u>, London, Labour Party, 1992.
94. Hughes, Colin., Wintour, Patrick., <u>Labour Rebuilt: The New Model Party</u>, London, Fourth Estate, 1990, p.70.
95. Hughes and Wintour: <u>Labour Rebuilt: The New Model Party</u>, p.71.
96. Hughes and Wintour: <u>Labour Rebuilt: The New Model Party</u>, pp.74-75.
97. Crick, Bernard., Blunkett, David., <u>The Labour Party's Aims and Values: An Unofficial Statement</u>, London, Spokesman Pamphlet No.87, 1988.
98. Hughes and Wintour: <u>Labour Rebuilt: The New Model Party</u>, p.65.
99. Butler and Kavanagh., <u>The British General Election of 1992</u>, p.61.
100. Driver, Stephen., Martell, Luke., <u>New Labour: Politics After Thatcherism</u>, Cambridge, Polity Press, 1998, p.15.
101. Marquand, David., <u>The Unprincipled Society</u>, London, Fontana Press, 1988.
102. Marquand: <u>The Unprincipled Society</u>, pp.63-88.
103. Marquand: <u>The Unprincipled Society</u>, p.213.
104. Marquand: <u>The Unprincipled Society</u>, pp.209-247.
105. Marquand: <u>The Unprincipled Society</u>, p.221.
106. Butler and Kavanagh: <u>The British General Election of 1992</u>, pp.284-285.
107. Butler and Kavanagh: <u>The British General Election of 1992</u>,Ibid. p.247.
108. The Commission on Social Justice, <u>Social Justice: Strategies for National Renewal</u>, London, Vintage, 1994, p.ix.
109. The Commission on Social Justice, <u>Social Justice: Strategies for National Renewal</u>, p.1.
110. The Commission on Social Justice, <u>Social Justice: Strategies for National Renewal</u>, p.398.
111. Labour Party, <u>1997 Labour Party Election Manifesto</u>, London, Labour Party, 1997, p.9.
112. Labour Party, <u>1997 Labour Party Election Manifesto</u>, pp.20, 25, 28.
113. Labour Party, <u>1997 Labour Party Election Manifesto</u>, pp.12-13.
114. Labour Party, <u>1997 Labour Party Election Manifesto</u>, pp.13-14.
115. Labour Party, <u>1997 Labour Party Election Manifesto</u>, pp.29-30.
116. Various accounts of the Blair-Brown leadership decision are discussed in Rentoul, John., <u>Tony Blair</u>, London, Warner Books, 1995, pp.349-375, Pym, Hugh., Kochan, Nick., Gordon Brown: <u>The First Year in Power</u>, London, Bloomsbury, 1998, p.2, and

MacIntyre, Donald., <u>Mandelson and the Making of New Labour</u>, London, Harper Collins, 1999, pp.305-306.

Chapter 5

1. Ludlam, Steve., 'The making of new labour', in Ludlam, Steve., Smith, Martin., (Eds.), <u>New Labour in Government</u>, Basingstoke, Macmillan, 2001, p.29.
2. Gould, Phillip., <u>The Unfinished Revolution</u>, London, Abacus, 1998, p. 219.
3. Gould: <u>The Unfinished Revolution</u>, p.219.
4. Gould: <u>The Unfinished Revolution</u>, p.219.
5. The new ideas and approaches are solely the inspiration of party modernisers and not based around a nation-wide Labour Party consensus. Although one could view the 1995 vote on the redrafting of Clause Four as the national Labour Party expressing its will democratically.
6. Mandelson, Peter., Liddle, Roger., <u>The Blair Revolution</u>, London, Faber and Faber, 1996, p. vii.
7. Mandelson and Liddle: <u>The Blair Revolution</u>, p.4.
8. These political values are the focus of chapters 6-8 of the book.
9. Smith, Martin., 'The complexity of new labour', in Ludlam., Smith., (Eds.), <u>New Labour in Government</u>, p.265.
10. Interview with Matthew Taylor, September 2002 at the IPPR.
11. Interview with Anthony Giddens, September 2002 at the LSE.
12. Interview with Michael Jacobs, November 2002 at the Fabian Society.
13. Interview with David Marquand, November 2002 in Oxford.
14. Interview with Neil Kinnock, December 2002 at the European Commission.
15. Interview with Giles Radice, February 2003 at the House of Lords.
16. Interview with Roy Hattersley, March 2003 at the House of Commons.
17. Matthew Taylor's interpretation of ideological groupings in the Labour Party is stated earlier in the chapter.
18. In chapters 3-4 I posited the following ideological distinctions in Labour Party thought in the post-war era: the 'Old left' or Bevanite left, the 'New left' or Bennite left, the 'Old right' or Gaitskellite/Croslandite social democratic right and I interpret the 'New right' of the Labour Party as being New Labour. For more on this see the introduction to (Eds.), Plant, Raymond, Beech, Matt, Hickson, Kevin, <u>The Struggle for Labour's Soul</u>, London, Routledge, 2004, pp.1-4.

19. Driver, Stephen., Martell, Luke., <u>New Labour: Politics After Thatcherism</u>, Cambridge, Polity Press, 1998, p.24.
20. Interview with Matthew Taylor, September 2002 at the IPPR.
21. Interview with Anthony Giddens, September 2002 at the LSE.
22. Gould: <u>The Unfinished Revolution</u>, p.236.
23. Gould: <u>The Unfinished Revolution</u>, p.237.
24. Interview with Michael Jacobs, November 2002 at the Fabian Society.
25. Interview with David Marquand, November 2002 in Oxford.
26. Interview with Neil Kinnock, December 2002 at the European Commission.
27. Interview with Giles Radice, February 2003 at the House of Lords.
28. Interview with Roy Hattersley, March 2003 at the House of Commons.
29. Gould: <u>The Unfinished Revolution</u>, p.216.
30. Gould: <u>The Unfinished Revolution</u>, p.221.
31. MacIntyre, Donald., <u>Mandelson and New Labour</u>, London, Harper Collins, 1999, p.315.
32. MacIntyre: <u>Mandelson and New Labour</u>, p.315.
33. Mandelson and Liddle: <u>The Blair Revolution</u>, p.52.
34. MacIntyre: <u>Mandelson and New Labour</u>, pp.317-318.
35. Mandelson and Liddle: <u>The Blair Revolution</u>, pp.53-54.
36. Labour Party, <u>Clause 4.4 of the Constitution</u>, London, Labour Party, 1995.
37. Smith: 'The complexity of new labour', p.264.
38. See, Hirst, Paul., Thompson, Grahame., <u>Globalization in Question</u>, Cambridge, Polity Press, 1996.
39. Giddens, Anthony., <u>The Third Way: The Renewal of Social Democracy</u>, Cambridge, Polity Press, 1998, p.30.
40. Giddens: <u>The Third Way: The Renewal of Social Democracy</u>, p.30.
41. Blair, Tony., <u>New Britain: My Vision of a Young Country</u>, London, Fourth Estate, 1996.
42. Blair: <u>New Britain: My Vision of a Young Country</u>, p.118.
43. Giddens: <u>The Third Way: The Renewal of Social Democracy</u>, p.31.
44. Giddens: <u>The Third Way: The Renewal of Social Democracy</u>, p.31.
45. Giddens: <u>The Third Way: The Renewal of Social Democracy</u>, p.31.
46. Labour Party, <u>1997 Labour Party Election Manifesto</u>, London, Labour Party, 1997, p.1.
47. Labour Party, <u>1997 Labour Party Election Manifesto</u>, p.1.

48. For a classic example of the 'means and ends debate' in social democracy see, Bernstein, Eduard., <u>Evolutionary Socialism</u>, New York, Schocken Books, 1961, pp.200-224.
49. Labour Party, <u>1997 Labour Party Election Manifesto</u>, p.1.
50. Labour Party, <u>1997 Labour Party Election Manifesto</u>, p.1.
51. Discussions of the Keynesian era and its policies, including its zenith and its nadir were outlined in chapters 2-3.
52. Mandelson and Liddle: <u>The Blair Revolution</u>, pp.12-13.
53. Giddens: <u>The Third Way: The Renewal of Social Democracy</u>, p.viii.
54. Blair, Tony., <u>The Third Way: New Politics for the New Century</u>, London, Fabian Society, Fabian Tract 588, 1998, p.1.
55. For a view which asserts the ambiguity of the concept of the 'Third Way' see Faux, Jeff., 'Lost on the third way' in <u>Dissent</u>, 46/2, (Spring 1999), pp.67-76 and Hall, Stuart., 'The great moving nowhere show' in <u>Marxism Today</u>, (November/December 1998), pp.9-14. For a view which argues that the Third Way is a reformed New Liberalism see, Ryan, Alan., 'Britain: recycling the third way', in <u>Dissent</u>, 46/2 (Spring 1999), pp.77-80. For a view which argues that the term 'Third Way' is inaccurate but that New Labour does hold to a variety of philosophical commitments see, Freeden, Michael., 'The ideology of new labour', in, <u>The Political Quarterly</u>, 69, Oxford, Blackwell, 1998, pp.42-51 and for a view which asserts that the Third Way is a political approach different from both neo-liberalism and traditional social democracy but still holds some but not all of the principles of tradional social democracy see, Plant, Raymond., <u>New Labour – A Third Way?</u>, London, European Policy Forum, 1998. For an argument advocating the legitimacy of the term and the merits of the Third Way see, Giddens: <u>The Third Way: The Renewal of Social Democracy</u>, Giddens, Anthony., <u>The Third Way and Its Critics</u>, Cambridge, Polity Press, 2000 and Giddens, Anthony., <u>Where Now for New Labour?</u>, Cambridge, Polity Press, 2002.
56. See, Blair, Tony., Schroder, Gerhard., <u>Europe: The Third Way - die Neue Mitte</u>, London, Labour Party, SPD, 1999 a statement of Third Way principles by the two leaders, and the public dialogue by Blair, Tony., Clinton, Bill., Schroder, Gerhard., Kok, Wim., D'Alema, Massimo., <u>The Third Way: Progressive governance for the 21st century</u>, The White House, Washington D.C, 25th April 1999.
57. Blair: <u>The Third Way: New Politics for the New Century</u>, p.1.
58. Blair: <u>The Third Way: New Politics for the New Century</u>, p.1.
59. However, as there is no contemporary survey of the political beliefs of the current Parliamentary Labour Party this is

speculation and not fact. For a defence of the ideas behind The Third Way see, Giddens: <u>The Third Way: The Renewal of Social Democracy</u> and Giddens; <u>The Third Way and its Critics</u>.
60. Labour Party, <u>2001 Labour Party Election Manifesto</u>, London, Labour Party, 2001, p.2.
61. It should be noted, that an aspect of the historiography of New Labour has been their determination to be viewed as competent economic managers. This is partly to dismiss the claim that Labour Governments cannot be trusted to run the economy and is an unfair reference to the difficulties experienced by the Wilson and Callaghan Governments and partly as an aspiration to demonstrate, that New Labour could be trusted as competent economic managers compared with the Conservatives under Major who had presided over the 1992 ERM crisis. See Mandelson and Liddle: <u>The Blair Revolution</u>, pp.74-81.
62. Labour Party, <u>2001 Labour Party Election Manifesto</u>, London, Labour Party, 2001, p.2.
63. Interview with Matthew Taylor, September 2002 at the IPPR.
64. Interview with Anthony Giddens, September 2002 at the LSE.
65. Telephone conversation with Michael Jacobs, March 2003.
66. Interview with David Marquand, November 2002 in Oxford.
67. Interview with Neil Kinnock, December 2002 at the European Commission.
68. Interview with Giles Radice, February 2003 at the House of Lords.
69. Interview with Roy Hattersley, March 2003 at the House of Commons.
70. Labour Party, <u>2001 Labour Party Election Manifesto</u>, p.3.
71. Labour Party, <u>2001 Labour Party Election Manifesto</u>, pp.2-3.
72. Blair, Tony., <u>Speech to Annual Conference of the Labour Party 2004</u>, London, 2004.
73. Crosland, Anthony., <u>The Future of Socialism</u>, London, Jonathan Cape, 1956.
74. See, Blair, Tony., <u>New Britain, My Vision of a Young Country</u>, pp.98-129.
75. These factors have been discussed at length in chapter 3 and therefore do not need repeating here.
76. Due to their tenure in office as New Labour ministers, I still regard to an extent Clare Short and Robin Cook as New Labour politicians even after their resignations over the recent war with Iraq and subsequent criticisms of the Blair Government.
77. Roy Hattersley raised this point in our interview in March 2003 at the House of Commons.
78. See, Ludlum: 'The making of new labour', p.28.

79. See, Hattersley, Roy., 'It's no longer my party', Observer, Sunday 24th June 2001.
80. Holland, Stuart., The Socialist Challenge, London, Quartet Books, 1973.

Chapter 6

1. I shall use the term liberty interchangeably with the term freedom.
2. I refer to the 'New Right' as a being a political and economic philosophy associated with conservative parties (particularly in Britain and the United States), but on the right-wing of conservative ideology. The term 'neo-liberal' is often used interchangeably with the term 'New Right' but can also hold subtle differences such as different social attitudes. I will also use the term 'New Right' to refer to the political and economic ideas of the Conservative Governments under the leadership of Thatcher and Major. Thatcher notes her principles in her autobiography as freedom, free markets, limited government and strong national defence. See, Thatcher, Margaret., The Downing Street Years, London, Harper Collins, 1993, p.15. For a good discussion of the ideological meanings behind the term 'New Right' see, Green, David., The New Right, London, Harvester Wheatsheaf, 1987 and Gamble, Andrew, The Free Economy and the Strong State, Basingstoke, Macmillan, 1988. For a taxonomy of political factions of MPs in the Conservative Party see, Norton Phillip., 'Electing the leader: the conservative party leadership contest 1997', Politics Review, April, 1998.
3. Bosanquet, Nicholas., After the New Right, London, Heineman, 1983, p.92.
4. Hayek, Friedrich., The Constitution of Liberty, London, Routledge and Kegan Paul, 1960, p.12.
5. For other negative libertarian accounts see Steiner, Hillel., 'Individual liberty', in Proceedings of the Aristotelian Society, London, 1974 and Berlin, Isaiah., Four Essays on Liberty, Oxford, Clarendon Press, 1969.
6. For more on this philosophical commitment to a negative conception of liberty see, Hayek: The Constitution of Liberty, ch.1.
7. Green: The New Right, p.113.
8. Green: The New Right, p.125.
9. Green: The New Right, p.129.
10. Brittan, Samuel., The Role and Limits of Government, London, Temple Smith, 1983, pp.74-75.
11. Brittan: The Role and Limits of Government, p.76.

12. Thatcher: <u>The Downing Street Years</u>, p.7.
13. Thatcher: <u>The Downing Street Years</u>, p.7.
14. Thatcher: <u>The Downing Street Years</u>, p.13
15. See, Joseph, Keith., Sumption, Jonathan., <u>Equality</u>, London, John Murray, 1978.
16. Joseph and Sumption: <u>Equality</u>, p.14
17. Plant, Raymond., <u>Modern Political Thought</u>, Oxford, Blackwell, 1991, p. 77.
18. See, MacCallum, Gerald., 'Negative and positive freedom', in Flathman, Richard., (Ed.), <u>Concepts in Social & Political Philosophy</u>, London, Macmillan, 1973.
19. MacCallam: 'Negative and positive freedom', p.294.
20. MacCallam: 'Negative and positive freedom', p.298.
21. MacCallam: 'Negative and positive freedom', p.299.
22. MacCallam: 'Negative and positive freedom', p.299.
23. MacCallam: 'Negative and positive freedom', p.300.
24. MacCallam: 'Negative and positive freedom', p.300.
25. MacCallam: 'Negative and positive freedom', p.300.
26. Plant: <u>Modern Political Thought</u>, p.250.
27. A further abstract point, which is not directly relevant to the present discussion of New Labour's conception of liberty is that Plant suggests that positive liberty can be understood in a maximalist and a minimalist conception. The maximalist conception seeks to secure the ends or goals sought by the agent whereas the minimalist conception seeks to secure the means of pursuing the agent's ends or goals. If the present discussion was attempting to work on a more abstract level it would probably be suggested in greater detail, that New Labour holds to a minimalist conception of positive liberty. See, Plant: <u>Modern Political Thought</u>, p.222.
28. However, there is a possible problem in citing Crossman as indicative of 'Old left' thought because by the early 1950s he was advocating what appeared to be a more decentralist form of social ownership and industrial democracy as opposed to the traditional state centrism of the Bevanite heritage. For more on this see, Foote, Geoffrey., <u>The Labour Party's Political Thought</u>, Basingstoke, Macmillan, 1997, p.276.
29. Crossman, Richard., 'Towards a philosophy of socialism' in Crossman, Richard., (Ed.), <u>Planning for Freedom</u>, London, Hamish Hamilton, 1965, p.57.
30. Holland, Stuart., <u>The Socialist Challenge</u>, London, Quartet Books, 1973.
31. Foote: <u>The Labour Party's Political Thought</u>, p.310.
32. Guy Howard Dodge claims that the French liberal thinker Benjamin Constant originally suggested that liberalism has an

ancient and modern tradition which expresses liberty in both the negative and positive sense: 'For Constant, then, ancient and modern liberty are two distinct historical experiences of liberty just as there are two historical experiences of democracy, the direct democracy of the ancients and the representative democracy of the moderns, with each type having its merits and risks...Constant contrasts, then, a negative and a positive type of liberty. One is the negative liberty of guaranteeism or protectionism against the state, and the other is the positive liberty of the people to govern itself.' See, Dodge, Guy., Benjamin Constant's Philosophy of Liberalism: A study in Politics and Religion, Chapel Hill, The University of North Carolina Press, 1980, pp.40-41.

33. See Hayek, Friedrich., The Road to Serfdom, London, Routledge and Kegan Paul, 1944, p.19.
34. Hayek: The Road to Serfdom, p.19.
35. Hayek: The Road to Serfdom, p.3.
36. Ignatieff, Michael., Isaiah Berlin: A Life, London, Chatto & Windus, 1998, p.298.
37. Berlin, Isaiah., 'Two concepts of liberty'. in Quinton, Anthony., (Ed.), Political Philosophy, Oxford, Clarendon Press, 1967.
38. Berlin: 'Two concepts of liberty', p.141.
39. See, Blair, Tony., The Third Way: New Politics for the New Century, London, Fabian Society, Fabian Tract 588, 1998.
40. A discussion of New Labour's conception of equality is provided in chapter seven.
41. See, Plant, Raymond., 'Social democracy', in Marquand, David., Seldon, Anthony., (Eds.), The Ideas That Shaped Post-War Britain, London, Fontana Press, 1996.
42. For more on the assumptions of structural and indirect coercion held by positive libertarians see, Plant: Modern Political Thought, p.233.
43. Berlin: 'Two concepts of liberty', p.148.
44. Arblaster, Anthony., 'Liberal values and socialist values', in Miliband, Ralph., Saville, John., (Eds.), Socialist Register, London, The Merlin Press, 1972, p.92.
45. Arblaster: 'Liberal values and socialist values', p.99.
46. For Green's conception of liberty see, Green, Thomas., 'Lecture on *liberal legislation* and freedom of contract' and 'On the different sense of *freedom* as applied to will and to the moral progress of man' in Harris, Paul., Morrow, John., (Eds.), T.H. Green Lectures on the Principles of Political Obligation and Other Writings, Cambridge, Cambridge University Press,1986 pp. 199-200, 241-242 and for Hayek's version of liberty see, Hayek: The Road to Serfdom, pp.18-23.

47. See, Arblaster: 'Liberal values and socialist values', p.99.
48. Green believed in the principle of social morality which was interpreted as community responsibility, and part of the New Liberal's conception of citizenship. See, Green, Thomas., 'Lectures on the principle of political obligation' in Harris, P., Morrow, J., (Eds.), <u>T.H. Green Lectures on the Principles of Political Obligation and Other Writings,</u> Cambridge, Cambridge University Press,1986. However, the principle of community did not appear to rate highly in Hayek's political thought.
49. In his Fabian tract of 1998, Blair cites the following principles: equal worth, opportunity for all, responsibility, and community. Therefore, all individuals have equal worth and are members of the community; in which they have responsibilities and rights and are entitled to certain freedoms to enable them to fulfil their chosen path. See, Blair: <u>The Third Way: New Politics for the New Century.</u>
50. See, Plant, Raymond., 'Blair and ideology', in Seldon, Anthony., (Ed.), <u>The Blair Effect,</u> London, Little Brown & Co. 2001.
51. The italicised words highlight the emphasis on social democratic themes and ideas.
52. Blair, Tony., <u>New Britain: My Vision of a Young Country,</u> Fourth Estate, London, 1996
53. Blair: <u>The Third Way: New Politics for the New Century,</u> p.2.
54. Brown, Gordon., <u>Mansion House Speech,</u> 12th June 1997.
55. Blair, Tony., <u>1997 Labour Party Election Manifesto,</u> London, Labour Party, 1997, p.1.
56. White, Stuart., 'The ambiguities of the third way', in White, Stuart., (Ed.), <u>New Labour: The Progressive Future?,</u> Basingstoke, Palgrave, 2001, p.11.
57. White: 'The ambiguities of the third way', pp.11-12.
58. White: 'The ambiguities of the third way', pp.11-12.
59. White: 'The ambiguities of the third way', pp.11-12.
60. White: 'The ambiguities of the third way', pp.11-12.
61. The only source listed in White's bibliography that comments on the ideology of New Labour is, Freeden, Michael., 'The ideology of new labour', in, <u>The Political Quarterly,</u> 69, Oxford, Blackwell, 1998.
62. White uses the term social liberal in conjunction with New Labour in the final chapter of the edited Volume, (See, White, Stuart., Giaimo, Susan., 'New labour and the uncertain future of progressive politics' in White, Stuart., (Ed.), <u>New Labour: The Progressive Future?,</u> Basingstoke, Palgrave, 2001) but not in his opening chapter when he is attempting to disseminate conflicting philosophical commitments regarding 'real opportunity'. This is either an oversight or an inconsistency in his analysis.

63. Certain types of Liberals hold a positive conception of liberty as a principled commitment; in Britain, they would traditionally be known as Social Liberals but in the nineteenth century they were known as New Liberals. Liberal Conservatives may also hold a commitment to a positive conception of liberty; in Britain they would be termed, One-nation Conservatives.
64. The nineteenth century New Liberals influenced social democracy significantly, but its tradition also came through the establishment of the Labour Party with its industrial working class base and a centralised view of the state to name just two individual characteristics. For more on the heritage of British social democracy see chapter 2.
65. For Tawney's influence on Gaitskell see, Brivati, Brian., Hugh Gaitskell, London, Richard Cohen Books, 1997, pp.16, 291, on Blair see Blair: New Britain: My Vision of a Young Country, p.239 and Rentoul, John., Tony Blair, London, Warner Books, 1996, p.52, on Brown see Brown, Gordon., Fair is Efficient, London, Fabian Society, Fabian Pamphlet 563, 1994, pp.3, 25.
66. For a discussion on the shared ends or goals of social liberalism and social democracy see, Carter, Matt., T.H. Green and the Development of Ethical Socialism, Exeter, Imprint Academic, 2003, Clarke, Peter., Liberals and Social Democrats, Cambridge, Cambridge University Press, 1978, Collini, Stefan., Liberalism and Sociology: L.T. Hobhouse and Political Argument in England 1880-1914, Cambridge, Cambridge University Press, 1979, Freeden, Michael., The New Liberalism: An Ideology of Social Reform, Oxford, Clarendon Press, 1978 and Vincent, Andrew., Plant, Raymond., Philosophy, Politics and Citizenship, Oxford, Basil Blackwell, 1984.
67. More will be said in chapter 8 (which is concerned with New Labour and community) of the possible difference in the connection between and practical outworking of the values of liberty and community by New Labour compared with traditional social democrats in the Labour Party.
68. Plant, Raymond., Equality, Markets and the State, London, Fabian Tract 494, Fabian Society, 1984 p.6.
69. This discussion is developed further in chapter 7.
70. Plant: Modern Political Thought, pp.91-93.
71. Plant: Modern Political Thought, p.94.

Chapter 7

1. See, Plant, Raymond., 'Social democracy' in Marquand, David., Seldon, Anthony., (Eds.), The Ideas That Shaped Post-War Britain, London, Fontana, 1996.

2. In 'Socialism Now' Crosland refers to his belief in equality as democratic equality and takes this from Rawls, John,. A Theory of Justice, Cambridge, Harvard University Press, 1971. See, Crosland, Anthony., Socialism Now and Other Essays, London, Jonathan Cape, 1974, p.15.
3. See, Plant, Raymond., 'Democratic socialism and equality' in Lipsey, David., Leonard, Dick., (Eds.), The Socialist Agenda, London, Jonathan Cape, 1981, pp.138-144.
4. However, when studying contemporary political theory it is apparent that there is another form of equality of opportunity which is discussed at length in the literature. It attempts to neutralise differences in individual's social circumstances such as their class, family background and culture. It is known as 'fair' equality of opportunity whereas the traditional reading of equality of opportunity is deemed to be 'procedural' equality of opportunity. Fair equality of opportunity attempts to ensure that individual's social differences do not translate into differences in chances of success and from this point of view it has some similarities with the idea of greater equality of outcome. For a wider discussion of the different types of equality of opportunity see, Rawls, John., A Theory of Justice, Oxford, Oxford University Press, Revised Edition, 1999, pp.73-78 and Flew, Anthony., The Politics of Procrustes, London, Temple Smith, 1981, pp.45-58.
5. See, Plant: 'Democratic socialism and equality', pp.138-144.
6. See, Brown, Gordon., Speech to the Child Poverty Action Group's Child Poverty Conference, London, 15th May 2000, and Brown, Gordon., A Modern Agenda for Prosperity and Social Reform, Cass Business School, London, 3rd February 2003, and interview with Senior Treasury Civil Servant, HM Treasury, December 2002.
7. See, Brown, Gordon., Budget 2003, H.M.Treasury, ch.5, pp.1-3, Prescott, John., Speech at World Seminar on Sustainable Development, Johannesburg, 17th May 2002, p.4 and Carvel, J., 'Chancellor offers more cash help for parents', The Guardian, 6th December 2000.
8. Ashdown, Paddy., The Ashdown Diaries: 1988-1997, London, Penguin, 2001, p.406.
9. See, Parfit, Derek., 'Equality and priority', in Mason, Andrew., (Ed.), Ideals of Equality, Oxford, Blackwell, 1998.
10. More detailed qualifications about these terms will appear later in the chapter.
11. I am concentrating on Hayek's thought and not other New Right thinkers such as Milton Friedman or Keith Joseph as Hayek's

philosophical thought is more sophisticated. I take Hayek to be the leading and most influential New Right thinker.
12. Throughout the chapter I will use the term 'socialist' as being synonymous with the term 'social democratic'.
13. In this chapter I regard the socialist notion of equality as any of the following: a 'generous sufficiency' conception, a 'priority' conception or a 'strict egalitarian' conception. This is because the New Right is hostile to any notion of equality which is concerned with more than preventing destitution and therefore, any notion other than a 'basic sufficiency' conception of equality.
14. More of this discussion was made in chapter 6.
15. Blake, Robert., The Conservative Party from Peel to Thatcher, London, Fontana Press, 1985, p.262.
16. Thatcher, Margaret., The Downing Street Years, London, Harper Collins, 1993, p.13.
17. Thatcher: The Downing Street Years, Ch. 14.
18. Thatcher: The Downing Street Years, Ch.1.
19. Hayek, Friedrich., The Road to Serfdom, London, Routledge and Kegan Paul, 1944, Chs.2-3.
20. Hayek: The Road to Serfdom, p.18.
21. Hayek: The Road to Serfdom, p.23.
22. Hayek, Friedrich., Law, Legislation and Liberty Vol.II: The Mirage of Social Justice, London, Routledge and Kegan Paul, 1976.
23. Hayek: Law, Legislation and Liberty Vol II, p.64.
24. Hayek: Law, Legislation and Liberty Vol.II, p.87.
25. New Labour has established a number of welfare measures that one can describe as based on the generous sufficiency conception of equality which are notably more widespread than previous Conservative Government policy. For example, New Labour has introduced the *National Minimum Wage*, increased *Child Benefit*, raised *Income Support* for younger children, introduced the new *State Second Pension* which is more generous than the *SERPS* scheme that it replaces and has introduced a 10p starting rate of income tax which means that the poorest earners pay less direct taxation. For a thorough evaluation of the welfare measures introduced by New Labour see, Hills, John., 'Beveridge and new labour' in Walker, Robert., (Ed.), Ending Child Poverty, Bristol, The Policy Press, 1999, pp.35-45.
26. A fuller discussion of the various strands of prioritarianism occurs later in the chapter when discussing New Labour's version of equality in more detail.
27. Bosanquet, Nicholas., After The New Right, London, Heineman, p.109.

28. Tawney, Richard., Equality, London, George Allen & Unwin, 1931, pp.228-229.
29. Tawney: Equality, p.35.
30. See, Shaw, George., The Intelligent Woman's Guide to Socialism and Capitalism, London, Constable, 1928.
31. As was stated in chapter 2 by 1901 the Marxist Social Democratic Federation had left the Labour Party. They held classical Marxist beliefs and therefore their political economy would have asserted the strict egalitarian conception of equality.
32. As was stated in chapter 2 by 1928 the Labour Party had banned all communists from being party members or affiliate members. Therefore, the belief in complete equality of outcome held by the Labour Marxists was present in the Labour Party for a very short period.
33. Tawney: Equality, p.118.
34. Tawney: Equality, p.132.
35. All of chapter 4 (pp.126-163) of Equality is spent dealing with the strategies that the state can use to increase equality in society. These include redistribution, communal provision and the extension of social services.
36. Crosland: Socialism Now and Other Essays, p.15.
37. The political theorist Amartya Sen has attempted to deal with the problem of determining what counts as inequality in his essay 'Equality of What?' See, Sen, Amartya., 'Equality of what?' in McMurrin, Sterling., (Ed.), The Tanner Lectures on Human Values, Cambridge, Cambridge University Press, 1980.
38. See, Crosland, Anthony., The Future of Socialism, London, Jonathan Cape, 1956, p.237.
39. Crosland: The Future of Socialism, p.296.
40. Crosland: The Future of Socialism, p.216.
41. Rawls: A Theory of Justice, 1999, p.53.
42. Rawls: A Theory of Justice, 1999, p.53.
43. Rawls: A Theory of Justice, 1999, p.72.
44. Interview with Roy Hattersley at the House of Commons, March 2003.
45. Although a benchmark which is often used is the European Union's measurement which suggests that individuals are living in poverty if they earn below half the average wage.
46. Legislation and social programmes that endorse the priority conception of equality may well also endorse the sufficiency conception of equality and vice versa. The *National Minimum Wage*, the *Pensioner Guarantee*, and the *Working Families Tax Credit* are all appropriate examples of this.
47. It is interesting to note the similarity between the strict prioritarians and the strict egalitarian conception of equality

mentioned earlier. Both conceptions of equality are underpinned with the assumption that inequality is objectionable because it is bad in itself, yet they differ in their remit.

48. Non-strict prioritarianism has more in common with sufficiency conceptions of equality. They each draw a line whereby the state ceases to have either as much responsibility or any special responsibility towards groups who have surpassed a specific level of need. Non-strict prioritarians, like those who hold a sufficiency conception of equality regard inequality objectionable only when it is unjust and because these specific conceptions of equality draw a finite level of wealth, opportunities and financial need that once it is surpassed these groups are then deemed to have 'sufficient' resources and do not warrant further priority.

49. For a thorough examination of New Labour's social legislation see, Toynbee, Polly., Walker, David., <u>Did Things Really Get Better?</u>, London, Penguin, 2001, pp.10-44.

50. Jeremy Paxman interviewed Blair on BBC's Newsnight, on 5th June 2001.

51. Before giving his speech Blair asked some academics to prepare briefing notes on the issue of poverty. One of the key points raised was that he must decide whether he is referring to absolute or relative levels of poverty. Blair did not cover this or make it clear in his speech on ending child poverty. Therefore, the figures that he gave as his intended targets are ambiguous and it is unclear whether they are either absolute or relative figures. For more on Blair's speech and the salience of stressing the absolute/relative levels of poverty see, Blair, Tony., <u>Beveridge Revisited: A Welfare State for the 21st Century</u> and Plant, Raymond., 'Social justice' in, Walker, Robert., (Ed.), <u>Ending Child Poverty: Popular Welfare for the 21st Century</u>, Bristol, Polity, 1999.

52. Interview with Senior Treasury Civil Servant, HM Treasury London, December 2002.

53. Interview with Senior Treasury Civil Servant, HM Treasury.

54. More will be said about New Labour and the concept of community in the following chapter.

55. Toynbee and Walker: <u>Did Things Really Get Better?</u>, p.38.

56. In the following chapter more will be said on how communities suffer varying forms of inequality of access.

57. According to the April 2002 Guardian/ICM poll, 72% of people asked said they approved of Brown's decision to raise national insurance contributions to fund more spending for the NHS. See, Travis, Alan., 'Popularity of budget halts tory revival', Guardian, April 23rd 2002.

58. The Commission on Taxation and Citizenship, Paying For Progress: A New Politics of Tax for Public Spending, London, Fabian Society, 2000.
59. The Commission on Taxation and Citizenship, Paying For Progress: A New Politics of Tax for Public Spending, p.235.
60. This is referring to the date when Crosland's seminal piece of revisionist social democratic thought, The Future of Socialism, was first published.

Chapter 8

1. Kingdom, John., No Such Thing As Society? Individualism and Community, Buckingham, Open University Press, 1992, p.87.
2. A discussion of the political principle of community is absent from Friedrich Hayek's main philosophical works. Notably, The Road to Serfdom, London, Routledge and Kegan Paul, 1944, The Constitution of Liberty, London, Routledge and Kegan Paul, 1960, and Law, Legislation and Liberty, Vol. II: The Mirage of Social Justice, London, Routledge and Kegan Paul, 1976.
3. The closest Hayek gets to critiquing the value of community is in his dismissive regard for concepts such as 'social goals', 'common purpose', 'common good', 'general welfare', 'general interest' as he believes that they are inaccurate and misleading because no complete ethical code exists which describes shared goals or communal values. He regards 'collectivism' in its many forms as atavistic and compares it to 'tribalism'. The 'Great Society' that he values is a liberal democracy with a free-maket economy and contains no ethical account of community or mutual citizenship. See Hayek: The Road to Serfdom, pp.42-43 and Law, Legislation and Liberty, Vol. II: The Mirage of Social Justice, pp.2-4, 133-136.
4. See, Hayek: The Road to Serfdom, pp. 100-113.
5. As defined by Ferdinand Tonnies. See Tonnies, Ferdinand., Community and Society, New York, Harper and Rowe, 1963.
6. Tonnies: Community and Society.
7. I define libertarians similarly to Mulhall and Swift, as extreme liberal individualists and therefore as occupying a strand of liberalism not existing independently from liberal thought. Libertarian thinkers such as Robert Nozick hold to the centrality of individual rights at all times and across a range of economic, social and political issues. See, Mulhall, Stephen., Swift, Adam., (Eds.), Liberals & Communitarians, Oxford, Blackwell, 1992, pp.xv-xvi.
8. See, Hayek: The Road to Serfdom, p.11.

9. Hayek: Law, Legislation and Liberty Vol.II: The Mirage of Social Justice, p.87.
10. Greenleaf, William., The British Political Tradition Volume II: The Ideological Heritage, London, Methuen, 1983, p.223.
11. A discussion of New Liberalism was presented in chapter 2.
12. Greenleaf: The British Political Tradition, p.224.
13. Greenleaf: The British Political Tradition, p.227.
14. Greenleaf: The British Political Tradition, p.277.
15. One could argue that the Conservative Governments of Churchill 1951-1955, Eden 1955-1957 and Macmillan 1957-1963 are indicative of various forms of Tory paternalism which is contrasted with the dominant neo-liberalism, in theory if not fully in practice, (especially regarding the Heath Government) of the Conservative Governments of Heath 1970-1974, Thatcher 1979-1990 and Major 1990-1997. The obvious exception to this observation is Douglas-Home's premiership of 1963-1964, as it is perceived by the historian Robert Blake that Douglas-Home was the first of the post-war Conservative Prime Ministers to lead the Party from the right of centre. See Blake, Robert., The Conservative Party from Peel to Thatcher, London, Fontana Press, 1985, p.294.
16. This includes Tony Benn and Shirley Williams. See, Foote, Geoffrey., The Labour Party's Political Thought, Basingstoke, Macmillan, 1997, p.72.
17. Winter, Jay., Joslin, David., (Eds.), R.H. Tawney's Commonplace Book, Cambridge, Cambridge University Press, 1972.
18. Greenleaf: The British Political Tradition, pp.442-443.
19. Greenleaf: The British Political Tradition, p.462.
20. Greenleaf: The British Political Tradition, p.461.
21. Chapter 4 of Equality sets out what, in Tawney's opinion, needs to be done to reduce inequality and thus promote liberty and chapter 5 sets out his philosophical position that suggests that equality and liberty are partners for the socialist. See chapters 4-5 of, Tawney, Richard., Equality, London, George Allen & Unwin, 1931.
22. Tawney: Equality, p.38.
23. Foote: The Labour Party's Political Thought, p.60.
24. Marquand, David., Ramsay MacDonald, London, Jonathan Cape, 1976, pp.83-84.
25. It has been argued in Chapter 7 that Crosland was confused in his expression of his main political values. It has been argued that Crosland was actually striving for greater individual liberty and that equality was an assisting principle, a vehicle for granting meaningful liberty to individuals.

26. Lipsey, David., 'Crosland's socialism', in Lipsey, David., Leonard, Dick., (Eds.), The Socialist Agenda: Crosland's Legacy, London, Jonathan Cape, 1981, p.38.
27. Lipsey: 'Crosland's socialism' pp.38-39.
28. Crosland's biographer Kevin Jefferys suggests that his 'hedonistic streak' (and thus his inclination towards liberalism and possibly social libertarianism) was a reaction to the conservative moral and social outlook of his parents' Plymouth Brethren faith. However, Jefferys also notes that the sect's egalitarianism, lack of ritual and formality and its Protestant work ethic were all positive influences on Crosland as an adult. See, Jefferys, Kevin., Anthony Crosland, London, Richard Cohen Books, 1999, pp.2-3.
29. Wright, Tony., Socialisms: Old and New, London, Routledge, 1996, p.144.
30. Plant, Raymond., Lesser, Harry., Taylor-Gooby, Peter., Political Philosophy and Social Welfare: Essays on the Normative Basis of Welfare Provision, Routledge & Kegan Paul, London, 1980, p.205.
31. Plant, Lesser and Taylor-Gooby: Political Phillosophy and Social Welfare, p.207.
32. Mason, Andrew., Community, Solidarity and Belonging: Levels of Community and Their Normative Significance, Cambridge, Cambridge University Press, 2000, p.20.
33. Mason: Community, Solidarity and Belonging, p.21.
34. Mason: Community, Solidarity and Belonging, p.21.
35. Mason: Community, Solidarity and Belonging, p.25.
36. Mason: Community, Solidarity and Belonging, p.27.
37. See, Blair, Tony., New Britain: My Vision of a Young Country, London, Fourth Estate, 1996, pp.215-222, Blair, Tony., Socialism, London, Fabian Society, Fabian Tract 565, 1995, p.4, Blair, Tony., The Third Way: New Politics for the New Century, London, Fabian Society, Fabian Tract 588, 1998, Blair, Tony., Clause IV: Labour Party Constitution, London, Labour Party, 1995, Brown, Gordon., 'The politics of potential: a new agenda for labour', in Miliband, D., (Ed.), Reinventing the Left, Cambridge, Polity Press, 1994, pp.113-122 and Blunkett, David., Civil Renewal: A New Agenda, The CSV Edith Kahn Memorial Lecture, 11th June 2003.
38. See, Tawney: Equality.
39. The *New Deal for Communities* promotes local communities firstly within the decision-making process of the programme; enabling them to speak as individuals, community organisations, churches, businesses and voluntary groups within their community instead of through a delegate or solely through a local government

officer. Secondly, because it provides local communities with a fixed grant to spend as they see fit.

40. Avineri, Shlomo., De-Shalit, Avner., (Eds.), Communitarianism and Individualism, Oxford, Oxford University Press, 1992, pp.2-3.
41. Levitas, Ruth., The Inclusive Society? Social Exclusion and New Labour, Basingstoke, Macmillan, 1998, p.90.
42. See, Levitas: The Inclusive Society? Social Exclusion and New Labour, Jordan, Bill., 'New labour, new community?', Imprints, vol.3, no.2, 1999, pp.113-131, Philips, Melanie., 'The father of Tony Blair's big idea', Observer, 24th July 1994, and Riddell, Peter., 'I'm a guru; are you one too?', The Times, 7th August 1996.
43. See, Etzioni, Amitai., The Spirit of Community: Rights, Responsibilities and the Communitarian Agenda, London, Fontana, 1995, The New Golden Rule: Community and Morality in a Democratic Society, London, Profile Books, 1997 and (Ed.), The Essential Communitarian Reader, Lanham, Rowman & Littlefield Publishers, 1998.
44. Taylor, Charles., Sources of the Self: The Making of the Modern Identity, Cambridge, Harvard University Press, 1989.
45. Sandel, Michael., Liberalism and the Limits of Justice, Cambridge, Cambridge University Press, 1982.
46. Walzer, Michael., Sphere of Justices: A Defence of Pluralism and Equality, New York, Basic Books, 1983.
47. This is the communitarian journal established in 1990 by Etzioni to act as a forum for new communitarian ideas.
48. Etzioni: The Essential Communitarian Reader, p.xi.
49. Etzioni: The Spirit of Community: Rights, Responsibilities and the Communitarian Agenda, p.4.
50. Blair: The Third Way: New Politics for the New Century.
51. Blair: The Third Way: New Politics for the New Century, p.12.
52. Etzioni: The Essential Communitarian Reader, p.xiv.
53. Etzioni: The New Golden Rule: Community and Morality in a Democratic Society, p.14.
54. Etzioni: The New Golden Rule: Community and Morality in a Democratic Society, p.17.
55. Etzioni: The New Golden Rule: Community and Morality in a Democratic Society, p.18.
56. Etzioni: The New Golden Rule: Community and Morality in a Democratic Society, p.29.
57. Etzioni: The New Golden Rule: Community and Morality in a Democratic Society, p.29
58. The social philosophy of the Labour Party in the mid-twentieth century had been exclusively linked to the theories of liberalism and according to the Right had in part led to the 'permissive

society' standpoint of the 1960s whereby the Wilson Labour Government under the guidance of the Home Secretary Roy Jenkins, passed a raft of liberal reforms of social legislation which modernised British law in line with cultural, sexual and economic changes happening in the western world.

59. For a good discussion of the liberal/communitarian debate see, Mulhall and Swift: Liberals and communitarians.
60. See, Driver, Stephen., Martell, Luke., 'New labour's communitarianisms', Critical Social Policy, 52, (1997), pp.27-46.
61. Etzioni: The Spirit of Community: Rights, Responsibilities and the Communitarian Agenda, p.15.
62. Etzioni: The Spirit of Community: Rights, Responsibilities and the Communitarian Agenda, p.15.
63. Etzioni: The New Golden Rule: Community and Morality in a Democratic Society, p.180.
64. Etzioni: The New Golden Rule: Community and Morality in a Democratic Society, pp.16-17.
65. Etzioni: The Spirit of Community: Rights, Responsibilities and the Communitarian Agenda, p.149.
66. Etzioni: The New Golden Rule: Community and Morality in a Democratic Society, p.180.
67. Etzioni: The New Golden Rule: Community and Morality in a Democratic Society, p.182.
68. Etzioni: The New Golden Rule: Community and Morality in a Democratic Society, pp.149-156.
69. Etzioni: The Spirit of Community: Rights, Responsibilities and the Communitarian Agenda, p.257.
70. Etzioni: The Spirit of Community: Rights, Responsibilities and the Communitarian Agenda, pp.61-62.
71. Levitas; The Inclusive Society?, pp.95-96.
72. These senior New Labour politicians are members of the Christian Socialist Movement which is an organisation within the Labour Movement.
73. Harris, José., 'Labour's political and social thought', in Tanner, Duncan., Thane, Pat., and Tiratsoo, Nick., (Eds.), Labour's First Century, Cambridge, Cambridge University Press, 2000, p.39.
74. See, Mandelson, Peter., The Blair Revolution Revisited, London, Politico's, 2002, p.xxii.
75. See, Hill, Dilys., 'Constitutional reform', in Plant, Raymond., Beech, Matt., Hickson, Kevin., (Eds.), The Struggle for Labour's Soul, London, Routledge, 2004.
76. For such a criticism see, Jones, Barry., Keating, Michael., Labour and the British State, Oxford, Oxford University Press, 1985.
77. For a further discussion on the trade-off between decentralisation and equality of services see, Plant, Raymond., Equality, Markets

and the State, Fabian Tract 494, London, Fabian Society, 1984,pp.14-16.
78. Blunkett: Civil Renewal: A New Agenda, p.20.
79. Blunkett: Civil Renewal: A New Agenda, p.21.
80. Blunkett: Civil Renewal: A New Agenda, p.21.
81. Brown, Gordon., Speech at the NCVO Annual Conference, London, 9th February 2000,p.1.
82. Brown: Speech at the NCVO Annual Conference, pp.7-8.
83. See, Dahrendorf, Ralph., Challenges to the Voluntary Sector, Arnold Goodman Lecture, London, 17th July 2001, pp.4-6.
84. Boateng, Paul., Speech at the New Economics Foundation, London, 7th May 2002, p.2.
85. Boateng: Speech at the New Economics Foundation, p.4.
86. Driver, Stephen., and Martell, Luke., New Labour: Politics After Thatcherism, Cambridge, Polity Press, 1998, p.15.
87. For a further discussion on the complexities of the debate surrounding liberals and communitarians and in particular, the areas of agreement see, Selznick, Philip., 'Foundations of communitarian liberalism', in, Etzioni, Amitai., (Ed.), The Essential Communitarian Reader, Lanham, Rowman & Littlefield Publishers, 1998.
88. However, there is no up to date survey of the social attitudes of MPs and in particular no specific study of Labour MPs therefore this issue is speculation and not fact.
89. See, Tawney: Equality.

BIBLIOGRAPHY

Arblaster, Anthony., 'Liberal values and socialist values', in (Eds.), Miliband, Ralph., Saville, John., Socialist Register, London, The Merlin Press, 1972.

Ashdown, Paddy., The Ashdown Diaries: 1988-1997, London, Penguin, 2001.

Avineri, Shlomo., De-Shalit, Avner., (Eds.), Communitarianism and Individualism, Oxford, Oxford University Press, 1992.

Beech, Matt., 'New labour' in (Eds.), Plant, Raymond., Beech, Matt., Hickson, Kevin., The Struggle for Labour's Soul: Understanding Labour's Political Thought Since 1945, London, Routledge, 2004.

Beer, Samuel., Modern British Politics, London, Faber & Faber, 1969.

Benn, Tony., Arguments for Socialism, London, Jonathan Cape, 1979.

Benn, Tony., Arguments for Democracy, London, Jonathan Cape, 1981.

Berlin, Isaiah., 'Two concepts of liberty' in (Ed.), Quinton, Anthony., Political Philosophy, Oxford, Clarendon Press, 1967.

Berlin, Isaiah., Four Essays on Liberty, Oxford, Clarendon Press, 1969.

Bernstein, Eduard., Evolutionary Socialism, New York, Schocken Books, 1961.

Bevan, Aneurin., In Place of Fear, London, William Heinemann, 1952.

Blair, Tony., New Britain: My Vision of a Young Country, London, Fourth Estate, 1996.

Blair, Tony., Schroder, Gerhard., Europe: The Third Way - die Neue Mitte, London, Labour Party, SPD, 1999.

Blake, Robert., <u>The Conservative Party from Peel to Thatcher</u>, London, Fontana Press, 1985.

Bosanquet, Nicholas., <u>After the New Right</u>, London, Heineman, 1983.

Brittan, Samuel., <u>The Role and Limits of Government</u>, London, Temple Smith, 1983.

Brivati, Brian., <u>Hugh Gaitskell</u>, London, Richard Cohen Books, 1997.

Brown, Gordon., 'The politics of potential: A new agenda for labour', in Miliband, David., (Ed.), <u>Reinventing the Left</u>, Cambridge, Polity Press, 1994.

Butler, David., Kavanagh, Dennis., <u>The British General Election of 1992</u>, Basingstoke, Macmillan, 1992.

Carter, Matt., <u>T.H. Green and the Development of Ethical Socialism</u>, Exeter, Imprint Academic, 2003.

Clarke, Peter., <u>Liberals and Social Democrats</u>, Cambridge, CUP, 1978.

Clegg, Hugh., et al, <u>A History of British Trade Unionism since 1889, Vol.I</u>, Oxford, Clarendon Press, 1964.

Clegg, Hugh., <u>A History of British Trade Unionism since 1889, Vol.II</u>, Oxford, Clarendon Press, 1985.

Cole, George., <u>The World of Labour</u>, London, G. Bell & Son, 1928.

Cole, Margaret., <u>Story of Fabian Socialism</u>, London, Heinemann, 1961.

Collini, Stefan., <u>Liberalism and Sociology: L.T. Hobhouse and Political Argument in England 1880-1914</u>, Cambridge, Cambridge University Press, 1979.

Commission on Social Justice, <u>Social Justice: Strategies for National Renewal</u>, London, Vintage, 1994.

Commission on Taxation and Citizenship, <u>Paying For Progress: A New Politics of Tax for Public Spending</u>, London, Fabian Society, 2000.

Crewe, Ivor, King, Anthony., <u>SDP: The Birth, Life and Death of the Social Democratic Party</u>, Oxford, Oxford University Press, 1996.

Cronin, James., <u>New Labour's Pasts</u>, London, Pearson Longman, 2004.

Crosland, Anthony., The Future of Socialism, London, Jonathan Cape, 1956.
Crosland, Anthony., The Future of Socialism, London, Jonathan Cape, Second Edition, 1964.
Crosland, Anthony., The Conservative Enemy, London, Jonathan Cape, 1964.
Crosland, Anthony., 'Socialism now', in (Ed.), Leonard, Dick., Socialism Now and Other Essays, London, Jonathan Cape, 1974.
Crossman, Richard., 'The affluent society' in (Ed.), Crossman, Richard., Planning for Freedom, London, Hamish Hamilton, 1965.
Crossman, Richard., 'Planning for freedom' in (Ed.), Crossman, Richard., Planning for Freedom, London, Hamish Hamilton, 1965.
Crossman, Richard., 'Towards a new philosophy of socialism' in (Ed.), Crossman, Richard., Planning for Freedom, London, Hamish Hamilton, 1965.
Dodge, Guy., Benjamin Constant's Philosophy of Liberalism: A study in Politics and Religion, Chapel Hill, The University of North Carolina Press, 1980.
Driver, Stephen., Martell, Luke., 'New labour's communitarianisms', Critical Social Policy, 52, (1997), pp.27-46.
Driver, Stephen., Martell, Luke., New Labour: Politics After Thatcherism, Cambridge, Polity Press, 1998.
Drucker, Henry., Doctrine and Ethos in the Labour Party, London, George Allen & Unwin, 1979.
Durbin, Evan., New Jerusalems: The Labour Party and the Economics of Democratic Socialism, London, Routledge & Keegan Paul, 1985.
Estrin, Saul., Le Grand, Julian., (Eds.), Market Socialism, Oxford, Clarendon Press, 1989.
Etzioni, Amitai., The Spirit of Community: Rights, Responsibilities and the Communitarian Agenda, London, Fontana, 1995.

Etzioni, Amitai., <u>The New Golden Rule: Community and Morality in a Democratic Society</u>, London, Profile Books, 1997.

Etzioni, Amitai., (Ed.), <u>The Essential Communitarian Reader</u>, Lanham, Rowman & Littlefield Publishers, 1998.

Faux, Jeff., 'Lost on the third way' in <u>Dissent</u>, 46/2, (Spring 1999), pp.67-76.

Finlayson, Alan., <u>The Making of New Labour</u>, London, Lawrence and Wishart, 2003.

Foote, Geoffrey., <u>The Labour Party's Political Thought</u>, London, Croom Helm, 1997.

Flew, Anthony., <u>The Politics of Procrustes</u>, London, Temple Smith, 1981.

Freeden, Michael., <u>The New Liberalism: An Ideology of Social Reform</u>, Oxford, Clarendon Press, 1978.

Freeden, Michael., 'The ideology of new labour', in, <u>The Political Quarterly</u>, 69, Oxford, Blackwell, 1998.

Gamble, Andrew., Walkland, Stuart., <u>The British Party System and Economic Policy 1945-1983</u>, Oxford, Clarendon, 1984.

Gamble, Andrew., <u>The Free Economy and the Strong State</u>, Basingstoke, Macmillan, 1988.

Giddens, Anthony., <u>The Third Way: The Renewal of Social Democracy</u>, Cambridge, Polity Press, 1998.

Giddens, Anthony., <u>The Third Way and its Critics</u>, Cambridge, Polity Press, 2000.

Giddens, Anthony., <u>Where Now for New Labour?</u>, Cambridge, Polity Press, 2002.

Gould, Bryan., <u>Socialism and Freedom</u>, Basingstoke, Macmillan, 1985.

Gould, Bryan., <u>A Future for Socialism</u>, London, Jonathan Cape, 1989.

Gould, Phillip., <u>The Unfinished Revolution</u>, London, Abacus, 1998.

Green, David., <u>The New Right</u>, Brighton, Harvester Wheatsheaf, 1987.

Green, Thomas., 'Lecture on *liberal legislation* and freedom of contract' in Harris, Paul., Morrow, John., (Eds.), <u>T.H. Green</u>

Lectures on the Principles of Political Obligation and Other Writings, Cambridge, CUP, 1986.

Green, Thomas., 'Lectures on the Principle of Political Obligation' in Harris, Paul., Morrow, John., (Eds.), T.H. Green Lectures on the Principles of Political Obligation and Other Writings, Cambridge, CUP, 1986.

Green, Thomas., 'On the Different Sense of 'Freedom' as Applied to Will and to the Moral Progress of Man' in Harris, Paul., Morrow, John., (Eds.), T.H. Green Lectures on the Principles of Political Obligation and Other Writings, Cambridge, CUP, 1986.

Green, Thomas., Prolegomena to Ethics, Oxford, Clarendon Press, 1906.

Greenleaf, William., The British Political Tradition Vol.II: The Ideological Heritage, London, Methuen, 1983.

Hall, Stuart., Breakthrough, London, Combined Universities CND, 1958.

Hall, Stuart., NATO and the Alliance, London, CND, 1961.

Hall, Stuart., 'The great moving nowhere show' in Marxism Today, (November/December 1998), pp.9-14.

Harris, José., 'Labour's political and social thought', in Tanner, Duncan., Thane, Pat., Tiratsoo, Nick., (Eds.), Labour's First Century, Cambridge, Cambridge University Press, 2000.

Haseler, Stephen., The Gaitskellites, London, Macmillan, 1969.

Hattersley, Roy., Choose Freedom, London, Michael Joseph, 1987.

Hayek, Friedrich., The Road to Serfdom, London, Routledge and Kegan Paul, 1944.

Hayek, Friedrich., The Constitution of Liberty, London, Routledge and Kegan Paul, 1960.

Hayek, Friedrich., Law, Legislation and Liberty, Vol. II: The Mirage of Social Justice, London, Routledge and Kegan Paul, 1976.

Healey, Denis., The Time of My Life, London, Penguin, 1989.

Hill, Dilys., 'Constitutional reform', in Plant, Raymond., Beech, Matt., Hickson, Kevin., (Eds.), <u>The Struggle for Labour's Soul</u>, London, Routledge, 2004.

Hills, John., 'Beveridge and new labour' in Walker, Robert., (Ed.), <u>Ending Child Poverty</u>, Bristol, The Policy Press, 1999.

Hirsch, Fred., <u>Social Limits to Growth</u>, London, Routledge and Kegan Paul, 1983.

Hirst, Paul., Thompson, Grahame., <u>Globalization in Question</u>, Cambridge, Polity Press, 1996.

Hobhouse, Leonard., <u>Liberalism</u>, London, Thornton Butterworth, 1911.

Hobson, John., <u>Imperialism: A Study</u>, London, James Nisbet, 1902.

Holland, Stuart., <u>The Socialist Challenge</u>, London, Quartet Books, 1975.

Hook, Sidney., 'Introduction to evolutionary socialism', in, Bernstein, Eduard., <u>Evolutionary Socialism</u>, New York, Schocken Books, 1961.

Hoover, Kenneth., Plant, Raymond., <u>Conservative Capitalism in Britain and USA</u>, London, Routledge, 1989.

Hughes, Colin., Wintour, Patrick., <u>Labour Rebuilt: The New Model Party</u>, London, Fourth Estate, 1990.

Hyndman, Henry., <u>The Record of an Adventurous Life</u>, London, Macmillan, 1911.

Ignatieff, Michael., <u>Isaiah Berlin: A Life</u>, London, Chatto & Windus, 1998.

Jefferys, Kevin., <u>Anthony Crosland</u>, London, Richard Cohen Books, 1999.

Jefferys, Kevin., <u>The Labour Party Since 1945</u>, Basingstoke, Macmillan, 1993.

Jones, Barry., Keating, Michael., <u>Labour and the British State</u>, Oxford, Oxford University Press, 1985.

Jordan, Bill., 'New labour, new community?', <u>Imprints</u>, vol.3, no.2, pp.113-131.

Joseph, Keith., Sumption, Jonathan., <u>Equality</u>, London, John Murray, 1978.

Keynes, John., <u>The General Theory of Employment, Interest and Money</u>, London, Macmillan, 1936.

Kingdom, John., No Such Thing as Society? Individualism and Community, Buckingham, Open University Press, 1992.

Kogan, David., Kogan, Maurice., The Battle for the Labour Party, Glasgow, Fontana Paperbacks 1982.

Laski, Harold., A Grammar of Politics, London, Allen & Unwin, 1925.

Laski, Harold., The State in Theory and Practice, London, Allen & Unwin, 1935.

Levitas, Ruth., The Inclusive Society? Social Exclusion and New Labour, Basingstoke, Macmillan, 1998.

Lipsey, David., 'Crosland's socialism', in Lipsey, David., Leonard, Dick., (Eds.), The Socialist Agenda: Crosland's Legacy, London, Jonathan Cape, 1981.

Ludlam, Steve., 'The making of new labour', in Ludlam, Steve., Smith, Martin., (Eds.), New Labour in Government, Basingstoke, Macmillan, 2001.

Ludlam, Steve., and Smith, Martin., (Eds.), Governing as New Labour, Basingstoke, Palgrave Macmillan, 2004.

MacCallum, Gerald., 'Negative and Positive Freedom', in Flathman, Richard., (Ed.), Concepts in Social & Political Philosophy, London, Macmillan, 1973.

MacIntyre, Alasdair., 'A mistake in causality in social science', in Laslett, Peter., Runciman, W.G., (Eds.), Philosophy, Politics and Society, Oxford, Basil Blackwell, 1964.

MacIntyre, Donald., Mandelson and New Labour, London, Harper Collins, 1999.

MacLean, Iain., Keir Hardie, London, Allen Lane, 1975.

Mandelson, Peter., Liddle, Roger., The Blair Revolution, London, Faber and Faber, 1996.

Mandelson, Peter., The Blair Revolution Revisited, London, Politico's, 2002.

Marquand, David., Ramsay MacDonald, London, Jonathan Cape, 1976.

Marquand, David., The Unprincipled Society, London, Fontana Press, 1988.

Marquand, David., The Progressive Dilemma, London, Heinemann, 1992.

Marquand, David., 'Moralists and hedonists' in, Marquand, David., Seldon, Anthony., (Eds.), The Ideas That Shaped Post-War Britain, London, Fontana, 1996.

Mason, Andrew., Community, Solidarity and Belonging: Levels of Community and Their Normative Significance, Cambridge, Cambridge University Press, 2000.

Masterman, Charles., (Ed.), The Heart of the Empire, London, T. Fisher Unwin, 1901.

Masterman, Charles., (Ed.), The Condition of England, London, Methuen, 1909.

Marx, Karl., Critique of the Gotha Programme, Peking, Foreign Languages, 1972.

McBriar, Alan., Fabian Socialism and English Politics 1884-1918, Cambridge, Cambridge University Press, 1963.

McMurrin, Sterling., (Ed.), The Tanner Lectures on Human Values, Cambridge, Cambridge University Press, 1980.

Meacher, Michael., Socialism with a Human Face, London, Allen & Unwin, 1982.

Mitchell, Austin., Four Years in the Death of the Labour Party, London, Methuen, 1983.

Mitchell, Austin., Competitive Socialism, London, Unwin Hyman, 1989.

Moore, Roger., The Emergence of the Labour Party 1880-1924, London, Hodder and Stoughton, 1978.

Morgan, Kenneth., Keir Hardie: Radical and Socialist, London, Weidenfeld and Nicolson, 1975.

Morgan, Kenneth., Labour People, Oxford, Oxford University Press, 1992.

Mulhall, Stephen., Swift, Adam., Liberals and Communitarians, Oxford, Blackwell, 1992.

Mullard, Maurice., New Labour, New Thinking, Huntington, Nova Science Publishers, 2000.

Norton Phillip., 'Electing the leader: the conservative party leadership contest 1997' Politics Review, April, 1998.

Nove, Alexander., The Economics of Feasible Socialism, London, Allen & Unwin, 1983.

Owen, David., Face the Future, Oxford, Oxford University Press, 1981.

Parfit, Derek., 'Equality and priority', in Mason, Andrew., (Ed.), Ideals of Equality, Oxford, Blackwell, 1998.

Parfit, Derek., 'Equality or priority' in Clayton, Matthew., Williams, Andrew., (Eds.), The Ideal of Equality, Basingstoke, Macmillan, 2000.

Pease, Edward., History of the Fabian Society, London, Fifield, 1916.

Pelling, Henry., A History of British Trade Unionism, London, Macmillan, 1963.

Pelling, Henry., The Origins of the Labour Party 1880-1900, Oxford, Clarendon Press, 1965.

Plant, Raymond., Lesser, Harry., Taylor-Gooby, Peter., Political Philosophy and Social Welfare: Essays on the Normative Basis of Welfare Provision, Routledge & Kegan Paul, London, 1980.

Plant, Raymond., 'Democratic socialism and equality' in Lipsey, David., Leonard, Dick., (Eds.), The Socialist Agenda, London, Jonathan Cape, 1981.

Plant, Raymond., Modern Political Thought, Oxford, Blackwell, 1991.

Plant, Raymond, 'Social democracy', in Marquand, David., Seldon, Anthony., (Eds.), The Ideas That Shaped Post-War Britain, London, Fontana, 1996.

Plant, Raymond., New Labour – A Third Way?, London, European Policy Forum, 1998.

Plant, Raymond., 'Blair and ideology', in Seldon, Anthony., (Ed.), The Blair Effect, London, Little Brown & Co. 2001.

Plant, Raymond., Beech Matt., Hickson, Kevin., (Eds.), The Struggle for Labour's Soul: Understanding Labour's Political Thought Since 1945, London, Routledge, 2004.

Przeworski, Adam., Capitalism and Social Democracy, Cambridge, Cambridge University Press, 1985.

Pym, Hugh., Kochan, Nick., Gordon Brown: The First Year in Power, London, Bloomsbury, 1998.

Radice, Giles, Labour's Path to Power, London, Macmillan, 1989.

Rawls, John., A Theory of Justice, Cambridge, Harvard University Press, 1971.

Rawls, John., A Theory of Justice, Oxford, Oxford University Press, Revised Edition, 1999.
Reid, Fred., Keir Hardie: The Making of a Socialist, London, Croom Helm, 1978.
Rentoul, John., Tony Blair, London, Warner Books, 1996.
Roberts, Benjamin., The Trades Union Congress 1868-1921, London, Allen & Unwin, 1958.
Ryan, Alan., 'Britain: recycling the third way', in Dissent, 46/2 (Spring 1999), pp.77-80.
Sandel, Michael., Liberalism and the Limits of Justice, Cambridge, Cambridge University Press, 1982.
Searle, Geoffrey., The Liberal Party: Triumph and Disintegration 1886-1929, Basingstoke, Macmillan, 1992.
Selznick, Philip., 'Foundations of communitarian liberalism', in, Etzioni, Amitai., (Ed.), The Essential Communitarian Reader, Lanham, Rowman & Littlefield Publishers, 1998.
Sen, Amartya., 'Equality of what?' in McMurrin, Sterling., (Ed.), The Tanner Lectures on Human Values, Cambridge, Cambridge University Press, 1980.
Shaw, Eric., Discipline And Discord in the Labour Party, Manchester, Manchester University Press, 1988.
Shaw, George., Fabian Essays in Socialism, London, Walter Scott Publishing, 1908.
Shaw, George., The Intelligent Woman's Guide to Socialism and Capitalism, London, Constable, 1928.
Skidelsky, Robert., John Maynard Keynes: Fighting for Britain 1937-1946, Basingstoke, Macmillan, 2000.
Smith, Martin., 'The complexity of new labour', in Ludlam, Steve., Smith, Martin., (Eds.), New Labour in Government, Basingstoke, Macmillan, 2001.
Steiner, Hillel., 'Individual liberty', in Proceedings of the Aristotelian Society, London, 1974.
Strachey, John., The Coming Struggle for Power, London, The Modern Library, 1935.
Strachey, John., The Nature of Capitalist Crisis, London, Victor Gollancz, 1935.
Strachey, John., The Menace of Fascism, London, The American League Against War and Fascism, 1933.

Tawney, Richard., The Acquisitive Society, London, G. Bell and Sons, 1921.
Tawney, Richard., Equality, London, G. Bell & Son, 1931.
Taylor, Charles., Sources of the Self: The Making of the Modern Identity, Cambridge, Harvard University Press, 1989.
Thatcher, Margaret., The Downing Street Years, London, Harper Collins, 1993.
Thomas, Hugh., John Strachey, London, Eyre Methuen, 1973.
Thompson, Edward., (Ed.), Out of Apathy, London, Stevens & Sons, 1960.
Thompson, Edward., The Making of the English Working Class, London, Gollancz, 1963.
Tonnies, Ferdinand., Community and Society, New York, Harper and Rowe, 1963.
Toynbee, Polly., Walker, David., Did Things Really Get Better?, London, Penguin, 2001.
Walker, Rob., (Ed.), Ending Child Poverty: Popular Welfare for the 21st Century, Bristol, Polity, 1999
Walzer, Michael., Sphere of Justices: A Defence of Pluralism and Equality, New York, Basic Books, 1983.
White, Stuart., 'The ambiguities of the third way', in White, Stuart., (Ed.), New Labour: The Progressive Future?, Basingstoke, Palgrave, 2001.
White, Stuart., Giaimo, Susan., 'New labour and the uncertain future of progressive politics', in White, Stuart., (Ed.), New Labour: The Progressive Future?, Basingstoke, Palgrave, 2001.
Williams, Phillip., Hugh Gaitskell: A Political Biography, London, Jonathan Cape, 1979.
Williams, Raymond., Culture and Society, London, Chatto & Windus, 1958.
Williams, Raymond., The Long Revolution, London, Chatto & Widus, 1961.
Winter, Jay., Joslin, David., (Eds.), R.H. Tawney's Commonplace Book, Cambridge, Cambridge University Press, 1972.

Wright, Tony., Socialisms: Old and New, London, Routledge, 1996.
Vincent, Andrew., Plant, Raymond., Philosophy, Politics and Citizenship, Oxford, Basil Blackwell, 1984.

Pamphlets and Lectures
Blair, Tony., Socialism, London, Fabian Society, Fabian Tract 565, 1995.
Blair, Tony., The Third Way: New Politics for the New Century, London, Fabian Society, Fabian Tract 588, 1998.
Blunkett, David., Civil Renewal: A New Agenda, The CSV Edith Kahn Memorial Lecture, London, 11th June 2003.
Brown, Gordon., Fair is Efficient, London, Fabian Society, Fabian Tract 563, 1994.
Crick, Bernard., Socialist Values and Time, London, Fabian Society, Fabian Tract 495, 1984.
Crick, Bernard., Blunkett, David., The Labour Party's Aims and Values: An Unofficial Statement, London, Spokesman Pamphlet No.87, 1988.
Dahrendorf, Ralf., Challenges to the Voluntary Sector, Arnold Goodman Lecture, London, 17th July 2001.
Plant, Raymond., Equality, Markets and the State, London, Fabian Society, Fabian Tract 494, 1984.
Plant, Raymond., Citizenship, Rights and Socialism, London, Fabian Society, Fabian Tract 531, 1988.

Policy Documents
Blair, Tony., Clause IV: Labour Party Constitution, London, Labour Party, 1995.
Blair, Tony., 'Foreword' in 1997 Labour Party Election Manifesto, London, Labour Party, 1997.
Brown, Gordon., Budget 2003, H.M. Treasury, 2003.
Labour Party, Programme for the Future, London, Labour Party, 1918.
Labour Party, Labour and the New Social Order, London, Labour Party, 1918.
Labour Party, Aims and Values, London, Labour Party, 1992.

Labour Party, Clause 4.4 of the Constitution, London, Labour Party, 1995.
Labour Party, 1997 Labour Party Election Manifesto, London, Labour Party, 1997.
Labour Party, 2001 Labour Party Election Manifesto, London, Labour Party, 2001.

Official Papers
White Paper on Unemployment, London, HMSO, 1944.

Interviews
Interview with Matthew Taylor, September 2002 at the IPPR.
Interview with Anthony Giddens, September 2002 at the LSE.
Interview with Michael Jacobs, November 2002 at the Fabian Society.
Interview with David Marquand, November 2002 in Oxford.
Interview with Neil Kinnock, December 2002 at the European Commission.
Interview with Giles Radice, February 2003 at the House of Lords.
Interview with Roy Hattersley, March 2003 at the House of Commons.
Telephone conversation with Michael Jacobs, March 2003.
Interview with Senior Treasury Civil Servant, HM Treasury, December 2002.

Speeches
Blair, Tony., Clinton, Bill., Schroder, Gerhard., Kok, Wim., D'Alema, Massimo., The Third Way: Progressive Governance for the 21st century, Washington D.C, 25th April 1999.
Blair, Tony., Speech to Annual Conference of the Labour Party 2004, Brighton, 2004.
Boateng, Paul., Speech at the New Economics Foundation, London, 7th May 2002.

Brown, Gordon., <u>Speech at the Mansion House</u>, London, 12th June 1997.

Brown, Gordon., <u>Speech to the Child Poverty Action Group's Child Poverty Conference</u>, London, 15th May 2000.

Brown, Gordon., <u>A Modern Agenda for Prosperity and Social Reform</u>, Cass Business School, London, 3rd February 2003.

Brown, Gordon., <u>Speech at the NCVO Annual Conference</u>, London, 9th February 2000.

Prescott, John., <u>Speech at World Seminar on Sustainable Development</u>, Johannesburg, 17th May 2002.

Articles in Newspapers and Periodicals

Carvel, John., 'Chancellor offers more cash help for parents,' Guardian, 6th December 2000.

Marquand, David., 'The blair paradox', Prospect, May 1998.

Philips, Melanie., 'The father of Tony Blair's big idea', Observer, 24th July 1994.

Riddell, Peter., 'I'm a guru; are you one too?', The Times, 7th August 1996.

Hattersley, Roy., 'It's no longer my party', Observer, 24th June 2001.

Travis, Alan., 'Popularity of budget halts tory revival', Guardian, 23rd April 2002.

Index

1832 Great Reform Act 10
1867 second Great Reform Act 10-11
1884 third Great Reform Act 19
1997 Labour Party election manifesto 100, 116, 118, 122, 127
1999 Pre-budget report 122-123, 127
2001 Labour Party election manifesto 122-123, 127
2005 Labour Party election campaign 128

Action Teams 172
Additional member system 200
Affluent society 37, 42
Allen, Arthur 43
American Civil Liberties Union (ACLU) 194
American communitarianism 177-178, 191-192, 195-196, 210
Anglo-American law 141
Anti-globalisation left 104
Arblaster, Anthony 147
Ashdown, Paddy 157
Asian Tiger economies 115
Atlanticism 40
Attlee Government 35, 38, 46
Attlee, Clement 26, 33, 39-41
Authoritarianism 79, 192, 194-195

Bad Godesberg 90
Balliol College 27-28
Basic Minimum 162
BBC 44
BBC Newsnight 173
Bebel, August 15
Beckett, Margaret 95, 98-99, 130
Bell, Richard 19
Benn, Tony 58-60, 62-66, 72, 76, 104
Bennite left 5, 58-59, 64, 93, 142
Berlin, Isaiah 144
Berry, Vaughan 35
Bernstein, Eduard 16, 21-23
Bevan, Aneurin 38-39, 41, 49, 60
Bevanites 5, 39-43, 50, 59, 142, 186
Beveridge Lecture 173
Bevin, Ernest 40
Birmingham 11
Bismarck, Otto von 161
Blair, Tony 4, 37, 58, 98-101, 105, 108-109, 111-114, 118-124, 127-130, 132, 144, 148-149, 151, 173, 191, 196, 198, 204, 206, 211
Blairites 90, 113, 126, 131, 206, 212
Bland, Hubert 18
Blunkett, David 90-91, 196, 199
Borrie, Gordon 96
Bracke, Wilhelm 15
Bretton Woods system 53
Britain 9, 13, 15, 17, 19-20, 32, 50, 52, 55, 78, 102, 107, 109, 115, 133, 158, 171-172, 179, 187, 193
British Idealists 12, 14, 27

British socialism 25-26
Brown, George 51
Brown, Gordon 4, 98, 101, 109, 120, 122, 124, 130, 148, 151, 156-157, 173, 196, 200, 202, 210
Brownites 126, 131, 208, 212
Budget 2002 4, 123-126, 175, 207-208
Budget 2003 156

Caird, Edward 27
Callaghan Government 102, 106, 131
Callaghan, Jim 51, 54, 74-76
Campaign for Labour Party Democracy (CLPD) 64, 72-73, 76
Campaign for Nuclear Disarmament (CND) 50, 59
Campbell, Alistair 101, 111
Capitalism 14-15, 17-18, 23-25, 27, 29-32, 34-36, 41-42, 46-47, 59-62, 65, 81, 129, 143, 156, 183
CATO Institute 194
Centrists 149-151
Centre-left 119
Chamberlain, Joseph 180-181
Chamberlain, Neville 180
Children's Fund 172
Christian fellowship 68-69, 177-179, 181-184, 189, 196, 210-211
Christian pacifists 50
Christian socialism 177-178, 182, 196, 205, 210-211
Christianity 28, 30-31, 182, 184
Churchill, Randolph 180
Citizen's Britain 157
Civil libertarians 194
Classical liberals 10, 12-14, 147, 159-160, 163, 179
Clause IV 21, 26, 49, 90, 100, 105, 111-113, 129-130, 190

Clinton, Bill 4, 101, 107, 109-110, 120
Clinton, Hilary 109
Cold War 116
Cole, G.D.H. 23-25, 68
Collectivism 11, 13-14, 24-25, 68, 70, 160, 179
Collectivist socialists 178
Commission on Social Justice 96-97
Common Market 65, 59
Communications revolution 115
Communism 20, 26-27, 32-33, 40, 117
Communist Party 27, 59, 175
Communitarian conservatism 181
Communitarian left 193, 204
Communitarian liberals 204
Communitarian social democrat 204
Communitarian socialism 82, 184-185
Communitarianism 1, 6, 14, 81-82, 93-94, 117, 177, 179, 187, 190-193, 197-198, 200, 204-205, 211-212
Community 1-2, 6, 14, 26, 68-72, 82-84, 94, 102, 133, 146-147, 165, 176-185, 187-191, 193-194, 196-197, 199, 201-202, 204-206, 208, 210, 212
Compact on Relations between Government and the Voluntary and Community Sector 203
Comprehensive Spending Review 4, 123-126, 207-208
Connexions 172
Conservatism 2, 11, 55, 145, 155, 180-181, 194-195
Conservative Party 6, 11-12, 16, 18, 46-49, 51, 54, 57, 66, 68, 79, 85, 89, 94-95, 102, 107, 112,

116, 118-119, 122, 126, 128, 137-138, 159
Cook, Robin 130
Crick, Bernard 77-78, 83-84, 88, 90, 139
Crosland, Anthony 14, 23, 43, 46-48, 54, 62, 66, 78, 86, 105, 129, 131, 154, 165-169, 176-177, 185-187, 209
Croslandites 60, 131, 151, 173, 197, 209
Crossman, Richard 41

D'Alema, Massimo 120
Dahrendorf, Ralf 203
Daily Mirror 41
Dalton, Hugh 35
Darwinian evolutionary theory 184
Davenport, Nicholas 35
Decentralisation 6, 68-69, 71, 88, 93-94, 103, 174, 177, 189, 197, 199, 200, 210, 211
Democracy 6, 15, 18, 22-23, 48, 60, 62-65, 71, 74, 77, 82, 90-91, 98, 103, 116, 119, 136, 160, 175, 177, 181
Democratic equality 43, 81, 155, 166-168
Democratic socialism 20-22, 37-38, 41-45, 78, 113, 120-121, 129, 160
Deputy Leadership 76-77, 95, 98-99
Devolution 69, 198, 200, 211
Dewar, Donald 130
Difference principle 168
Disraeli, Benjamin 10, 180
Durbin, Evan 35
Dutch 108

Eastern Europe 50, 116
Edwardian era 185, 196, 205

Egalitarian conception of equality 154, 158, 161, 164-172, 176
Eisenachers 15
Electoral college 74-76, 98
Ends group 42-43
Engels, Friedrich 15-17
England 16, 85, 197, 199, 203
Equality 1-2, 6, 22, 26, 43-44, 62, 69, 71, 81, 83-84, 87, 102, 133, 139, 154-155, 158-159, 161, 164-165, 169, 171, 175-176, 183, 199, 206, 208-209, 210, 212
Equality of opportunity 81, 85, 145, 154-158
Equality of opportunity and fairness of outcome 154, 156-158, 176
Equality of outcome 81, 154-156, 158
Exchange Rate Mechanism (ERM) 92
Ethical socialism 21, 28
Etzioni, Amitai 177-178, 191-195
Euro 115
European Commission 105
European Community (EC) 78, 92
European Economic Community (EEC) 64
European Parliament 200
European Union (EU) 94, 107, 109, 111, 115

Fabian Society 3, 16, 18-19, 23-25, 27, 33, 68, 104, 175
Far left 58
Far right 104
Fascism 31-32, 117
Figgis, J.N. 33
Foot, Michael 74, 76, 106
Fourth Party 180
French Revolution 10

Gaitskell, Hugh 14, 25, 35, 37, 39-40, 43-44, 49, 51, 78, 112, 151, 206
Gaitskellites 5, 23, 37, 39-40, 43, 129-131, 186, 206
Galbraith, J.K. 57
Gang of Four 5, 58, 66-67, 70, 72, 75, 206
Gemeinschaft 179
General Association of German Workers 15
Generous sufficiency conception of equality 1, 161-162, 164-165, 172, 176, 209-210, 212
German Social Democratic Party 15-16
Germany 15-16, 32
Gesellschaft 178
Giddens, Anthony 103-104, 108, 119, 121, 123-124, 126
Gladstone, William 12, 181
Globalisation 61, 70, 100, 104, 113-116, 129, 175
Gordon-Walker, Patrick 43
Gore, Charles 27-28
Gotha Programme 15
Gould, Bryan 77-78, 87-88, 95, 139, 144
Gould, Philip 101, 108-111, 113
Great Debate 5, 26, 39, 186, 207
Great War 26
Greater equality of outcome 23, 53, 68, 70, 72, 78, 82, 85-86, 146, 154-156, 158, 163, 166, 169-170, 172-174, 182, 185-187, 197
Greater London Assembly (GLA) 200
Green, T.H. 12, 14, 27-28, 147, 151
Guild socialism 24-25, 29, 68

Hall, Stuart 59
Hard left 58, 103
Hardie, Kier 19
Hattersley, Roy 85-86, 89, 95, 104-105, 109, 125, 131-132, 139, 144, 154, 168-169, 175-176, 209
Hayek, Friedrich von 56, 134-137, 143, 147, 152, 159-160, 162, 179
Healey, Denis 76
Hegel, G.W.F. 14
Hobhouse, L.T. 13, 151
Hobson, J.A. 13-14, 33, 151
Holland, Henry Scott 28
Holland, Stuart 59-62, 65, 132, 143
Hyndman, H.M. 17-18

Independent Labour Party (ILP) 19
Individual freedom/liberty 87-88, 90, 136, 163, 176, 179, 182, 187 Individualism 82, 159, 175, 192, 197, 212
International Marxist Group 77
IPPR 3, 96, 103
Iraq War 127
Irish Home rule 181
Italy 61

Jacobs, Michael 104, 106 108, 110, 124, 126, 207-208
Jay, Douglas 35
Jenkins, Roy 43, 66-67, 75
Joseph, Keith 54, 56, 138
Justice as fairness 168

Keep Calm group 39
Keynes, John Maynard 32-35, 51
Keynesianism 10, 34-36, 51-53, 55, 59, 61-62, 80, 85, 92-94, 103, 114, 117-118, 143

Kinnock, Neil 89-90, 95, 105-106, 109-111, 113, 125, 130-131, 207-208 Kok, Wim 120

Labour left 29, 33-34, 37, 39-40, 42, 49-51, 59, 64-65, 72, 75-76, 79, 81, 102, 112, 121, 164
Labour Marxists 17, 29, 31, 156, 164, 176, 209
Labour Movement 1-2, 9, 17-18, 69, 129, 181, 185, 193
Labour Party 1-3, 6, 9, 11, 14, 17, 21, 25-28, 33-37, 39-43, 47, 49-51, 54-55, 57-59, 62-64, 66-67, 69-70, 72, 74, 76-79, 82, 85-91, 94-97, 100-102, 104-106, 108, 110-113, 117, 120, 125, 128-130, 132, 141-142, 149, 151, 156, 159, 163-164, 176, 184-187, 193, 197, 204-209
Labour Party Constitution 20, 42, 49, 59, 64-66, 74, 90, 111, 129, 148
Labour Party Young Socialists 77
Labour Representation Committee (LRC) 5, 16, 19
Labour Representation League 11
Labour right 5, 33, 37, 39, 43, 50-51, 58, 60, 65-67, 74-77, 102, 121, 130, 132, 178-179
Labourism 17, 19-20, 39, 103
Laissez-faire 10, 12, 14, 45, 47, 144, 150
Laissez-faire conservatives 194
Lansman, John 76
Lasalle, Ferdinand 15
Lasallians 15
Laski, Harold 27, 29, 32-33
Left Book Club 27, 33, 45
Leftists 149-151
Lenin, V.I. 33
Levitas, Ruth 190, 195

Liberal 2, 55, 117, 119, 121, 138-139, 143, 145, 147, 152, 164, 166, 178-179, 181, 187, 189, 194, 197
Liberal communitarians 204
Liberal conservatives 155
Liberal democracies 137
Liberal Party 10-13, 15, 18-19, 28, 35, 63, 68, 181
Liberal social democrat 197, 204
Liberalism 14, 20, 28, 43, 120-121, 147, 150, 160, 181, 186, 190, 193, 204, 211
Libertarian socialism 24, 82
Libertarianism 179, 181, 192-194
Liberty 26, 42, 44, 68-69, 71-72, 83-87, 102, 133-136, 138-139, 141-143, 145-146, 148, 152-154, 158-160, 164, 169, 170, 181, 183, 198, 206, 208-209, 211
Liberty Bell 194
Liberty principle 168
Liddle, Roger 112, 119, 131
Liebknecht, Wilhelm 15
Limehouse Declaration 75
Local-level community 1, 178-179, 189-190, 197, 211-212
Locke, John 14
London 11, 173, 197
London Mayoral elections 200
Lord Salisbury 180
London School of Economics (LSE) 103

MacCallum, Gerald 139-141, 208
MacDonald, Ramsay 177-178, 184-185, 196
MacIntyre, Alasdair 9
Macmillan, Harold 51
Major Government 192

Major, John 94, 102, 107, 137, 179
Manchester liberals 10, 150
Mandatory reselection 73, 77
Mandelson, Peter 98, 101, 108-109, 112, 119, 130-131
Marquand, David 104, 108-109, 124-125
Marx, Karl 15-17, 22-23, 32-33
Marxism 15, 17, 21, 26-27, 30-31, 78, 81, 83-84, 117, 160
Mason, Andrew 188-189, 198, 210
Masterman, C.F.G. 13-14
Mayhew, Christopher 43
Means group 44-45
Miliband, David 96
Militant Tendency 77, 89
Minimum Income Guarantee 156
Modern left 103-104, 149
Modernised social democracy 95, 102, 119, 121, 197, 205
Modernisers 4, 39, 95, 100, 105, 107, 111-112, 129-132
Monetarism 54, 80
Moral Majority 194
Moralized concept of community 188-189, 210-211
Morris, Dick 110
Morris, William 68
Morrison, Herbert 38

NAFTA 115
National Council for Voluntary Organisations (NCVO) 200
National Executive Committee (NEC) 38, 40, 49, 61, 64-65, 72-74, 77, 113
National Insurance contributions 47, 175
National Minimum Wage 170, 210
Nationalisation 18, 20-21, 23-26, 31, 38-39, 42-44, 47-49, 60, 62, 68, 86, 89, 92, 121, 142-143

NATO 40, 50, 59
Nazism 32
Negative libertarians 134, 139, 146, 148, 179
Negative liberty 1, 13-14, 71, 82, 87, 133-135, 137-140, 143-147, 212
Neo-liberalism 45, 54-57, 66, 79-82, 84-85, 92-93, 96, 120, 137, 143, 145, 147, 151, 155, 164, 173, 178-179, 192-193, 212
Neutralism 41
New Deal 51, 172
New Deal for Communities 174, 190, 211
New Deal Plus 172
New Democrats 4, 100-101, 107-111, 119, 207-208
New Labour 1-6, 9, 26, 36-37, 54, 57-58, 75, 91, 96-98, 100-114, 116-133, 139, 141-142, 144-145, 147, 149-150, 153-154, 156-158, 162, 167-177, 182-183, 185, 187, 189-191, 193, 196- 200, 202, 204-212
New left 5, 50, 58-60, 62, 64-67, 72-74, 76-79, 82, 98, 106, 130, 132, 142-143, 207
New Liberal 13-14, 81, 147
New Liberalism 12, 28, 150-151, 180
New Right 1, 6, 54-55, 57, 88, 95, 101, 119, 133, 135, 138, 144, 154, 159-163, 175, 177-180, 202, 208
New right-wing of the Labour Party 107, 132, 207
NHS 47, 115, 175
Non-conformists 10
Non-strict egalitarianism 210
Non-strict prioritarianism 1, 169, 171-172, 176, 210, 212
North 116
Northern Ireland 197

INDEX

Northern Ireland Assembly 200
Nove, Alec 77-79, 139
Nozick, Robert 178

Old Labour 4, 91, 94, 100, 102-106, 112, 120, 123-126, 202, 207, 208
Old left 59-60, 64, 74, 79, 106, 116, 119, 132, 142-143, 207
Old Right 106, 141, 207
One-Member One-Vote 98-99, 131
One-nation Conservatives 10
OPEC 115
Opportunity 139, 148
Opportunity for all 133, 144-145, 153, 209
Opportunity society 127-128
Ordinary concept of community 188-189, 198, 210
Owen, David 66-72
Oxfam 200
Oxford University 12, 23, 28

Parfit, Derek 154-155, 158, 209-210
Parliamentary Labour Party 38-40, 43, 49, 60, 64, 73-74, 98
Party Conference 26-27, 73-74, 76, 88, 91, 95-96, 96, 127-128
Party Leader 43, 74-76, 95, 98, 129
Paxman, Jeremy 173
Pensioner Credit 156
Pensioner Guarantee 172, 210
Permissive society 197
Plant, Raymond 77-78, 80-83, 87-88, 139
Policy Review 89-92, 94, 96, 131
Policy Unit 96
Positive libertarians 145

Positive liberty 1, 14, 56, 71, 80, 82, 84, 86-87, 133, 138-147, 153, 208, 209, 212
Post-Thatcherite 6, 54, 133, 175
Post-War Consensus 45
Post-war Era 37, 85
Prentice, Reg 65
Prescott, John 95, 99, 111-112, 130, 190, 211
Priority conception of equality 145, 150-151, 154-155, 158, 161-162, 164-165, 167-171, 176, 209-210
Progressive left 151, 187
Progressive universalism 154, 156-158, 176

Radical individualists 194
Radical liberals 10-11, 103, 106, 180
Radice, Giles 105, 109-110, 121, 125, 208
Rawls, John 43, 81, 167-169, 210
Real opportunity 149-151
Regional Development Agencies 190, 197, 211
Regional lists 200
Regional-level community 1, 189-190, 197, 211-212
Religious Fundamentalism 117
Representation of the People Act 26
Republican Party 55
Revisionist right 14, 23, 29, 37, 39, 42-43, 48-49, 53, 206, 212
Reynolds News 41
Robens, Alf 43
Robbins, Lionel 32
Rodgers, Bill 66-67, 131

Sandel, Michael 191
Save the Children 200
Saville, John 59

Scandinavians 108
Schroder, Gerhard 120
Scotland 85, 197, 200
Scottish Parliament 199, 200
Second Term Ideas 100, 122
Second World War 33, 40, 46, 51, 186, 196
Shaw, George Bernard 18-19, 156, 164, 176, 209
Shore, Peter 76
Silkin, John 76
Single transferable vote 200
Skidelsky, Robert 51
Smith, Adam 45, 178
Smith, John 92, 95-96, 98, 105, 131-132, 198
Snowden, Philip 34
Social conservatives 187, 192
Social democracy 1-2, 4, 6, 14, 17, 23, 32, 36, 47, 60, 67-68, 71, 75, 79, 81, 85-87, 91, 93-94, 100, 102, 104-105, 111, 116-117, 122, 125, 127, 133, 138-139, 144, 157, 161, 164, 166, 169, 175-176
Social democrat 39, 56, 66, 69-70, 80, 82-85, 88, 92, 96-97, 103, 106, 109, 117, 120-121, 128, 143, 145, 148, 150-151, 155, 158, 167-168, 170-172, 177, 181, 183, 185, 187, 189-191, 195-197, 205-210
Social Democratic Federation (SDF) 17-19, 26, 156, 164, 176, 209
Social Democratic Party (SDP) 5, 67, 69-70, 75, 84, 176, 206-207
Social Democratic Workers' Party 15
Social justice 10, 12-13, 15, 22, 55-56, 83, 96-97, 119, 121, 136, 148, 153, 155, 160-161, 163, 178-179, 199

Social liberal 121, 147, 150-151, 155
Socialism 9, 11, 13, 15-16, 18-19, 22-24, 33-34, 39, 43, 63, 66, 72, 80, 82-83, 87-88, 90-91, 93, 138, 143, 151, 158-161, 163, 182, 184
Socialist Workers' Party 77
Socialist Workers' Party of Germany 15
Soft left 103, 106
South 116
Soviet Communism 79-80, 87, 144
Soviet Union 20, 50
State-level community 1, 178-179, 189-190, 197, 211-212
Stewart, Michael 39
Strachey, John 27, 29, 31-32, 39
Strauss, George 39
Straw, Jack 130, 196
Strict prioritarianism 169, 171, 210
Strict-egalitarian conception of equality 154-155, 158, 161, 164-168, 170-172, 176, 209-210
Sufficiency conception of equality 154-155, 158, 161-162, 164-165, 167-168, 170-172, 176
Sunday Pictorial 41
Supplementary vote 200
Surestart 172-173
Switzerland 16
Syndicalism 23, 25, 29

Taverne, Dick 65
Tawney, R.H. 27-30, 69-70, 151, 154, 163-165, 176-177, 181-185, 196, 205, 209
Taylor, Charles 191
Taylor, Matthew 103, 106-108, 110-111, 123, 126, 207-208
Thatcher Government 192

Thatcher, Margaret 5, 54, 79-80, 102, 104, 118, 137-138, 159, 179-180
Thatcherism 57, 70, 93, 101, 124
The Red Cross 200
The Workers' Revolutionary Party 77
Third Way 100, 108-109, 119-121
Thompson, Edward 59
Tory democracy 180
Tory Reform League 180
Totalitarianism 160, 179
Toynbee Hall 173
Trade Union Congress (TUC) 15, 19
Trade unions 15, 17-18, 20, 27, 39-40, 42, 49, 52, 63, 65, 74-76, 92, 95-96, 98, 106, 113, 185
Traditional social democracy 1, 5, 133, 147, 151, 154-155, 166
Transport and General Workers' Union (TGWU) 112
Treasury 156, 173, 203
Triangulation 108, 110, 208
Tribune 41, 112
Trickle-down theory 173
Trotskyite 77, 103, 106

Ultra-modernisers 132
Unilateralism 50, 60
Unilateralist-multilateralist debate 50
Unison 112
University College, Oxford 173
USA 40-41, 52, 55, 60, 107-109, 111, 119
USSR 27, 40-41, 50, 60
Utopianism 22, 46

Voluntary sector 177, 200-203

Wales 85, 197, 200
Waltzer, Michael 191

Webb, Beatrice 18, 27
Webb, Sidney 18, 27
Welsh Assembly 198-200
Wembley Conference 75
Western democracy 136
Western world 109, 114, 116
Whigs 10-11
White, Stuart, 149-151
Williams, Philip 23, 44
Williams, Raymond 59
Williams, Shirley, 66-67, 131
Wilson-Callaghan Government 53, 65, 175
Wilson Government 48, 65, 102, 106, 131
Wilson, Harold 51, 72
Workerist right 103, 106
Working Families Tax Credit 172, 174, 210
Wyatt, Woodrow 43

XYZ Club 35